The

"I LOVE this book! No matter the stage of your relationship, the Couples' Castle is a must read! I felt like I truly knew these characters and identified with so many of their struggles. It pulled my heart, then showed me exactly what I need to challenge within myself for the sake of our marriage. I'm truly grateful for this book." —**Patty McMinn**, *Married 15 years, Mom of 4*

"If you're seeking the answers to having the ultimate relationship, look no further! The relatable characters and compelling story make it easy to apply the lessons to your own life and finally reach your happily-ever-after. Deep down, everyone is wanting their marriage and relationship to be a success, but it's hard to find the right guidance you need. Aaron's book covered it all, and is very universal for everyone, no matter what they are going through in their relationship! I'm so thankful for this book and for the truly life-changing experience it gave me!!" —**Adrianna Petrie**, *Found the Love of My Life*

"Consider The Couples' Castle a reset button for your relationship. An excellent read that holds invaluable information; a book that will surely stand the test of time." —**Katlin Cox-Moore**, *Owner-Operator at SHEA Studio*

"Ready for an adventure in relationships? Couple's Castle takes you on a poignant clue hunt for a fresh perspective on self-evaluation and a grid to assess your marriage and relationships. Whether pre-, mid-, or post-relationship the reader will leave encouraged, motivated, and prepared for greater fulfillments. This book is awesome!" —**Scott and Judy Reichard**, *CPA, QPA, QKA, Movie Producers, Authors, Philanthropists, 37 years married*

Marriage is a journey of both ups and downs and every couple would benefit from reading this book. Thanks to Aaron and his inspirational words to help every couple on this blessed adventure called marriage!
—**Kelly Trask**, *married 22 years, 4 kids*

"Hands down the best book I've read on relationships." —**Jonathan McMinn**, *MD, Emergency Medicine*

"You will be drawn into the fictitious lives of the characters. Through their journeys in the Couples' Castle you will discover ways to help your own relationship become all that it was intended to be. Whether you are just beginning a relationship or have been married decades there is something to be gleaned from the strategies discussed in this book."
—**Rod and Lisa Hoewing**, *Married with nearly 20 years experience*

"The Couples' Castle is an instant hit! While reading it, I got the satisfying sense that I was not only being captivated by a compelling tale about characters with whom I immediately connected, but also learning powerful lessons about how to elevate my life and relationships. I spent equal time laughing, crying and taking notes! There was something written in the pages of this book that educated and inspired the wife, mother, daughter, sister, colleague and friend in me. It is by far the best book on relationships I have ever read. It is truly the go-to resource that should be read and experienced time and again." —**Tiffany Barnett White**, *PhD, TEDx Talk Presenter, Award Winning Professor*

"This book is truly inspiring and captivating from beginning to end. Wherever you are in your marriage, read this book!" —**Skylur and Jessica Orwick**, *Happily Married*

To learn more about the author and to receive your free resources, visit aaron-bird.com

THE Couples' CASTLE

THE

Couples'

CASTLE

*An Inspiring Tale to Experience the Ultimate
Relationship, Find the Love of Your Life,
& Make Your Marriage a Masterpiece*

AARON B. BIRD, PHD

Copyright © 2017 by Aaron B. Bird, PhD.

Library of Congress Control Number:		2017905709
ISBN:	Hardcover	978-1-5434-1563-6
	Softcover	978-1-5434-1564-3
	eBook	978-1-5434-1565-0

Print information available on the last page.

Rev. date: 06/29/2017

To order additional copies of this book, contact:
Xlibris
1-888-795-4274
www.Xlibris.com
Orders@Xlibris.com
757715

Contents

To my seventh grade sweetheart.
Convincing you to marry me is the
greatest achievement of my life.

Chapter 1

The Red Treasure Chest

"Happily ever after—w-what a joke." Titus, a well-built, rusty-haired, country-music fan looked down at the dirty dish in the sink and sighed.

Emma spun around, her sunkissed blonde hair moving like liquid. *O.M.G! If anyone's listening up there in heaven, please tell me he doesn't know.*

Tick. Tick. Tick. *Three hours until our fifth anniversary. How could you have been so stupid, Emma?* "Um, what'd you say, honey?"

Titus shut the stainless steel dishwasher and scratched his forehead, "N-nothing."

The dark cherry hardwood floors camouflaged his composite-toe boots as they thudded across the room. His presence was so powerful.

"Titus?" Her quivering voiced reflected the terror in her heart.

He stopped, facing the opposite end of the arched hallway in their modest one-story home.

Titus had never been good with words, but if she could just get a sense of what he's feeling—some reassurance even. Something, *anything*.

Nothing.

What'd she expect? They went for such long stretches in their marriage these days without any sort of spark. It used to be different, so romantic and cuddly. An "I appreciate you" or "it's okay" would've worked every now and then—especially tonight, just so she could know whether he knew the shocking secret she'd withheld from him.

The air filled with such thick desperation, that she picked at her index fingernail so deeply and didn't even notice she cut into her skin and drew blood.

Titus pivoted.

Was he pinching his lips tight to keep them from trembling? Were his eyes really watery?

Emma froze. She was the crier in this relationship. She'd never seen him shed a tear. Not even at his mom's funeral four years ago, and her death broke his heart.

But there he stood. The tall strong mountain that he was now sending out a long pained look and then breaking eye contact.

Should I go to him? Her feet wouldn't move from the scratched-up hardwoods that now mirrored her life. Slowly, her disbelief turned to distress.

He must know something. Her head hung down toward her feet when she thought of all they'd gone through, all the trust built up over the years, and the wonderful memories stored in her heart that were now about to come crashing down.

The doorbell rang.

Who would drop by unannounced this late at night? *Just ignore it.* But what if one of the evening's guests left something behind? She walked over to open the mahogany front door.

Emma opened the door but didn't see a soul. She stepped outside onto their wraparound porch and into the cool fall evening and almost tripped over a little brown gift box.

A small box, with a yellow ribbon wrapped around it and tied in a bow, it read, "Titus and Emma Parker. *Open immediately.*"

"What's that?"

Emma had a heavy feeling in her stomach.

If he knows, why's he so close to me? "I don't know," she said.

"You didn't see anyone?"

She bent over to pick it up. "No, just this box. I thought maybe Larry or Linda left something here and came back to get it, but I didn't see anyone."

"L-larry, huh?" His trembling chin betrayed his pain.

She studied his face. The way Larry's name rolled off his tongue settled it. How he knew, she didn't know. It only happened one time, and that was two years ago.

"Well, are you going to bring it in?" He moved out of her way.

They sat at the long table where they'd just entertained their best friends, Larry and Linda, for two hours. Maybe he saw Larry smile at her. She loved Titus so much. He'd always been loyal, and she couldn't bear the thought of losing him.

The once high-school sweethearts stared at the unopened box while Titus's finger tapped the table. Each tap felt like another crack in her heart.

My sins are coming back for me. Our entire history is about to go up in flames.

She remembered when it all started—at the high-school Halloween dance, when they separately showed up in homemade cowboy and cowgirl costumes. That look on his face when they announced his name over the speakers for best costume—she'd never forget it. *Then me, he picked me—even when I wore those hideous yellow glasses. What was the tradition? That the male and female costume winners must dance together and yet he politely declined, walked over to grab my hand, and picked me, an underclassman.*

She couldn't say much for his dance skills—he was like her golden retriever trying to stay upright on their wet hardwood floors. Still, he picked her. She'd take his unswerving devotion over hip dance moves ten out of ten times.

"Emma?"

But the slow dance . . . the slow dance, that's where it really started. When we started to fall in . . .

"Emma?"

She looked up at him, hands on the table—trembling—recalling their early years.

An introverted, strong boy who grew up on a farm, marrying a buoyant carefree person like her. His quiet strength always made up for his failure to get a joke. His fierce friendship always overshadowed his inability to pick up on social cues. Those horseback rides he took her on behind his farm to watch the sunset reflected his purity.

"Emma, your hands are shaking."

"Titus, do you remember when we first dated? How we spent so much time together?"

He pushed away from the table and stood up. "I can't t-talk about this right now."

"Do you remember the state fair?" She raised her head, her eyes searching his.

"I said . . ." His voice cracked. "I can't t-talk about us."

Leaning in, she said, "That was our first kiss."

Titus scrubbed his hands over his face and let out a deep sigh.

"When I found out you'd never kissed anyone, sometime in our first week of dating, I decided right then and there that I wanted to make your first kiss special."

Titus's eyes flooded, and his breathing slowed.

She calmly stood in hopes to keep him from leaving. "Ya, I had insider information that you hadn't kissed anyone. Your mom of all people. Such a sweet woman. She told me you thought kissing me would either be magical or a hot mess."

Titus covered his mouth with two fingers, his eyes frosting over.

"Remember, Titus? We entered the hall of mirrors and bumped into the mirror and laughed so hard we cried. And we couldn't stop laughing all the way through the exit where we tripped over each other and barreled down the ramp—and I fell into your arms?"

She looked up and to the left, then back at him and smiled. "And you said, 'hey,' and I said, 'right back at ya, mirror man,' and we burst out laughing so hard that the people standing in line accused us of drinking?"

"Emma, just stop." Titus sat down near the box.

She reenacted the scenario. "And how the ticket taker said, 'You guys need to get up and keep moving, please. So I grabbed your hand, and we ran through the nearby trees, onto the other side where the moon was reflected on the quiet, still lake."

"Emma."

"And you flipped your shoes off first. Then I did too, and we stood on the bank with our toes touching. Do you remember what happened next?"

"Emma, I mean it. Stop."

Her voice quieted but persisted out of desperation. "You put your arms around me and asked me for a dance, one that I bet even made the gods jealous."

She took a soft step his way. "I was always at my happiest when dancing with you."

Titus rested his chin on his palm, bit his lip, and shook his head.

"I put my arms around your neck, and you wrapped your strong arms around my waist. I scooted myself close and leaned in for our first . . ."

He'd had enough. "Stop!" He stood up and glared at her from the corner of his eyes, his breaths intensifying.

"Kiss." She craned her neck. "And do you remember what you said?"

He shook his head at her in disdain.

"Magical. You said, 'magical.'"

"Well, so much for that, huh?" He dropped the kitchen chair he didn't even know he'd been clutching onto.

"What happened to us, Titus?" she pleaded with him, opening her arms, palms face up.

"You stopped loving me when the doctors told us I was s-sterile—that's what happened."

She slumped into one of the chairs. "No, that's not it. I would never do that."

"Well, I saw the way you looked at me in the doc's office. I knew right there you felt different about me." He looked down at the floor.

"Titus, that was two years ago—you've thought that this whole time?"

"Don't act like your feelings toward me didn't change that day." He started to make his way to the office but then turned. "Why am I even having a c-conversation with you?"

She jumped up and pleaded, "My feelings never changed. In fact, the opposite was true. That's why we keep trying. Who cares what the doctors say?"

"What, you pitied me? Ya, no thanks. You can keep your pity."

"That's not what I'm saying, Titus." She was getting close enough that she could almost feel the hair standing up from his arms.

"You actually think I care what you're saying? You've lost the right to say a-anything to me."

"That's just it. After the doctor shared the news, I felt closed off from you, like we couldn't say anything to each other. I needed you to share your feelings with me. I mean, anything. Just say something, Titus. You just stay quiet, walled up and closed off. I needed your love, something. I couldn't get you to talk about it. God knows I tried. I cried myself to sleep at night thinking, 'What's a relationship if we can't connect about the most important things?' That's why we never talk anymore. It may have even been the cause of your stuttering, you know, when you started taking antidepressants."

The way he glared made her want to hide behind her hair.

Emma put her hands over her mouth. "I don't know what to say." *He'll never forgive me. All's I ever wanted for us was to be happy. One misstep and just like that, my marriage is done—the love of my life, gone.*

Only one thing could distract from the impending marital disaster. The mysterious brown box with the tied yellow ribbon and bow on top. Emma leaned over to open it before he could walk away.

*   *   *

"So do you want to have sex?" Oliver wore a blue Dallas Cowboys cap, a faded Mickey Mouse shirt, and a playful grin across his chiseled African American jaw. Unfortunately for him, his boyish looks and charm held little spell-binding effect with his wife, Olivia, these days.

Seriously, he's doing this again? Olivia couldn't understand the male species in this regard, much less her husband's inability to connect the dots between making love and helping out around the house. Bearing the brunt of the household responsibilities had left her feeling worn out and overwhelmed.

"Well?" His eyebrows moved quickly up and down three times.

"I'm paying the bills, Oliver."

"Well, maybe you shouldn't pay the bills on our bed. You're tempting me, O. C'mon, let's do it. It's been like, I don't know, foooooooorever." He moved his arms out like a band director.

"How can you even talk about sex right now?" Olivia narrowed her eyes, squinting, then placed a blanket over her long luring legs.

"What do you mean?"

"Are you kidding me? You don't even know?"

"Know what?"

"Do I have to say it?" Her eyebrows raised.

"Well, I'm not a mind reader."

"Nothing." She pinched her lips together.

"C'mon, don't do that. Just say it." He lifted himself in his desert boots and leaned in.

She sized him up and thought better of it. "No. Never mind. It's not worth it."

"Try me."

He just doesn't get it. Does he need me to spell it out for him?

"C'mon, spell it out for me. Whatcha got?"

Apparently so. "Okay then. I feel overwhelmed and, if I'm honest, underappreciated for what I do around here."

"Maybe sex will help take the pressure off?" His eyes glistened with the light of a car salesman pitch.

"Oliver, I'm serious. Way more serious than you think." Bills were sprawled all over the bed, hair accessories were scattered all across the bathroom counter, and the dirty laundry was piling up in the corner basket. *Does he not even see it?* "Look at all this."

"Look at what?"

She shook her head. *Breathe, Olivia. Breathe.*

"Look at what, Olivia?"

"Everything!"

Oliver took one step back. "You okay, O?"

She was like a volcano ready to erupt. "No, Oliver, I'm not. For the last several years, I've been Mom, maid, and missus. I sacrifice sleep to get up with the youngest—every night. In the morning, I'm the one who bathes, dresses, and feeds them. I help them brush their hair and teeth, pack their lunches and backpacks, sign their parental forms and permission slips, and my reward? I get to go to work." She didn't even pause to catch her breath. "Afterward, I pick them up from school, take them to gymnastics, swimming, or piano, depending on the night, and then bring them home where I make dinner and help them with homework. Saturday's my one free night, and I'm in here paying bills. I'm tired, Oliver, worn out." *There, I've connected the dots for him. Maybe now he'll show some appreciation.*

"I help."

Her jaw dropped in disbelief, and her toes curled. *You've got to be kidding me. What is it with men? How can he not understand?*

She tilted her head and her nose flared. "The one time you did dress them for school, they wore mismatched clothes and shoes, with knots in their hair. The teachers thought it was cute because they heard you oversaw the clothing disaster, but I'm judged differently. If I did that, they'd think I'm crazy mom. I have to make sure our kids look, act, dress, and smell somewhat normal, so their peers and teachers will accept them."

Oliver tapped the dresser. "I did the dishes last night."

"You gotta be kidding me, Oliver, that's just it. You expect me to throw you a party whenever you do something around the house, but I'm just expected to do it all the time—the dishes, dusting, vacuuming, sleep deprivation for the kids, and the list goes on."

Her cry for help went sailing over Oliver's head. Although well intended, he just had one thing on his mind tonight. Oliver calmly sat down at the end of the bed, removed the blanket, grabbed her foot, and began massaging it.

"No, Oliver. I know what you're doing."

"I can't help it, O. You've got those deep brown eyes and long gorgeous lashes that take me prisoner."

"Nice try."

"And the symmetry of your face would make a runway model jealous, though I know, I know, you have no aspirations of becoming one." He pressed deeper into the foot, just the way she liked it.

"Stop. You're not getting anywhere."

"The way your long brown hair lays gently on your shoulders. Other guys trip over themselves just to be around you, O. I see them. And the closer I get to you, the more your beauty intoxicates me." The way he smiled did make her feel beautiful.

"Oliver, I'm in sweats and a T-shirt. Besides, it's been a long day." She drew her foot back and put her hands on her temples to rub her head, feigning a headache in hopes that he'd leave.

"You do look a bit worn out."

"Gee, thanks." She felt a tightness in her chest and tilted her head to the side and squinted.

"Well?" He put his hand on her leg and leaned forward.

"Well, what?"

He gave her the sexy eyes. "Maybe cuddling will help you relax."

"Cuddling? Do you even know what that means?" Olivia's cheeks blew out and then released. Some of the bills went flying off the bed when she grabbed a pillow to place behind her back. She leaned over to pick them up and gave out a grunt.

"You sound angry."

"I'm feeling bitter and alone, and that's worse. Anger's a secondary emotion of love and subsides. Bitterness lasts." *Hold your tongue, psychologist Olivia, so you don't feel the need to unsay something later.*

Oliver adjusted his cap and scooted closer. After a moment, he placed his hand on hers.

She withdrew. "Stop. I told you, I'm paying the bills."

He stood up, exasperated, and said, "When then?"

"What do you mean *when*?"

"Well, you keep saying, 'not right now.' So when's a *good time*?"

"Later."

"When's later?"

"Oliver!" She took the pillow behind her back and threw it at him.

He dodged it. "Hey, wouldn't it be cool if our pillows collected our dreams by osmosis, and then we could plug our pillows into our computers to watch the dreams? That way, I could see if you were thinking of me, and then I'd know which days to ask about making love."

She looked at him like he was from outer space. "Did you learn that in your transcendental meditation class?"

"Nah, I stopped going. I was the only black person there in a class of fifty white people. I felt like a chocolate chip in a bag of marshmallows. Plus, my belly couldn't handle the downward-dog pose."

"Isn't that yoga?" She grabbed the calculator to begin paying the bills again.

He shrugged. "They mixed and matched."

"Hmm." She picked up her spreadsheet, disinterested in his gym time.

"Anyway, I only went to the class to see if the devil would get me."

She glanced up. "The devil?"

"Yeah, where I come from, meditation, yoga, all that stuff is hocus-pocus, new agey-type devil stuff."

"So did he get you?"

"Only when I slipped during downward dog."

I wish I could've seen that.

"So, anyway, back to the subject at hand. Later then?" Oliver tilted his head.

"Maybe later, later."

"When's later, later?"

He's insufferable. Olivia let out a dismissive sigh.

"We ate dinner, and the kids are in bed. It's just us, babe. Now's our, you know, rare - mmmm - alone time."

"I know they're in bed. I'm the one who gave them a shower and put them to bed . . . by myself as usual." She gave him the once-over. "Have *you* even showered today?"

Oliver leaned against the dresser. "Hey, in the course of all seven books, Harry Potter bathed just once, and people liked hanging out with him."

Her eyes slowly looked up at him like he suddenly had started talking Mandarin, then back down to the spreadsheet. "Will you please just let me pay the bills? *Someone* in this house has to do it."

"You said *do it*."

She rested her head in her hands. "I'm a person, not a product, Oliver."

"Ya, but we're also married, so what's that supposed to mean?"

She grabbed her hair in clumps and looked up to the ceiling. "It means I need help. Honestly, Oliver, I don't know how much longer I can go on like this." Soft tears fell from Olivia's eyes. She let out a deep sigh, then talked like she was the only one in the room. "I feel like my world's disappearing in the vortex of cleaning, cooking, working, and parenting. I play the part that people expect, that *you* expect. My chameleon identity is a reflection of what everyone else wants."

Oliver squinted. "But we hosted your friends two weeks ago. Wasn't that for you?"

She shook her head, amazed with his lack of understanding. "When we entertain guests, I spend hours cleaning because there's a standard for how our house should smell and look. I'm not saying we should do what everyone else does, but you know people have certain standards, and we do too. Why am I—by default—the one in charge of this? And you continue to leave those orange peels on the floor."

Before Oliver could defend himself, O continued. "When's the last time I sat down to read a good book, Oliver? When's the last time I did . . . anything for myself?"

Why do I even try to spell this out for him? We go through this every three months or so. If he only knew my heart's light switches are flickering off.

She spun to the side of the bed, sat up straight, and said, "Look, this isn't the kind of relationship I imagined us having. I feel like we're growing apart. And please don't like you don't feel it too."

Oliver flinched. "Does this have anything to do with your job and that one patient at the hospital?"

Her head fell into her hands. "No. Maybe. I don't know." She looked up at him. "That patient inspires me. He lives life on purpose despite his disabilities. It would be nice if we shared goals about redesigning our marriage. If we lived with purpose. We have no sense of direction. Let me grab my Bible, so I can show you something."

Bills flew off the bed again, but she didn't care. This held top priority. *I just want us on the same page, living with purpose and moving in the same direction. Why does that feel like so much work?*

While she thumbed through the scriptures, Oliver pivoted to leave the room. "Let's just live and let live."

"Please just listen for a minute."

He came back and placed his elbow on the brown dresser to prop up his head, pretending to listen.

Two minutes in, Oliver drew a desperate breath and this time, with an annoyed tone, said, "Look, I just want us to make love more. I assumed the frequency slowed way down because of the kids and life feeling so hectic, but even with the kids at summer camp two weeks ago, nothing, nada, zilch. The only time we get close to making love is when I initiate. What happened to our passion? Call me a pig, lame, 'a man,' whatever you want. Just know that's when I feel most connected to you, O." He rubbed his forehead. "What I want—*need*—is I want you to want me, O."

Olivia leaned back against the headboard and sighed. "I don't know."

"Don't know what?"

"Never mind." *Ugh, these bills could've been paid by now.*

He took a step closer. "Are you hearing me, O? We both have needs. You say 'later' and 'later, later,' and 'tonight,' but you say that and then half the time when it becomes 'tonight,' you tell me you're too tired. Then you say 'try again tomorrow,' but you're out the door in the morning, and besides, why is it always *me* who's required to 'try'?"

"Honestly?" She sighed and rolled her eyes.

"Yes, be honest."

"Okay, Oliver. You make sex feel like a chore." She thought that'd get him out.

"So I'm a chore, huh?" His mouth twisted. "That's what you think of me?" His head shook, hurt, like a bobble head doll. "Figures."

"I didn't say that."

"Ya. Ya, you did. *You* said, 'you make it feel like a chore.'"

She got up off the bed and faced him. "No. What I'm saying is that I feel like it's just one more thing I have to do."

"Mmm, that makes me feel so much better." He slipped his hands into his jean pockets.

She pressed a fist against her mouth and puffed out her cheeks. "Look, I'm just not in the mood, okay?" She gazed at her pillow, longing for a good cry to put her to sleep.

"Mmm, hmm. Let me ask you . . ." He lifted his hands, palms up. "Seriously, a serious question. Are you ever in the mood anymore? I mean, like, do you even know what sex is?"

Olivia dropped her head and rubbed her temples, feeling like she wasn't enough—even while feeling like she did so much. "I told you I'm exhausted . . . I'll let you know when I am."

Oliver shrugged, then nodded and twisted his mouth. "So . . . will that happen prior to the next presidential cycle or . . . some other cycle?"

She spun back around, pointing her finger at him. "Okay, I can't take it anymore. You think you're funny, but you can be so cruel sometimes."

His eyebrows arched. "Maybe it's you who's acting cruel. You ever thought about that?"

"Oh, all the time, Oliver." She nodded affirmatively, then picked up a dirty towel and threw it over to the laundry basket, an air ball.

Oliver kicked at the carpet. "Look, O, I'm just trying to be honest. I have needs."

"Yes, I know. I can tell by the porn sites I found on the Internet's history page."

He froze. His face went pale, a huge contrast to Mickey Mouse's smile on his shirt.

"What's wrong, cat got your tongue?" She leaned in.

His voice faltered. "You saw those?"

"Yes, and I have feelings, you know." She picked up her Bible and put it close to his chest. "Maybe if you started coming to church with me, things would be different."

Oliver was biting his thumbnail. "So you're saying that if I go to church with you, we'll have more sex?"

"That's not what I'm saying, Oliver. Ugh!" She fell to the bed in exhaustion.

Oliver stepped forward and lowered his voice. "Truth be told, I didn't even care if we had sex tonight. I just want to remind you that my love language is touch, and all I'm hearing is complaints about how bad *you* have it. 'Woe is me.' Why can't you just look on the bright side of things, O?"

He so infuriating I just want to wring his neck sometimes. He doesn't see what I do around here, much less show any appreciation. Her heart pounded against her ribcage. *Just breathe, Olivia. Don't say anything you'll regret.*

She sighed. "Do you want me to just be a hollow plastic doll with a fake smile?" She sprawled herself on the bed and offered up her best Barbie doll impersonation. "Oh, take me Oliver!"

"Whatever." He rolled his eyes.

She sat up. "Look, Oliver, my asking for help hasn't reached you clearly. I take responsibility for the weak manner in which I've cried out for help, but hear me loud and clear now: I'm drowning!" She waved around the room to the pile of dirty clothes, myriad of bills, and dirty bathroom.

"You don't think I carry heavy responsibilities at work?" Oliver blinked rapidly and rubbed the back of his neck.

Olivia briefly closed her eyes and gritted her teeth, taking in a slow breath through the nostrils. She couldn't believe she kept having to repeat herself. "Of course, but I go to work too. I cook, clean, chauffeur, and clock in at work. After working, I come home to a pigsty, which somehow you don't see, make dinner, help with homework, put dishes in the washer, clean the kitchen, get our kids ready for bed, all while you're what? Watching TV or reading a book. Because the game is soooo important. Why is it always game seven or in the last two minutes of overtime? You spend your life watching the end of games, but lately I feel like we're nearing our own end."

"Did you just threaten me?"

"Maybe if you treated me like you did at the start, there'd never be talk of an end. All I do is keep this house moving forward while you focus on your games, your porn, your pleasures, your whatever. Then you have the gall to come in here and ask me about making love. Making *love*? I don't even know who you are anymore. Love is the last thing I feel right now."

Oliver wagged a finger, berating Olivia for her accusations. "So what do you want? You want me to tell you I appreciate you every time you pay a bill or check the mail?" He reenacted opening the mail. "Oh, look at me, my name is Olivia and I open the mail and do the dishes. Give me a gold medal everyone!"

Olivia felt her body temperature rise and wanted to scream. She did. "You are so full of hate, Oliver!"

It grew silent, like a country park with only the slightest of wind blowing an empty swing.

Olivia burst out sobbing.

Oliver rushed to put his arm around her. After a few moments, Olivia sat straight up to remove the notion that he could hurt her.

"Oliver, it's not just about the house responsibilities. I miss the mini moments of kindness you used to give, like a reassuring touch, a kind word, and a loving hug. I know you do a lot at work. I just need you to pitch in at home, you know, to show some, I don't know."

Oliver started breathing again, then adjusted his ball cap. "Well, I thought I did. I remove spyware off the computer, make sure Netflix is working, and pick out the right electronics."

Olivia pulled her knees in and hung her head, letting out a long exhale. "Oliver, I'm at a breaking point. I can't do this anymore."

A long dark silence enveloped them.

"Are you saying you want me to move out so that you can live alone with the kids?" He stood and reached for his clothes in the closet, like he'd start packing those first.

"I already *feel* all alone." She looked away and her voice trailed off.

He sighed loud enough for the neighbors to hear. "Oliva, I haven't had an affair, dragged us into debt, abused you, become a drug dealer, or drank us into poverty, and you're threatening me with this nonsense?"

"I'm not threatening you. I just feel . . . alone. Really alone. I can't keep playing second fiddle."

Oliver placed his hands on his knees and leaned forward. "What, like you feel invisible or something?"

Her head cocked to the side, and she clamped her hands around her waist. "It's not that I feel invisible, but that I feel visibly ignored, and I have way too many responsibilities demanding my energy that I'm not living the life that matters most to me. Time is ticking and we're not getting any younger. What the heck are we doing, Oliver? Are we living with purpose? Do we *have* a purpose—together? I don't think we're designed to just pay bills, clean dishes, and watch the last two minutes of games."

He raised his eyebrows like he was hearing her talking like this for the first time.

"Please don't act like this is coming out of the blue. I keep calling out for help. Days turned into weeks and months. I still have the second half of my life, and I'm not going to keep living this way, Oliver. It's not a threat. It's just the way it is. I won't do it."

The doorbell rang.

Oliver turned toward the door. "Are you expecting someone?"

"No, are you?" She scooted off the bed.

They walked to the front room, opened the door, and didn't see anyone.

Just a brown box with a yellow ribbon tied around it with a yellow bow.

Oliver bent over, grabbed it, and shook it.

"What is it?" Olivia leaned in.

"If I knew that, I'd be a magician in Vegas."

She shook her head and blew out a breath that rattled her lips. "Just bring it in, and let's open it."

Once the box hit the kitchen island, Oliver tore into it.

"Be careful of the bow." Olivia craned her neck to see.

I wish he wouldn't look at me like I'm crazy.

With the box now open, Olivia asked again, "What is it?"

"A treasure chest!" His eyes opened like he just found the answer for how to quit his job.

"What? Let me see." She grabbed his shoulder and leaned over to get a peak.

Oliver took the small red treasure chest out of the brown box and passed it to her. The chest looked a half foot long and couldn't have weighed more than five pounds. *Wow, this feels like walnut, and these are iron hoops, with a gold key attached.* "Look at the top. It says, 'Take this key to room 7. *Happily-ever-after* awaits.'"

"What?" Oliver cocked his head back in disbelief. "Let me see it. Someone's pulling our chain." Oliver leaned on the island.

"It could be true." Olivia tugged and pulled at the key. "I can't seem to get the key off this chest."

"Here, let me try." When Oliver couldn't remove the key, he set the chest down. "What the heck does this mean?"

"How am I supposed to know?" She eyed the chest.

"Well, where's room 7 supposed to be? A hotel? Oh, you want to go to a hotel with me?"

"Stop it, Oliver. I'm serious. That key probably opens something special." Olivia bit her nails.

"Hey, look, there's more in the box. It's a scroll." Oliver reached for it.

Interesting.

The scroll was sealed with a royal logo cast in red wax. He broke the seal and unrolled the scroll. Out fell a golden ticket with the words "The Couples' Castle" on the front and "The Relationship Blueprint to Experience the Ultimate Relationship, Find the Love of Your Life, and Make Your Marriage A Masterpiece" on the other side.

"This is kinda like a Willy Wonka ticket," Oliver said.

Her eyes turned to the scroll while Oliver read out loud,

Dear Oliver and Olivia Keets:

We are pleased to offer you this golden ticket for a three-day experience at *The Couples' Castle*. It's where people get the best strategies to experience the ultimate relationship, find/keep the love of their life, make their marriage a masterpiece, and live an authentic *happily-ever-after*. To receive these benefits, you must find the red treasure chest similar to the model chest next to you. It's in room 7, and you'll need your gold key to open it. Find the real treasure chest, unlock it with your key, and what's inside will sprinkle you with power beyond fairy tales and pixie dust. What awaits you in the red treasure chest is the best thing you will ever experience in your whole life.

Should you choose to accept this invitation, please get your blood work done (our safety first policy) at the local hospital and send the results to the return address. Then dress in business casual attire, wear comfortable walking shoes, and meet at the North Street lamp in Evermore Park one week from Wednesday, a little before midnight. A driver will pick you up. Bring the golden ticket for entrance and the key attached to your red treasure chest for room 7. Everything's been building toward this.

Olivia picked up the treasure chest and gripped the key in her hand.

*   *   *

"Do you believe in Heaven?" Isabella sat on the lakeside bench watching the sunset bounce off the creamy blue waters.

Zeb knew the real reason she asked the question. She had that look in her eyes again. Instead of offering up a verbal solution this time, he let her words float up into the air over the water. He looked in the opposite direction toward the kids and rolled his lucky half dollar coin over his knuckles.

"Well do you?" Isabella's voice trailed off like she was seeing things.

Zeb's compassion for her was real, but he just couldn't deal with this again - not right now. He knew she needed him, really needed him, but he had his own issues and so he quickly changed the subject. He pinched his belly together and said, "I've really let myself go, haven't I, hun? Jeez, my abs look like layered Jell-O." The office made Zeb feel locked up like a caged animal at the zoo. All his promotions over the years were a disguised path to a prison from which he could find no escape. He was stuck in his job and barely had time for anything interesting anymore, let alone the gym.

"You're not that out of shape, Zeb, and hey, you're jogging again, and you've lost twenty pounds!"

"I know, but doc says I still have twenty-five more to go before I'm out of the danger zone. And that's not even my healthy range." Although relieved to have successfully changed subjects, Zeb's downturned mouth revealed his depression about being overweight.

"Like a caterpillar turning into a butterfly. All good things take time." She kissed him on the cheek.

"Do caterpillars know they're going to turn into butterflies, or are they sitting in those cocoons thinking, 'What the heck am I doing with my life?'" He couldn't take his eyes off his belly.

"I like this." Her feet rocked back and forth over the grass.

"Like what?" Zeb knew she was putting on a front.

"Us spending time together. Taking walks together." She looked up into his eyes, then rested her head on his arm.

"Me too. The more I stay at home, the more homeless I look. You know, babe, your husband here, back in the day, was once in shape."

"I know. I've seen your old family photos. Speaking of family, my mom will be over soon, so we need to get home."

Zeb pushed himself up off the bench, knowing full well that if Isabella wasn't ten minutes early to every appointment, she'd experience shortness of breaths and flashbacks - even after all these years. He called out, "Yo, kids, time to go."

Adella and Nathan giggled about something they saw in the water, then managed their way up from the water banks to follow their parents around the lake's path toward home. Their golden cairn terrier, AJ, followed close behind the kids.

Isabella's hair was blowing in her face. "It's windy, but the trees sure are gorgeous this time of year."

"I agree, but fall would be that much prettier if the grass also changed colors."

"Ha ha, that would be colorful! By the way, have you and Cindy worked out how we're going to get all the kids under our roof for Thanksgiving?" She rubbed her elbow.

"No, have you worked it out with Mike yet?"

"Touché. This whole blended family thing's a lot tougher than I expected. Your kids are doing better adjusting than mine though." She took a deep breath and sighed.

"You're telling me. I need a better-paying job. The alimony and child support payments are taking their toll." Zeb scratched the back of his neck.

Isabella stopped. "What do you mean? Are the finances under control?"

Zeb heard a bird flapping its wings as it took flight from a nearby tree. "For now. I have some buyers interested in the homes listed." *If she only knew the weight I carry on my shoulders with providing for the family.*

The kids pointed out the frogs and flowers along the path while Isabella wondered out loud, "I bet neither of us ever thought growing up that we'd go through divorce, remarriage, and a blended family."

"I'm glad I found you though."

She smiled, and they started walking again. "It's crazy. We're just a year in, and we rarely put our marriage first anymore. Sometimes I feel like I'm losing my mind, especially when Cindy comes over to get your kids."

You think you have it bad? "Try being stuck in a job you hate."

She didn't seem to hear him, like she talked just to talk so that she didn't have to think how close October 19th was. "Our kids must've grown accustomed to us putting them before our relationship because they're sure vying for our attention more than I can remember at any time in the past."

"Seconded." Zeb helped her step over a tree branch on the sidewalk.

"And we became so set in our own ways before marrying again."

Ahh, the days when I had more money. Crazy, I make more now but see less. Explain that formula to me, Albert Einstein.

Isabella called out, "Kids! Get away from the edge."

The wind rustled the leaves of the nearby trees. Zeb knew her hypervigilance was justified from her perspective, but it was keeping their kids from feeling free. "Honey, just a gentle reminder that if our kids don't start feeling more free they're going to have a lot to unlearn from us before they grow into their true selves - and it'll probably be through therapist payments." He let go of her hand and looked off in the distance at two squirrels scrabbling around tree trunks.

"Well, if we don't keep them safe, they may not grow up at all."

"Let's not do this again."

"You can be so insensitive, Zeb."

Zeb knew he couldn't say anything. He could never say anything. Her problem always overshadowed anything he had going on. "Nobody ever warned us about meshing parenting styles and methods of discipline, did they? Maybe we should've discussed all that prior to marrying."

Isabella cupped an elbow with one hand and tapped the lips with the other. "What do you think about adding more structure, maybe with color-coded magnets, chore charts, and a centralized calendar? You know, something to unify the family and keep us on the same page?"

There's her high J from the Myers-Briggs coming out again, trying to dominate the family routines. Why am I being so critical? This job stress is going to kill our marriage—if not me first. "Maybe we could try it out. I'll tell you what. You organize it. Then we'll have a family meeting. I can't wait to see how the kids take it." He laughed at the thought of their wrinkled noses and lame excuses.

Isabella kicked a rock, then raised a finger like she had a new idea. "That reminds me, and you feel this way too, so I'm genuinely asking what we can do about it. Whenever you're critical of Adella's piano lessons, I feel like there's a murderer rising up in me. I know there's a double standard, since I'm critical too. So I guess, I'm just wondering how we move past feeling that way when one of us is critical about the other's kids? Is it possible?"

"Anything's possible," he said, clearing his throat. He felt a sudden pain in his chest.

The smell of burning leaves was just around the corner, and they turned to look at the lake one last time before finishing their walk. The slight breeze felt nice on the skin.

"Hey, before we get home, I'd like to bring up just one other thing?"

Zeb wondered if she'd ask for something that would cost more money, like another vacation or car, and his chest pain intensified. He wished more than anything that he could provide better. He hated his job, but knew he couldn't just up and quit with all his family responsibilities. Zeb felt so stuck and the energy drained from his already pale face. He turned his head away from her, sighed, and searched the sky in quiet desperation. "Of course, honey."

She rubbed his arm with her other hand. "Please don't think less of me, but, and I know I shouldn't be, but sometimes I find myself jealous of Cindy. Knowing you chose her and me in this lifetime sometimes drives me crazy, especially since you had children together." She crossed her arms in front of her chest. "I know, I did too. I'm just being honest."

"I understand." *Why can't we just walk in peace for these last few blocks? Where's* Star Trek's *beam-me-over thing when you need it? I'd like to beam myself over to my recliner, get some stress-free time in front of the TV before I have to go back to a dead-end job.*

"Again, I'm just trying to be honest."

Zeb's own insecurities bubbled to the surface, but he kept them to himself. How could he adequately provide for Isabella and the new family unit? He kept making more money but it never seemed to be enough. She didn't have to work in her previous marriage. And those comments she made about missing seeing her kids grow up and not being able to participate in their school functions crushed him. *It's like I'm never enough.* Since abandoning Isabella and the kids wasn't an option, Zeb wondered how he could die where the insurance company would still leave his family the money. What he really wanted to do was turn around and walk straight into the lake until he just... disappeared.

He rubbed his forehead and encouraged her to finish the walk. "You know, honey, I read a statistic the other day that 65 percent of blended families end in divorce."

"Really?" Her eyes widened.

"I don't want that to happen to us." But if this stress kept up, he wouldn't live much longer anyway.

"Wow, that's a high number." She looked sideways at him. "I wonder what the other 35 percent do to stay married and if they're even happy or just too tired to divorce again."

A man raking fallen leaves near the sidewalk paused long enough to let them walk by.

"That'd be nice to know. Is there anyone we can sit down with and get advice from? Or a couple we could model after? A couple where the man is working a lot?"

Isabella thanked the man with the rake and then turned back to Zeb. "Let me ask you, and be honest, on a scale of 1-10, how happy are you with our marriage?"

If it was just us, and we didn't have to worry about income? A 7 or 8. But as it stands, a 2. "You're a 10, Isabella."

"That's not what I asked." She squeezed his hand and smiled.

"Well, what do you think?" *Ah yes, a question with a question—Socrates style.*

"Our relationship feels like a yo-yo. The number fluctuates, anywhere from an 8 to a 2. Don't you think so?"

"Sure, I guess."

They turned a corner and entered their subdivision. AJ ran right past them after a stick the kids threw.

"I wonder if it's possible to be truly happy, like most of the time you know? To flourish again, this time in a blended family marriage. I just never thought about our situation while growing up."

Zeb thought about how her getting a salaried job would help them feel happier. *I doubt she'll ever talk about that. They start the feminist movement and demand rights for salaried jobs, then all the prices in the marketplace significantly increase to handle a dual income household, but then where's that leave those of us where the woman wants to stay at home and raise the kids?*

The kids and AJ ran until they were a block ahead, now chasing orange and black butterflies—safe as long as they stayed on the sidewalk and paused to look both ways before each driveway.

"Well," Zeb answered, "I know psychologists and counselors talk about relationship stages that include the honeymoon stage, accommodation stage, challenge stage, and uh . . . the crossroads stage, maybe . . . something like that. Oh, and the rebirth stage, which is something about how there's a time when you realize who you *really* married and accept it. So I guess it depends on what you're looking for."

She studied his face. "Do you think it's possible to flourish in any of those stages or do you have to go through stages in order to flourish?"

"Flourish in any stage." *The summer of my first love proves it. I wonder what ever happened to her.*

When they were about one block from home, Isabella started talking faster, while Zeb was lost in thought about that romantic summer fifteen years ago. When he looked up, a man in a black tux was walking away from their porch and climbing into a black limousine.

"What in the world?" Isabella squinted to get a clearer view.

"Who's that?"

Their pace quickened, and a moment later, Adella shouted, "Mom! Dad! There's a brown box with a yellow bow sitting on the front porch! Can we open it?"

Chapter 2

Evermore Park

At eleven thirty, Zebediah and Isabella, after making arrangements with Cindy and Mike to watch the kids, stepped out the front door to make the fifteen-minute hike to Evermore Park.

When they approached the lamplight, Isabella whispered, "Are those *people*?"

"It appears so," Zeb said in a soft whisper. He prayed Isabella would hold it together on this trip. October 19th was rapidly approaching. "They look safe."

She clutched his arm. "Maybe more couples were invited."

Royal buzz sailed through the warm fall air. *Golden tickets, treasure chests, and an escort to a Couples' Castle.* As they drew nearer, the faces became visible under the lamplight. *What the . . . ?* Zeb's head jerked back, eyes widened, and his mouth fell open. He stopped dead in his tracks, squeezed his eyes shut and then opened. *Olivia?*

She saw him too.

Olivia's hand flew to her chest, spreading the fingers out in a fan across her breastbone. She shuffled back a step or two and tripped over the outer wooden beam that enclosed the playground, landing hard on the woodchips adjacent to the swing set.

Everyone rushed to her side—everyone, that is, except Zeb.

Could it really be Olivia? His pulse raced, and he walked in circles while raking his fingers through his hair. His mind sifted through past images of the powerful first love they shared years ago.

They first bumped into each other in the small Colorado town where, fresh out of college, he visited his widowed mom. It'd been two years since he'd last seen his mom, but when she found out the doctor's report, she requested he visit at once.

Zeb sauntered through a Colorado park, enjoying the memorial outdoor concert and festivities, when Olivia's striking beauty caught his eye. They were walking in opposite directions—she toward the concert and he toward the food trucks—when their shoulders brushed just enough for them both to pivot and say "Sorry, excuse me."

Her eyes were so deep and full of promise and pleasure that he babbled his way through the apology while the crowds of concertgoers swirled around them like butterflies.

"C'mon!" Olivia's friends hollered. Keeping her eyes locked onto his, she cracked a smile while back stepping toward her friends.

He couldn't figure out what it was about her that made him feel alive again. He'd never dated someone of a different skin color before. Was it her smile? Her wavy hair? The way she looked at him? He thought his face might melt off, and he scrambled to say something, anything before she disappeared forever.

Above the hustle and bustle of the crowd, he hollered, "Can I buy you a funnel cake?" *That's the best you could come up with? Idiot!*

Olivia's friends giggled and grabbed her arms. "C'mon, the new band just jumped on stage. Hurry, let's find a good seat!"

Olivia joined her friends but turned again and gave him a warm wave.

He felt such a fire in his heart that he wasn't even upset with the gruff middle-aged man in overalls who tumbled into his backside. Life seemed to make complete sense in Olivia's smile.

Later that night, he found her sitting on a blanket with two of her girlfriends, enjoying the last band of the evening. He was glad he'd put on his good purple shirt this morning. "Is this seat taken?"

Her friends started whispering.

"It's public property." She offered him a divine smile, followed with a refined shrug.

Pull yourself together, Zeb. You can do this. He sat next to her on the blanket, swallowing hard.

"I didn't say public property extended to the blanket." She raised one eyebrow with a grin lighting up her face.

"Oh, I'm sorry." He moved over to the grass and crossed and uncrossed his arms.

She had her hair pinned in a hippie hairstyle with a modern messy braid and beautiful flowing waves. The flower crowns are a little strange, but the way her lavender summer dress flowed around her body made up for it. She was picture perfect for this summer festival.

"Is the band any good?" Zeb picked at the dandelions.

"They're all right."

They looked up at the stage, then at each other. This band put the finishing touches on the day's festivities. Hundreds of people surrounded them on this Memorial Day weekend, sitting on blankets, wavy grass, and each other's laps. The temperature felt like a May sixty-five degrees.

"What's your name?" Zeb threw a dandelion straight ahead.

"What's yours?" Olivia countered, shifting her head askance with eyebrows raised.

"Zebediah, but people who like me call me 'Zeb.'"

"Oh, that's a nice name, 'Zeb . . . ediah.'"

Ah, she's witty too. Brains and body. "Aren't you going to tell me your name?"

"What, and remove the mystery?" She smiled.

I can't believe I'm talking to her. You need to get over your cottonmouth, quick. "Okay, how about, if I guess your name, you have to dance with me when the band plays its next slow song?"

She flinched. "That's crazy. Nobody around here is even standing, let alone dancing. Not happening."

"But what if it turns out to be the greatest dance of your life?"

Her head flinched. "That's a big 'if.'" She pressed her dress down her legs.

His confidence was unwavering. "I just want what's best for you, and this could be the best dance you ever experience. Will you take me up on the deal?"

"Okay, deal, but you get two minutes max to figure out my name. If you don't guess it, you have to buy all those kids over there some cotton candy."

He sat up and looked past the crowd. "What? Those kids playing jump rope?"

"Yes, and the smaller ones watching them."

He turned to face her. "Deal." He felt a lightness in his chest every time they made eye contact.

"Starting now." She set the timer on her phone.

C'mon, Zeb. You can do this. "Is it Cinderella?"

She rolled her eyes. "Cheesy."

"Okay, Tyra." He pointed his index finger at her like he got it right. She shook her head no, trying to hide her smile.

"Victoria?"

"Nope."

"Jasmine?"

She shook her head again.

"Caiden?"

"Oh, you got it . . . wrong again."

What'd Mom always say? Women like guys who make them laugh? "Well, can you tell me how you spell it?"

"N. I. C. E. T. R. Y."

"Is it Bailey? Becky? Faith?" He looked to the sky for answers. "Tonya? Chloe? Heaven?" *Please, God, help me out here.*

"One minute left." She picked one of his dandelions and twirled it in her fingers.

Just then the band stopped playing their version of Lynyrd Skynyrd's "Free Falling" and announced their next song, Shania Twain's, "From This Moment."

"Okay," Zeb said in a rush, "clap three times and tell me your mom's maiden name."

"Telfer," she said, amused.

"Now think of a number between twelve and thirty-seven."

"Got it." She gently bit her lip.

"Now add seven to the number you picked," Zeb suggested like a mind reader.

"Okay," Olivia replied, sneaking a look over at her friends.

"Hey, look back here, into my eyes. I'm about to get it." He moved to his knees.

Olivia sat up straight, cleared her throat, looked into his eyes, and said with a straight face, "Thirty seconds, hombre."

"Is your name . . ." *Oh, I got nothing.* "I'd do better if you'd put the palms of your hands in mine."

She tilted her head to the left. "You don't think I know what you're trying to do?"

"C'mon. Trust me." He placed his hands in front of her.

"Okay, give it a shot, but you have fifteen seconds. Those kids are going to get a sugar high tonight." When she grabbed his hands, he felt like he could do anything, be anyone. She appeared ready to confess an answer, like she wanted him to get it so she could dance with him, when, instead, she started counting down, "Eleven. Ten. Nine. Eight . . ."

He spit out names in rapid fire.

The band was just under way with "From this moment on . . ." Couples everywhere looked on from their seated positions, an enchanted charm in the air. He could sit there forever with their hands touching.

"Seven. Six. Five."

When she got to five, one of Olivia's friends shouted, "Olivia. Say 'Olivia'!"

Zeb stole a quick glance at the friend to say thank you.

"Olivia." The name rolled off his tongue like a slow kiss.

"Not fair!" She pulled her hands away, spun around, and smacked her friend. He couldn't help but look at the back of her legs when she did.

Her friends bellowed out such loud laughter that nearby families coughed in annoyance. Zeb stood and offered her his right hand in an invitation to dance.

"I'm not getting up in front of all these people." She shook her head and held her breath, eyes darting left to right.

She likes you, Zeb. She's just indecisive right now. "You either dance with me, or I go up to the stage and ask the band if I can sing a song that's dedicated to you."

Her jaw dropped. "You wouldn't."

"I would." He turned toward the stage.

The band's lyrics echoed throughout the park.

She reached to hold on to her friends, but her smile betrayed her. *You can do this, Zeb.*

He motioned toward the stage, his eyes ping-ponging between her and the band.

She didn't say anything, and her arched eyebrows looked like she was calling his bluff.

Olivia's friends gave her a friendly push in the shoulder. "Olivia!"

But she kept looking at him with that face that said "Go ahead."

Fine then. What was the worst that could happen? He stepped toward the stage.

"Wait!" She shook her head and drew a deep breath.

The people around her cried out, "Shhh!"

Yes! "Wait, what?"

"I'll dance with you."

Oh my gosh. This is the best day of my life. He tried to play it cool when walking back over to help her up, but underneath—his heart beat faster than he could ever remember.

In a park buzzing with families and food vendors, they danced. They were the only ones dancing, and Zeb couldn't help but flash the biggest smile of his life.

The rest of the summer, Zeb spent romancing her into a relationship—everything from showing up unannounced with beautiful flowers to writing sweet nothings and delivering them to her at work to serenading her from her front lawn at night. Despite the looks they received from others regarding the interracial relationship, he swept her off her feet. They took long strolls under the stars, danced in the quiet meadows, talked weekend nights until 2:00 a.m. on her porch swing, and even took an intensive two-week crash course in French for their planned trip to Paris together.

Their most exciting night landed on the Fourth of July, when they sneaked away from her family at the park to a nearby lake, just when the fireworks were about to light up the sky. Lying there looking at the stars, they noticed a vine hanging down from a tree, just over the water's edge. They joked about jumping in, but neither wanted to get their clothes wet.

"Have you ever been skinny-dipping?" Olivia lay motionless.

"Uh no." A flush of adrenaline tingled through his body, his breathing momentarily suspended.

"So you probably haven't been with anyone before either? Or have you? You don't have to answer if you don't want to."

His ears burned. "No, that's okay. I'm a . . . virgin. That okay?"

"Of course," she said. "I am too. I plan to stay that way until marriage. I made a promise to God."

"Oh." *A Christian girl. Hmm.*

"Does that scare you?" She moved to get closer.

"No, not at all." After all this time dating, they still hadn't kissed. His mouth became moist, his fingers ached with the need to touch her.

The fireworks sailed through the sky. She nestled under his arm, and he interlaced their hands. When she tilted her head to gauge him from the corner of her eye, he lowered his face to hers and leaned in, his lips coming close. As her lips parted, Zeb stopped inches away and stroked her cheek until his thumb traced a line along her lower lip so that he could savor the experience. A wave of warmth flowed through his heart when he rested his forehead against hers. He leaned in again until their lips met. Wrapping his hands around her waist, he drew her closer.

Her lips feel soft, like a strawberry candy sucker.

When he pulled away, she said, "Well . . ."

"Well, what?" His breathing quickened.

"What do you think about a night swim?" A wide grin grew across her face.

"A night swim?" *Seriously? It's cold in the water.*

"Skinny-dipping, but we'll keep our undergarments on." She pushed him to the side, then jumped to her feet.

With flushed skin and a high-pitched voice, he said, "Ya, of course."

She'd just taken off her shoes, and he began to unbutton his shirt when they heard her friends call out, "Olivia, are you back there? Olivia?"

They quickly glanced at each other and giggled. Wanting an evening to themselves, Zeb and Olivia rushed to put their shoes and shirt back on and raced back to the park before the end of the fireworks display. Once there, they jogged to the baseball diamond, leaned against the centerfield fence, and laughed. The sky lit up with promise about their bright future.

In late July, Olivia took Zeb out to her countryside house when her parents were out of state. *What's this? Candles, wine glasses, and is that a framed picture of us from our first dance, the night I met her in the park?* He bounced lightly in place and felt a tingling in his hands.

After dinner, they moved to the living room and snuggled on the couch in front of the crackling fire. He placed his hand on her leg, and she turned her eyes to meet his. "I don't know what will happen from here on out, but I want you to know something."

"What is it?" She rubbed his leg.

"Promise me you won't laugh?" He felt weightless.

"I pinky swear." She stretched out her pinky for him to grab.

"I love you."

She lifted her chin to expose her neck, then looked up into his eyes.

A warm flutter swirled in his stomach. He craned his head to kiss her on the forehead.

They cuddled there, her head on his chest, feet kicked up on the ottoman, eyes reflecting the crackling fire.

"Zeb."

"Yes?"

"I love you too."

They fell asleep in each other's arms.

* * *

The next morning Olivia awoke—surprised to find herself alone on the couch. She stretched her arms, moseyed to the kitchen, and found a note on the table.

> Dear Olivia, thank you. Thank you for being you. Thank you for the best summer of my life. This is hard to say, so I wrote it. I had to leave. Back to Virginia. I know this seems out of the blue and really crazy, but it's for a reason best left unsaid, something important. Please trust me. I'm not running from us. In fact, this is best for you. It's not fair to tell you why. I'm sorry.

"What am I supposed to do with that? This whole summer was perfect. I don't understand," she muttered to herself and dropped the letter.

Olivia searched for answers, including reaching out to Zeb's mom, since she lived in the area. Ashamed that she'd never visited her home, she found her number listed online and called, but when no one answered, she drove over to meet with her. When Olivia pulled up, she noted a *For Sale* sign in the yard. She rang the doorbell anyway. When no one answered, she peeked in the window—vacant. She continued to search for Zeb on social media, but nothing. She thought about taking a flight to Virginia but didn't want to look desperate. After weeks of confusion, sadness, and anger, everyone, including her mom and friends, encouraged her to move on. So she did, as much as one could move on from a first love.

*   *   *

"Zeb, Zeb! Help us!" Isabella called out.

Zeb couldn't stop walking in contemplative circles. *There she is, and that must be her husband. What the heck?*

"It looks like she'll be okay. I don't think we'll need to phone an ambulance or anything." Olivia's husband took a deep breath through his nose and helped her to her feet.

A white stretch limo rolled around the corner at midnight right on time.

The oncoming headlights blinded him, and the thought of getting in the limo with Olivia made him feel like his insides were vibrating. Zeb had never told Isabella about her. He swallowed hard.

Out of the driver's seat stepped a tall Albino man with a black top hat, black cane, and a red bow tie. He walked to the rear of the limo, opened the door, and said matter-of-factly, "If you're coming to the Couples' Castle, please introduce yourselves to one another, if you haven't already, then step into the vehicle."

While the couples exchanged pleasantries, Olivia and Zeb shot a look of disbelief to each other. Under the light, Zeb could see her eyes go wide, showing the whites. He felt his ulcer acting up.

He turned to Isabella and lowered his voice. "I just don't think this is a very good idea—this limo and Couples' Castle stuff. What if something bad happens? Let's go home."

Her head flinched back slightly. "Maybe you're right, honey. It's just . . ."

"Just what?" He tapped her elbow to get them going.

"We need help. We talked about this. No matter how crazy this gets, it can't be crazier than our blended family right now. So maybe this is a little bizarre, but right now, I can tell the family's driving you crazy. And now look. We didn't even think a limo would actually show up. Maybe getting in the limo isn't safe, but thinking it's all going to work out at home without any help or new strategies . . . that's more dangerous."

Oliver stepped forward. "Maybe Zeb's right. I mean, who's ever heard of a Couples' Castle?"

*   *   *

Oh boy, now they're all looking at us. Olivia felt like her insides were quivering.

"You're all asking the wrong questions," the Albino said, scanning the group. Oliver turned toward the driver. "What are you talking about?"

"Inside the Couples' Castle is the relationship blueprint for living happily ever after in today's world. Your relationship is the most important part of your life and yet the least mastered. By coming to the castle, you're going to find something that will prove to be the best thing you've ever experienced. You'll get the world's best strategies on how to experience the ultimate relationship, find the love of your life, and make your marriage a masterpiece. To prove it, I'll give you one strategy right now, even if you decide not to get into the limo."

Isabella gave him a sideways glance.

The limo driver walked toward them so they could hear clearly. "The couples who ask better questions of one another are the couples who experience the best relationships. Whether in speaking *to* each other or when thinking *about* each other, make sure your questions are framed the right way."

Olivia's lips were slightly parted and she wondered where this limo driver—this stranger with a red bow tie—was going.

He stopped ten feet in front of them, with the playground about twenty feet behind them, and gestured calmly. "Your brain is always, always, always . . . asking questions—all day long, every day—whether to yourself or to others, so make them helpful questions, ones that generate pleasurable feelings for each other."

"What do you mean?" Emma formed a steeple with her hands and pressed them to her lips.

"Well, the brain, like a computer, can only find answers to match the kinds of questions you employ. So when you're over here emptying questions like 'What if something bad happens at the castle?' your brain will only look for negative answers to match the negative question."

He walked over to Oliver and Olivia and turned them to face each other. "If Oliver here questions Olivia 'Will you make love to me?' her brain will find an answer to mirror the question asked—she will answer that question and only that question and in the tone with which he asked. In other words, she won't come up with an answer about the Cold War, not in a political sense anyway. My hypothesis is she'll say no because of how he asked. One's energy even matches the way the question is posed. That is because she framed his question negatively, she gave a negative answer."

Olivia's face turned beet red, and her knees locked tight together. She wished she'd worn the coat with her hood as she glanced around for a place to hide.

"But do take note," the driver insisted, "if Oliver changes the way he questions, Olivia will change her response."

"Why didn't my dad tell me about this when he talked to me about the birds and the bees?" Oliver shook his head.

This was getting more embarrassing by the second. She closed her jacket tighter and gritted her teeth, pressing her lips tight.

"Say Oliver approaches Olivia in a kind, warm, and understanding way. Body language is part of our communication, after all, so it's part of the question."

"Okay," Olivia said hurriedly, hoping to speed this conversation up.

"And if Oliver then said, 'Honey, I see you're paying the bills'—"

"Word? Have you been spying on us?" Oliver sized the driver up.

"Let's just say we know a lot more than you think." The driver continued, pretending to be Oliver's voice. "Honey, I see you're paying the bills. Thank you. I appreciate you. You do so much around here, and I don't tell you that enough. I bet if I did just half of what you do, I'd be worn out. I'm going into the kitchen now to do the dishes, and maybe later you'll let me rub your shoulders before I put the moves on you to demonstrate how grateful I am for you."

"Put the moves on?" Olivia raised her eyebrows.

The driver winked at her with his ocean-blue eyes. "Baby steps."

Oliver chimed in. "That sounds like a lot of work just to, you know."

Olivia put her hands on her hips and gave him the side eye. *I can't believe he just said that in front of everyone, especially Zebediah. And what the heck is he doing here after all these years anyway?*

The driver added, "It's less work than you *putting the moves* on Olivia when you first dated. You went all out to woo her. You just operated with a different enthusiasm for her back then, but I get ahead of myself."

"No, go ahead," Olivia prodded, hoping to get Oliver to understand how she feels.

The driver tipped his cap. "The spark, chemistry, and amazing feelings for each other are always accessible, just like they were when you first fell in love. The primary difference between then and now is simple: the questions you ask yourself about each other have changed."

> The chemistry you felt when you first fell in love is always accessible. The primary difference between then and now is the questions you're silently asking about each other.

He gestured more freely now. "Look at couples who've been married for a long time sitting at a restaurant table, and many of them are either not talking at all or they're playing on their phones. Conversely, observe couples who are dating—they're exploring and flirting with each other. The primary reason for this is each person—in both examples—is leveraging certain types of questions in their minds."

"What kinds of questions?" Olivia stole a gaze at Zeb.

*   *   *

He adjusted his bow tie. "Well, the first couple employs questions like 'Why does she always have to play on her phone? Why is he eating fatty foods? Why can't she dress like my secretary? Why can't he be more attentive like my fitness trainer? What's her problem?' Or take Zeb and Isabella here with their blended family."

He knows a lot about the couples. Thank goodness he hasn't called out Titus and me. Emma looked over at the limo and prayed a silent prayer for her marriage.

The driver rested his hand on Zeb's shoulder. "There's a reason why remarriages and blended families have over a 65 percent chance of failing: They use negative questions like 'Why's this so hard? Why can't the kids ever get along? Strangely, it was easier in my first marriage (an implied question). When will we ever have enough money, given child-support fees?' Because of the way the brain is wired, negative questions lead to negative energy—felt by the partner—and negative conversation. The results are anything but pleasurable. They're downright disastrous."

"And couple two?" Zeb was pinching his bottom lip.

The driver patted his shoulder, then stepped in front of the group. "Couple two is using feel good questions like 'How can I help? What can I do to bring the joy today? What if life with my husband keeps getting better? What kind of positive impact can our family make today? What new opportunities exist to expand our cash flow? What's something fun we can do today? What excites us about how our kids interact? How did I get so blessed to wake up next to her?'"

He paused and looked across the street at the houses. "Most couples mix and match negative and positive questions, and that's a major problem because it plants seeds of doubt rather than certainty. You need to believe in your relationship—with the strongest sense of certainty, regardless of circumstance—if you're going to experience the ultimate relationship. No matter the fight, no matter the finances, no matter the family drama, the couple must maintain feelings of certainty for each other. Don't wait for feelings of certainty to surface, generate them on your own every day with intentional questions."

The driver took his hat off and pointed to the brain. "Anyway, because the way the brain's wired, when you frame questions positively it searches for positive answers. This shifts the couple's energy and emotions to feel good about each other—inducing feelings of certainty. If both couples begin their conversation at a five, on a scale of one to ten, in terms of good feelings for each other, the first couple's number plummets, while the second couple's number improves.

"At some point down the road, the first couple's questions break their relationship without them even understanding what's going on. They think they've fallen out of love, but in reality, they're using different questions that create doubt. Conversely, the second couple's relationship thrives—thanks to finding better questions that create certainty."

Are we getting in the limo already, or is he going to talk all night? Room 7. Room 7. Room 7. Emma inhaled deeply through the nose and slowly released through her mouth.

The driver bounced lightly on his feet. "This is just one of the powerful strategies you'll discover at the Couples' Castle. Asking better questions can breathe new life and energy into your relationships. And here's the kicker: Your brain is always, always, *always* consumed with questions. Even your statements are embedded with questions. So the idea is to catch them in midthought and then rewrite them into enjoyable and energizing questions that will bring forth positive answers so that you'll get enjoyable and energizing relationship experiences."

Emma wandered a short distance toward the limo before returning. She opened her mouth, then closed it. *A better idea would be to take this conversation to the limo.*

The driver pressed the lock button on his car keys, and the group heard the resulting beep. "Think about it this way: You're always thinking—perhaps an overstatement for some—and your thinking always revolves around a question, whether it's the past, present, or future. You just need to recondition your brain to find better questions, ones that'll create the ultimate relationship experience. Put it this way, if you're feeling miserable about your relationship—in a state of doubt or annoyance about your partner—realize you're asking negative questions. Flip how you frame your questions for better feelings. Here are three questions we at the Couples' Castle recommend to all our couples: one for whenever you are thinking about your past, another whenever you are talking about the present, and the final question is for when you're planning for your future."

Emma recalled how good their past was until they discovered their infertility issue. Now it all just seemed hopeless.

The driver waved his hand behind him. "When thinking about the past, ask 'What did we really enjoy about our relationship then, and how does that makes us feel?'

"We've discovered at the Couples' Castle that asking this question improves the relationship tenfold, so try it. Go ahead, take ten seconds to think about it. What did you enjoy about your relationship? We also tack on 'How does that make you feel?' because human beings are emotional creatures. Here's proof: Tell me your partner's current emotion, and I'll tell you the direction of your relationship in the next ten minutes. Your actions always follow your emotions. That's why questions are so important. They change your emotional state—and your emotional state is how you get to happily ever after because marriage is an amplification of your emotions."

Oliver cleared his throat. "What do you mean?"

The driver's arms dropped to his sides. "It works like this: Questions trigger emotions, your emotions spur your actions, and your actions lead to your results. Results are what matter. Most couples give reasons why they're struggling, reasons why they can't improve, reasons for their loneliness, reasons for their exhaustion. Those who enter the Couples' Castle get results, not reasons. It all starts with finding better questions. It's how two people find the love of their life—because they're asking exciting questions about what could be. Again, you're always using questions about the past, present, or future. Leverage question one for your past.

"Now here's question two, the one for the present. *What's really fun about our relationship right now, and how does that make us feel?*"

There's nothing Emma could think of. Then it hit her to ask, "Does that mean even if there's some bad energy between us, this question will force our brains to find answers that make us feel good about each other?"

The driver gave her an assuring wink. He then raised three fingers. "The third question when thinking about your relationship in all its tomorrows is *what are we really excited about* and *how does that make us feel?* This question puts a smile on your face.

"Partners who generate fun and exciting experiences with each other are the ones who stay together. I've just given you one strategy to do that—turn everyday questions into enjoyable and empowering questions. Then I gave you three starter questions that'll help generate exciting and empowering emotions, actions, and results, whether thinking about the past, present, or future. Use them enough, and watch your relationship become a masterpiece. Guaranteed."

Isabella grabbed Zeb's hand. "I think we should get in the limo. Scratch that. Honestly Zeb, I have to get in that limo."

Ya think? Let's go already. Emma checked her pockets for a Tic Tac. "I agree," Zeb said.

The limo driver smiled, bowed in service, and motioned toward the car. "Happily-ever-after really is within your grasp and the Couples' Castle will show you how."

Oliver and Olivia followed.

This limo was spacious. *Wait, where's?* Emma turned to see him standing back at the lamppost, bumping her head on the door when getting back out.

C'mon, Titus, please don't do this. Please get in. "Are you coming?" Emma's hair lifted on the back of her neck.

Silence.

Emma thought about the worst-case scenario and turned to the limo driver. "Can you give us just a moment, please?"

The driver checked his watch. The color of his watch matched the color of his bow tie.

I'm getting closer, and he's not moving away. Maybe everything's okay. "Titus, are you coming?"

Titus studied her.

"Titus?"

A big tear rolled down his left cheek, like the first water leak from a broken dam. "How c-could you, Emma?"

She saw the look of distrust in his eyes. *Oh no. It's over.* "I'm sorry, Titus. Please don't leave. I didn't mean . . ."

"I don't c-care that it was two years ago. How c-could you?" Titus repeated. He stood there, broken, giving a slow disbelieving head shake.

Emma felt a painful tightness in her throat and spots flashed in her vision. *Hold on, Titus. I can't stop crying long enough to answer. C'mon, Emma. Breathe. He's about to leave you . . . forever.*

Titus turned his back on her and walked home.

I can't breathe. I can't breathe. She sank to the ground. *How did I go from finding the love of my life to wheezing on the ground?* "Titus, *please!*"

He was getting further away.

The limo driver shut the rear door and walked toward the driver's seat.

Emma lay in the fetal position, wrapped in the consequences of her affair. The tears poured so thickly; she couldn't wipe them away fast enough. Her nose clogged, and her lungs searched for unavailable oxygen. *Stand up, Emma. Go get him. Beg. Do whatever it takes.* She put her hand on the ground to push herself up, but her legs gave way, and her body crumpled in on itself.

The crying drowned out the buzzing of the park's insects. The couples in the limo fell silent and just stared out the window, eyewitnesses to a painful marital collapse.

Emma lay there in the dark, crying herself to death and bargaining with God. A light turned on at a house across the street, while several dogs barked throughout the neighborhood.

The driver put the key in the ignition and started the limo. Just then Emma felt a tap on her shoulder.

He came back for me. She wanted to say "I'm sorry" but couldn't get past the wheezing. *Please stay.* Only slobber came out.

He helped her up, his face like a distrusting stranger. *He's moved from brokenness to numbness. He doesn't love me anymore.* Titus was the most loyal person she knew, but she'd breached his trust. Her only hope was to get the key and Titus to the Couples' Castle—to room 7. They promised the red treasure chest held the answers.

Emma could sense—everyone in the limo could sense—that this relationship had moved beyond resuscitation. There was no Couples' Castle. He only helped her up because Titus stood for all that was right in the world. He didn't want Emma—now on the path to becoming his ex-wife—crying all alone at the park in the middle of the night. But nor could he sleep in the same house with her again. That left one option.

The limo driver knew too. He checked his watch, got out, jogged to the back of the limo, and opened the door. They got in.

When the limo drove off from Evermore Park, into the night, the house light across the street turned off.

*　　*　　*

Chapter 3

The Couples' Castle

Whatever you do, Olivia, don't let him see you look his way. Except for some added weight, Zeb had barely changed. Still handsome. But what was he doing there, and where had he been?

Everyone remained button-lipped for the first five minutes, giving Emma time to pull herself together.

"Here." Isabella, after picking lent off her pretty purpose blouse, handed Emma a Kleenex.

"Thank you. I'm so sorry, you guys." She cleaned up her running mascara.

Isabella squeezed Emma's shoulder. "Oh no, no. It's okay." Isabella seemed at home in a motherly role.

Titus sat still as a board, staring out the opposite window. Next to Emma, yes, but a barrier thicker than the old East Berlin wall rose between them, and it would take far more than a president's tear-down-that-wall speech to bring reconciliation. *Wow.*

Oliver switched subjects, probably to lighten things up. "Can you believe we're all out at midnight? When's the last time that happened? And in a limo on our way to a *castle* of all things."

The limo did have a calming effect, cruising down the country road. The Couples' Castle lured Olivia in a way she hadn't felt since, well, since their wedding day when the officiant pronounced them a couple who could live happily ever after—an authentic happily-ever-after. She recalled the way that made her feel when it rolled off the officiant's lips. *If only.*

At one time, she thought it'd be with Zeb. Why did he leave her that summer morning, and what was he doing here? She should tell Oliver that she knew him. *No, that'd be weird to do right now.* On the other hand, not telling Oliver felt wrong. She'd never said anything about Zeb. Why would she have? A woman could only talk about her first love to certain people, sometimes just to herself. She rubbed her ear instead. *Shift your focus, Olivia, before you say something stupid.*

"Okay," she said, leaning forward, "my husband, Oliver here, believes someone's pranking us, but when we saw the rest of you at the lamppost, we couldn't put together the pieces of the puzzle. Is there someone who knows all of us? I mean, we don't even know one another." *Why did I just say that last part? The point was to avoid saying something stupid. C'mon Olivia!*

"Yeah," Oliver added, "is there someone who would want to prank us all? We've never heard of this Couples' Castle before." Oliver shook his head and laughed. "I think it's Scott."

"Who?" Olivia and Zeb said simultaneously, then glanced at each other.

I don't know whether to hug or slap him. Given our situation, I can't do either yet.

"Scott, that prankster. He's a guy at the office who's always coming up with mind-blowing practical jokes." Oliver grabbed the sides of his head in an I-can't-believe-he-got-me gesture.

Isabella sat up straight like a mother trying to keep control. "But do you think he could pull this off? And why on the rest of us? *We* don't know Scott."

"Yep, he sure could. He'd relish it. He's just trying to get me for the fish I put in his drink last spring. Why he pulled you guys in on it, I'm not sure—perhaps to make it more plausible. But I can tell you this much: There's no castle."

"Couples' Castle," Olivia corrected.

"*Couples'* Castle." Oliver rolled his eyes. If they weren't in the company of other couples, that eye-roll would've been met with backlash. Olivia wanted to ring his neck whenever he rolled his eyes at her and this time was no different. Right now a cold shoulder would have to do. "No way it exists. We'll arrive, and there'll be some sort of surprise, or worse, the limo will drop us off in the middle of nowhere, in the middle of the night, and we'll have to find our way back on foot in the dark. That's so Scott."

Five minutes passed. Then ten. Each person created a plausible narrative about what the night might hold.

Titus found a compartment in the door. When he opened it, out popped a bowl of mini candy bars and breath mints. He seemed surprised, a nice change from his constant cadaver-like state.

"Hey, look at this. Would anyone like some breath mints or fun-size candy bars?" Titus asked.

"Sure." They all reached out their hands like scavengers.

Oliver said thank you and turned the candy with his fingers. "These mini candy bars shouldn't be called fun size. Now a candy bar the size of my sofa would be fun size!"

Olivia was too caught up in her thoughts to even be dismissive of Oliver's lame jokes. *Zeb's still got that freckle on his right earlobe.* She remembered seeing that freckle the night she rested her head on his shoulder in the park where they first danced. *Looks like he married well. Good for him. I hope he's found happiness.* He looked so calm over there rolling the half dollar over his knuckles. But he did owe her an explanation. And how did they randomly come together on this night? What the heck was that all about?

An hour passed since they'd snacked on the candy bars, and it'd grown quite while they contemplated the evening's mysteries, just the smell of leather seats and the soft humming of the limo's tires.

"I have to pee." Oliver locked his knees together and leaned forward, then exhaled.

"Me too." Emma put her hand in the air. "Okay, I just want to say again that I'm sorry about earlier, guys. I'm so sorry."

Olivia felt uncertain about what else she could say to make Emma feel at ease, but did give her an understanding nod that was well received.

"This limo is smooth," Oliver announced. He glided his outstretched hand along the interior lighting. "Gotta hand it to Scott. He's got style."

"I wonder how much farther. We've been riding in here for . . . what, does anyone have the time?" Emma scanned the interior, looking for a clock.

"No, the driver collected our phones when we stepped into the limo," Isabella replied, "but I'd say we've been in here almost two hours. I really hope we're not late."

"About the driver," Oliver pursed his lips in thought. "He seems like he knows something, like this isn't his first rodeo. I wonder how much he's getting paid and how often he helps with these pranks. Let's find out."

Oliver scooted to the font of the limo and knocked on the partition. "*Ahem*, excuse me, Mr. Limo Driver." He always pushed the boundaries.

The tinted window didn't budge.

"Excuse me!" Oliver hollered, now pounding. "Anyone up there?"

Nothing.

"Well, look at that. The dude seemed cool enough . . . till now."

Just then flashes of purple and gold surrounded the vehicle and appeared to lift the vehicle slightly in the air. Olivia gasped, grabbed her seat, then glanced around to see if the others were experiencing the same thing. Titus widened his eyes and pressed his hands against the window. Zeb shook his head vigorously, like he'd just seen a ghost.

A few moments later, the limo hit the ground and screeched to a sudden stop, jolting them against their seat belts. The treasure chests sailed through the air and bounced around, landing on the dark custom floor mats.

"What the heck was that? Is everyone okay?" Oliver reached for his seat.

Emma seemed shaken but gave a thumbs-up. By the way she looked at her legs, she seemed relieved to be wearing slacks instead of a dress.

"My key! Where is it?" Isabella looked around in a panic like a mom who lost sight of her kids at the mall.

"They're all on the floor in the back." Oliver motioned.

While they busied themselves with their treasure chests, Oliver knocked on the privacy window again. "Hey, Mr. Driver, you okay up there? What was that? Did Scott pull off some magic trick show? You know, someone could've gotten seriously hurt. Either way, you aren't fooling us."

All the windows, including the privacy window, came down at once, and the limo driver said with a sly smile and without apology, "We're here."

The group looked out the windows at the massive structure lighting up the sky.

"A castle?" Oliver rubbed his eyes in disbelief.

"Whoa!" Emma's hand covered her mouth.

Olivia wished she'd worn a dress. She fumbled through her purse for a hand mirror and checked and rechecked her hair and makeup when she found it. When she looked out the window again, her neck grew goose flesh.

The driver stepped out and opened the door facing the massive structure, motioning for them to exit the vehicle.

The castle's light illuminated the inside of the car. Stunning. The castle pulled at Olivia's imagination, but she couldn't move her legs. Fear of the unknown bound her to her seat.

Ten long seconds passed. Then twenty. Everyone else seemed to be feeling the same way. The driver waited.

"I'm going in." Oliver, in his white button-down and khakis, tumbled out of the car. "I don't know how Scott pulled it off, but this is just cool."

That snapped everybody from their stunned silence.

"Well, if he's going in, we should all go in," Isabella said.

While the others piled out, Zeb questioned the driver, "Is this place safe?"

Safe? That's not the wild and free Zeb I knew.

The limo driver chuckled. "Not by a long shot, but if you'd like me to take you home, tell me now. Or you can go in and discover what's on the other side of the front door."

Before Zeb could reason things out, Isabella whispered, "Zeb, now's our chance for more. We both know something's off with our relationship and let's be honest, you're feeling overburdened with the finances. I can tell. Now look at this place, Zeb. I don't know if we're dreaming or if this is real, but let's give this Couples' Castle thing a shot."

Olivia couldn't help but wonder what was off with their relationship. Olivia seemed to click with Zeb when they were together. They were like the perfect puzzle.

Zeb stepped out.

For a few minutes, they stood in awe under the castle's towering brilliance.

The whole estate felt like a combination of something futuristic and ancient, creating an insatiable curiosity about whether they would be beamed from one spot to another or knights on white horses would ride out to escort them around the royal grounds.

The castle stood on a hill and radiated multicolors. Instead of peaks in the roof, there were four domed towers designed in brilliant gold, one for each of the four corners. Instead of featuring arrow slits for archers, the protruding towers featured engraved words in bold white, *The Couples' Castle.*

The group stood, heads tilted upward, like mesmerized tourists visiting Florence, Italy. Captivated, Olivia didn't notice the limo pull away, but when she turned around, it's disappearance left her feeling like a college kid who's come home on break only to find her old room transformed into an office - cut off and alone. She looked over at Isabella who seemed to be counting the windows on the castle.

The castle walls were built of white stone that radiated warmth and power. The solid blocks on top of the wall were decorated with Xs and Os, which wrapped with perfect symmetry around the castle. Straight down the middle, blue and pink banners crisscrossed. Dazzling crystals illuminated the drawbridge over the moat that flowed with ocean-like blue water.

"No way your friend Scott pulled this off," Isabella bellowed in a dubious tone.

"Yeah." Oliver tipped his head from side to side, weighing the hole that was just punched in his own theory.

The place felt magical. The luminous lights hanging from the castle's walls revealed a blaze of colorful royal gardens. Fresh fragrant blooms with stunning Mediterranean gardens filled with Tuscan olive trees and green spires of Italian cypress, giant water lilies, and rose gardens flowed all around. The perfumed air filled Olivia's lungs.

The gentle air caressed her skin, and the ground was soft and spongy beneath her feet.

"Where are we?" Zeb looped his fingers into Isabella's.

"Somewhere special." Isabella shook with excitement and squeezed his arm.

Interesting. They did look happy together. Or maybe it's the castle's effect.

"I wish we had our cell phones so we could take some selfies. No way anyone's going to believe us." Oliver kept shaking his head in disbelief.

Olivia craned her neck to the left. She couldn't see through the dark, but she could hear the sound of flowing water on the other side of the mammoth trees. It made her feel alive. She felt like running, and she would've, but the uncertainty about whether it was an enchanted area suited for royalty or a haunted forest filled with monsters kept her feet planted to the ground.

As they crossed the bridge together, she noted the curtain wall wrapping around the center structure. It looked at least twenty-five feet thick and fifty feet tall. The whole castle itself towered well above the tree line, and the trees were massive. It was a thing of wonder.

Projecting upward were two large structures made of stone, standing tall on each side of the front gate. The center portion between the two structures was imprinted with yellow words, *Golden Tickets*. Olivia really hoped Oliver remembered the tickets.

It appeared someone had built this castle to withstand relationship pain more so than cannon fire. Nobody here intended to fortify treasure, more like to strengthen relational certainty. It promised tremendous security, but the security had nothing to do with fears of oncoming raiders and bandits. It was like some kind of command center for serving couples, dominating the landscape with the perfect mixture of promise and love.

They approached the massive entryway, and Oliver quipped, "I wonder if a green leprechaun will stick his head out and tell us that a wizard lives here.'"

Someone did stick his head out to greet them, just not a green leprechaun.

*   *   *

A tall man, dressed in butler attire, emerged. "Do you have your Couples' Castle golden tickets?"

Olivia handed the butler their ticket. "Thank you." He gave each person a white sheet of paper. "Before entering, you must fill these out. Also, this isn't random. Not just anyone may fill out this assessment or enter the Couples' Castle. Only those ready to improve their relationship in every possible way—all the way to the ultimate relationship experience—get exclusive access. It's designed to help you find the love of your life by transforming you into an irresistibly attractive person, irrespective of race, class, length of relationship, or history. It works for married couples, too, for those who want to make their marriage a masterpiece anyway. Just follow the instructions."

An irresistibly attractive person, huh? It sounded farfetched, and definitely more geared toward singles. These people seemed to know what they were doing, and it felt safe enough—for now. Before Olivia sat on a bench to fill out the questionnaire, she asked, "Isn't this more for singles? I mean, we're all married."

The butler pivoted her way. "We have singles come through here all the time. Yes, you're married, but whether single or married, wouldn't you agree that becoming an irresistibly attractive person fulfills both you and your partner's desires?" Before she could answer, he continued. "The bigger question is 'Are you worthy of the relationship you expect to have?'"

That was a question Olivia had never considered. After all her dating and marriage experience, she just realized how helpful it would've been to have that question remain on her mental dashboard. *Am I worthy of the relationship I expect to have?* Olivia sat down on the bench, visibly shaken a bit by the question.

> Always be asking, 'Am I worthy of the relationship I expect to have today?' It'll help you find the love of your life and make your marriage a masterpiece.

While handing out pens, the butler instructed, "You should ask that question of yourself everyday—married or not—'Am I worthy of the relationship I expect to have today?' Keeping that question on your mind will elevate your standards and move you to take massive action so that you'll transform into a person that attracts the kind of relationship you dream of.

Zeb raised his hand, "Um, excuse me."

"Yes, what is it?" The butler said.

"Just wondered if you all got our blood work you had us send in?" The butler nodded.

Zeb rubbed his nose. "Well, I'm not trying to start any kind of argument, but, um, isn't having our bloodwork done a little excessive? And are we all healthy?"

"Safety first policy. No exceptions. And, yes, you're all fine."

Fine? That's it, just "fine?"

"Now please turn the assessment in when finished. It gives everyone inside the Couples' Castle a gauge of the new couples entering. You'll get it back in room 5, should you make it that far. By the time you're finished with your journey through the Couples' Castle, again, should you make it that far, you'll have improved the quality of your relationship to a consistent nine out of ten. Okay, enough talking. Start the assessment now."

FIND/KEEP THE LOVE OF YOUR LIFE
BY BECOMING AN IRRESISTIBLY ATTRACTIVE PERSON
AND WORTHY OF THE RELATIONSHIP YOU EXPECT TO HAVE

GOAL: The idea is that you attract who you become. Want to find the love of your life? Grow into a ten, and you'll attract tens. Want to feel like your spouse is the love of your life again? Grow into a ten, and your spouse will model you via her mirror neurons alone, if nothing else.

Answer the questions according to whether you're single or married. What doesn't get measured, doesn't improve, and when you measure your life to the level of a nine, you attract others of the same quality who want to be with you. This will help you become worthy of the relationship that you expect to have today or someday.

INSTRUCTIONS: Circle the dots when you can answer yes "Y." Be honest. The more Ys you have, the more irresistibly attractive you become. Do this monthly until you're getting 18–20 Ys. Then review it quarterly.

**FIND/KEEP THE LOVE OF YOUR LIFE
BY BECOMING AN IRRESISTIBLY ATTRACTIVE PERSON
AND WORTHY OF THE RELATIONSHIP YOU EXPECT TO HAVE**

WHO ARE WE BECOMING?

Number of Yeses (20 max) _____

- We don't have any unfinished business or unresolved issues.
- We're obsessed about loving each other.
- We spend time with couples that we want to be like.
- We always have three shared big goals we're working toward.
- We're excited about our future.
- We create one growth challenge to accomplish per month, e.g., dance, painting class.
- We know what we believe, and we live in alignment with that truth.
- We have more than we need.
- We practice meditation, prayer, or some form of calmness together once per day.
- We both have outlets to manage our stress.
- We meet once per week to talk/agree about wins, losses, and responsibilities.
- We have marriage mentors that we talk to at least once per month.
- We both do cardio workouts two to three times a week.
- We both do strength workouts two to three times a week.
- We both take a thirty-minute walk every day, sometimes together.
- We read one personal development book per month.
- We have an abundance of time to do what matters most to us.
- We are at peace with who we are in life.
- We are at peace in all our relationships.
- We attract people and couples who are either one step behind or one step ahead of us.

> **FIND/KEEP THE LOVE OF YOUR LIFE**
> **BY BECOMING AN IRRESISTIBLY ATTRACTIVE PERSON**
> **AND WORTHY OF THE RELATIONSHIP**
> **YOU EXPECT TO HAVE**

THINK YOUR WAY TO A NINE RELATIONSHIP

Number of Yeses (20 max) _____

- At least once per day, I bring a smile to my partner's face.
- I guard my thoughts, and I'm careful about what I dwell on.
- I often tell myself, "Life's getting better with my partner. Our future's bright."
- I often tell myself, "I have the resourcefulness within to shape my relationship."
- When a challenging circumstance overwhelms me, I remind myself that *life is easy.*
- I take 100 percent responsibility for all my actions and all my results.
- I believe love is unlimited and unconditional.
- I am one of the most positive people I know.
- I believe I am right with God.
- Money does not own me, and I have enough of it (can still want more).
- There are facts and interpretations of the facts, with space between the two. I choose to interpret everything with empowering meanings.
- I remind myself often that abundance is flowing into my life.
- I have great energy; knowing the kind of energy I send out is the kind I get back.
- I attract people to me who are making similar choices in life—in how they think, in what they love, in how they treat their bodies, etc.
- I believe God is *for* me, that life doesn't happen *to* me but *for* me.
- I believe I'm a person of extraordinary confidence and courage.
- When my inner voice asks questions of myself, I choose to ask empowering questions rather than disempowering questions.
- When I think about the past, I think about what I'm grateful for.
- When I think about the present, I think about what I'm committed to.
- I say at least one positive thing about/to my partner each day.

**FIND/KEEP THE LOVE OF YOUR LIFE
BY BECOMING AN IRRESISTIBLY ATTRACTIVE PERSON
AND WORTHY OF THE RELATIONSHIP YOU EXPECT TO HAVE**

SET HIGH STANDARDS

Number of Yeses (20 max) _____

- When my partner is sharing with me, I don't "one-up" him with a similar story.
- I find ways to be grateful for something in every circumstance.
- I no longer gossip, meaning I never talk about my partner in neutral or negative ways when she's not present.
- I no longer tolerate drama or messes in my relationship.
- I do not argue.
- I do not complain, shame, or blame.
- I do not make excuses. Instead, I turn my *shoulds*, *coulds*, and *woulds* into *musts*.
- I do not procrastinate.
- I do not say *yes* when I want to say *no*.
- I do not compromise our relationship's agenda.
- I do not let distractions take over my days.
- I do not let doubts fill my mind about our relationship.
- I do not abuse my body or my thought life.
- I don't waste time.
- I don't watch a lot of television.
- I don't eat much sugar.
- I no longer believe in the law of scarcity but instead believe in abundance.
- I no longer partake in pity parties for myself.
- I don't have any debts outside of my mortgage.
- I don't feel the need to carry the weight of other people's problems on my shoulders.

*   *   *

Looks like I'm the last one finished. Emma handed her assessment to the butler.

"It's time to master the skills of a sustainable relationship and the laws of love." He led them through the gated entrance, up a walkway that circled to the front entry.

Okay, here we go. He opened the door, and they followed him down a long straight hall decorated with knights' armor and royal portraits in gold frames on either side. The red carpet that lay on the marble floor had large golden seals woven into it. The smell of the botanical gardens reached the Victorian-style hall while candles adorned the wall fixtures.

Am I dreaming, or is this real? "Pinch me," Emma whispered to Titus. Maybe this place really could help them. Unfortunately Titus looked numb, ignoring everything she said. *It's going to take a miracle.*

Straight ahead, at the end of the long hall, hung a gigantic painting of a prince and princess dancing. The prince's right arm held her in a deep dip, face-to-face, eyes-to-eyes, in storybook swooning fashion.

The last time she felt like a princess was at their wedding or maybe earlier in life when she and her sister played dress up and twirled in the living room in front of Dad.

Just before the end of the hall, the butler turned left and led them up a grand spiral staircase made of ornate mahogany. Once to the top, they rested to catch their breath. The carpet up here was a darker red, still with the same royal seals. The room was circular with a Juliet balcony and an enormous wraparound window. The group was drawn toward this massive awe-inspiring window. It looked hundreds of years old yet breathtakingly beautiful. Below them were people dressed in royalty, one couple even wore crowns like a king and queen, and all of them danced underneath chandeliers like they were at a royal ball. Emma rubbed her eyes in disbelief. She still didn't know whether the castle was real or fantasy.

"What in the world is going on down there?" Oliver placed his hands on the window and leaned in for a closer look.

Olivia joined him. "Where the heck are we?"

"It's like a fairy tale." Isabella's eyes widened like saucers.

No, it's perfect. This reminds me of dancing with Titus near the lakeside, the night of our first kiss.

"Can they see us?" Olivia asked. She pressed down her light green blouse.

"No, this is a tinted window," Oliver said. He double-checked the entire window to be sure.

Emma glanced at Titus. "I wonder if they'd let us dance with them."

Oliver tossed his shoulders back and puffed out his chest. "Want me to go ask? I will."

"You sure are confident," Isabella said.

Olivia giggled. "Don't you know it?"

Oliver shrugged and smiled. "Hey, I just assume that all women like water, and if that's the case, then all women already like 75 percent of me."

Isabella felt around for a way to open the window but found nothing.

Oliver pointed to the far side of the ballroom. "Is that a fondue fountain over there by the knight statues?"

"Where are we?" Olivia repeated.

"Maybe a better question is 'When are we?'" Isabella's fidgeting made Emma feel nervous about the answer.

"I know this sounds bizarre, but do you think maybe the limo drove us through some portal in time?" Isabella was now biting her nails.

Everyone considered the crazy possibility.

Zeb ran his hand through his hair. "Well, we did see those flashes of purple and gold lights. And I know I'm not the only one who felt the limo lift in the air a bit, am I?"

"Or maybe it's a dream?" Oliver said.

"How's that even possible?" Olivia's eyebrows narrowed.

Emma didn't much care at this point whether it was real. She had to act like everything was real and at stake in her marriage—because it was.

"This is where couples come to discover how to live an authentic happily-ever-after, not the pack of lies happily-ever-after you were sold back where you're from," said a soft clear voice behind them.

They turned to see a tall beautiful woman wearing a full-length red dress embellished with hundreds of diamonds. She wore platinum guild stilettos with more diamonds encrusted in the straps. Her flowing dark hair lay gently on her shoulders.

Wow, I bet Titus thinks she's beautiful.

"Uh hello," Oliver stammered.

Olivia jabbed him in the side.

Zeb looked around. "Where'd the butler go?"

"What butler?" replied a short pudgy man standing next to the tall woman. He donned a light blue top hat and light blue tuxedo and gripped a white cane. His chin had a chin, with a life of its own.

"You'll never guess why, but they call me Blue and my beautiful friend here, Red." His eyes sparkled when he smiled.

"Oh okay. Hello, Blue and Red." Oliver gave Olivia a suspicious side-eyed look.

Blue got right to the point. "Welcome to the Couples' Castle. We only have three rules. Rule number one: You only have a limited amount of time to find the real red treasure chest. As you know, it's in room 7. We can't tell you why, but you must find it within the three days' time frame or seventy-two hours. You either find it or fail." He cleared his throat. "Starting now at 6:00 a.m.—no exceptions.

"Rule number two: You'll enter seven rooms. Before you exit each room, please ask your partner, 'On a scale of one to ten, how would we rate the quality of our relationship relative to this room's purpose? If the answer is less than a ten, ask, what would it take to make it a ten?' It's critical that you talk to each other about your answers."

"Uh, excuse me?" Oliver stepped forward. "Will you be going with us?"

Blue tilted his head and studied him.

"What?" Oliver shrugged.

"Rule number three: You must go through rooms 1 through 6 before entering room 7. And the only way you can leave a room is if the hosts in each room initial your model treasure chest. Doing so indicates that your hosts think you're ready."

"Can I ask why?" Isabella placed her hands on her hips, slowly tapping her foot.

Red moved closer to erase the distance. "So many people only dabble in relationships, playing at the surface level. As such, they find themselves successful in many areas, except the one that matters the most—their intimate relationship. We aren't about dabbling but about relationship mastery. You get that right and so many other areas of life get easier and more exciting. Even if you found room 7 before experiencing the other rooms—which you won't—you wouldn't be ready for what awaits you there."

Zeb looked over his shoulder and scanned his surroundings. "What awaits us there?"

Blue rocked slightly. "Let's just say it's not for the faint of heart."

Isabella barraged the older gentleman with questions. "Are couples allowed to enter each room at the same time, or do we take turns? What's in the rooms? Will there be food? How long will it take? Our kids will worry if we don't touch base via phone—will we do that soon?"

"One question at a time, please." Red motioned with her hand, unfazed with Isabella's curiosity.

"Will the rooms be safe?" Zeb's gaze flitted around the room, never settling on a person or object for long—except for Olivia.

Why does that Zeb guy keep looking at Olivia?

"Safe enough." Red spoke in a flat voice.

Titus appeared to be paying attention during this question-answer session. Emma walked back to the window to watch the royal dancers again and to offer up a quick prayer. *God, hear my prayers. Please forgive me for my recklessness, and please, please soften Titus's heart. This'll probably be our final night together, unless you answer my prayer or some Couples' Castle pixie dust falls on us. God, I'm begging you. Please.*

Behind Emma, Red mentioned something about Abraham Maslow, how relationships improve when certain human needs are met, how people are driven to behave in ways to meet certain intrinsic needs, but when Emma couldn't make out the rest, she moved closer to the group.

Red stroked her cheek. "Your needs determine your marital behaviors. These rooms are a gift to you, and if you find the red treasure chest in room 7 in time, the ultimate relationship experience will be yours."

Emma didn't know if any of what Red was saying was true, but she hoped the part about what existed in the real red treasure chest was for her marriage's sake. She held the key like it was her newborn child she never had. Maybe it really did hold the cure to her dying marriage.

Looking down at the royal ball with her lips parted slightly, she wished on the key that she and Titus could dance together again. She found herself swaying with the treasure chest in her arms, staring at the royal dancers with quiet desperation, longing to feel fulfilled with Titus again. *We gotta make it to room 7. And find that red treasure chest.*

"All relationships have needs." Blue gestured enthusiastically. "But in this new world, the way in which you satisfy those needs is new. People are flocking to various forms of pornography. Others are isolating themselves with whatever the latest social media platform, and how you interact with your partner is changing—you communicate via your phones while you're in the same house, for crying out loud. You give each other thumbs-up and thumbs-down on a Facebook screen, and how you're spending time together—driving kids to event after event or sitting in front of a television—is reshaping relationships."

"Yes, I agree with that." Olivia blew out a breath that rattled her lips. The others nodded.

Blue leaned on his cane. "The old 'togetherness' has dissolved into a fragmentation of activity where parents sign their kids up for every opportunity while they take on extra jobs to support the new ideal vision of marriage and family. In other words, what drives a relationship is changing. The old days of providing four walls and a roof with dinner served promptly at 5:00 p.m. isn't enough anymore."

"With the world's rapid changing," Red stepped forward, "your relationships have changed in order to survive. Whereas in the past, most relationships were confined to one state, city, or town, limited by the constraints of the factory or corporate world, many people are becoming self-employed and leading start-ups. With that comes more travel, experiences, and explorations. With more of that comes desire for more stimulation and significance. Unfortunately, most couples feel worn out and unfulfilled. The opportunities and choices are limitless, and we want to help you figure out how you can thrive in your own way, according to your own needs and wants, at a consistent nine. You can fight the pace of the culture and struggle to survive or figure out how to adapt so that your relationship can thrive."

"I think you're right. The demand to make more money is crazy." Zeb leaned back against the wall. "If I'm being honest . . . Can I be honest? The chaos and rat race at work causes stress in our relationship, and that, in turn, creates more stress back at work, and so goes the cycle of stress."

"How much did they pay you to give up on your dreams?" Red said.

"What?" Zeb crossed his arms over his chest and squinted his eyes.

Red looked at Zeb like he was the only person in the room. "Relationships are no longer only driven by what they need: leave the cave, catch some food, and the family is happy about surviving. Most couples and families now have food, shelter, safety, and security. But you have dreams and desires too right?"

Zeb shook his head and shrugged slightly. "Yes, but ... at some point, you have to be realistic."

Red nodded. "Check your heart, Zeb. Your dreams are still there. Any healthy marriage encourages the pursuit of shared and individual dreams. Just look at the dissatisfaction your current trajectory has caused you. I bet you blame your job, but how is it your job's fault? Did your job pick you? Couples are discovering—at an alarming rate—that just satisfying their basic needs does not create a happy relationship. It's a huge blessing to live in such times, but in an age of abundance, more marriages are now seeking after what they *want*. They just go about finding fulfillment in dysfunctional ways. Conversely, we want to help your relationships become healthy and happy."

When the questions ended ten minutes later, Red called Emma's name, "Emma."

"Yes?" She turned, startled.

"Are you ready to enter the first room? The others already left."

Emma's cheeks flamed. Her eyes darted around the room, searching for Titus and the others. The far side door was just closing. She ran to catch up, stopping only to read the sign above door: PLAYFUL PLEASURE ROOM. Emma stole one last glance at the royal dancers, nestled her treasure chest close to her body, and pulled the door open. "Titus, wait!"

When she stepped through the door, she dropped into thin air, and a scream ripped from her chest as she fell into nothing.

Chapter 4

Room 1

Once through the door, the floor gave way, and gravity took care of the rest. Emma found herself screaming all the way down the giant yellow slide.

She felt like her stomach was in her throat and she tried to catch her breath.

Emma hadn't felt this euphoric since childhood when she played with her dad at the park. Those slides only took three seconds, but this slide had been going on for ten seconds or more. After letting go of the fear about where she might land, she screamed, "This is awesooooooommmmmmme!"

Kerplunk!

She landed in a pit full of colorful foam balls in the middle of all the other couples. Everyone was laughing. *Where's Titus?*

"That was dope!" Oliver sat on the edge, tossing balls in the air like a juggler. His white dress shirt now un-tucked.

Zeb was seated to the left, legs hanging over and kicking the balls with his brown shoes. "I had a near-death experience there, but I haven't had fun like that since," he scratched his head, "well, since I don't know when."

She spotted Titus, running his hand along a built-in bookcase on the far wall. A bookcase seemed out of place in this room, and she knew that was why Titus was investigating it.

"Guys, I think I f-found something." Titus pressed into the wall with both his hands. It turned. The wall was some kind of secret passageway. With the adrenaline of her fall still rushing through her body, Emma's sense of adventure kicked in.

Oliver ran over first, but it didn't take long for the others to join him. They could hear faint music coming from the other end of the hidden entrance, but they hesitated stepping in because it was pitch-black. Titus went first, with Emma and the others close behind. Emma felt her way through the complete darkness by running her hand along the dusty wall for balance and navigation. When her shoulder scraped the wall in the one tight spot they passed through, she prayed with all her might nothing would skitter across her skin.

"Look, there's a light up ahead." Emma let out a huge sigh of relief and reached out to Titus for comfort, but he flinched and kept walking. *All right, Emma, try to be patient. God only knows how much you've betrayed him. One foot in front of another until Room 7. Just get to Room 7 in time. Keep moving.*

At the end of the passageway, she heard a woman's voice. "Welcome to the Playful Pleasure Room. Keep walking this way." It was Red, standing tall and relaxed next to Blue. Behind them was a white gate that served as an entrance to a lighted room the size of a mall with soft hip-hop music coming from surround-sound speakers. The massive room behind the gate appeared to have dozens of other different-shaped sections built into it.

Zeb looked at Red, puzzled. "I didn't see you on the slide. How'd you get down here?"

"I took the elevator." She acknowledged their presence with firm eye contact.

"There's an elevator in this place?" Zeb raised an eyebrow and chuckled.

"There are a lot of things in the Couples' Castle. Now c'mon, follow me to the gate."

Emma walked across the marble floor while admiring the high ceiling and displays of artwork that hung on the side walls. She pinched her hand to make sure she was awake.

It was a lobby area that included cabinetry and fixtures, a wine fridge, freshly cut flowers, a bar, and ambiance lighting. When Emma leaned up against one of the chairs, she heard a soft *whump* of a gas fireplace turned on. As nice as the lounge was, she still couldn't get over the room on the other side of the gate. The closer she got, the more it looked like a classy banquet hall—only artistically divided up into sections.

Oliver was the first to walk over to the drinking fountain, and a line soon formed behind him. Cold water had never tasted so refreshing to Emma. She let it run over her lips for a couple extra seconds.

Blue leaned forward on his white cane. "Shall we get started?

Emma turned, clasped her hands under her chin and nodded. She felt a tingling in her legs and a flutter in her belly.

"Now the only way you're allowed to enter the Playful Pleasure Room is for you to hug your partner for five seconds first."

What? She knew that would be the last thing Titus would want from her. Just the thought of it had him rubbing the back of his neck.

Isabella's head flinched back slightly, and she scratched her cheek. "Um okay. Seems kinda odd. Can I ask why?"

Blue tugged down at his shirt sleeves. "You're going to have more fun in this room than you've had in a long time, maybe ever. We designed it that way because everyone's looking for her relationship to bring massive fulfillment, but what most couples don't do is intentionally choose to mentally link their partner to pleasure. This leaves you linking monotony to your partner, and pleasure to events and other people, ultimately eroding the spark in the relationship. You want to link massive pleasure to your partner because that's your way to relationship fulfillment on a large scale. He couldn't contain his grin.

Isabella stood on her tiptoes to look over the white gate at the room. "What do you mean?"

Blue tapped his foot to the rhythm of the music in the background. "Your brain subconsciously associates certain behaviors with pleasure and others with pain. Everyone wants to feel more pleasure than pain, yes?"

Yes, but what if there's no way out of the pain? Emma stole a glance at Titus.

Blue spoke with conviction and kindness. He always seemed to be in a good mood. "The good news is you hold the power to view your relationship—and the majority of your partner's behaviors— through the lens of pleasure rather than pain. Over time, couples tend to mentally link their partner first to monotony, then to pain – emotionally and otherwise. To change this, go back to like when you were first dating. Many couples end their relationships but they never would if they treated each other the way they did in the beginning. Treat each other in your present like you did at the start and there would never be an end. And what did you link your partner to at the start? Pleasure! My friends, that's the secret to feeling fulfilled. Implement that one idea into your relationship, no matter how long you've been married, and you'll have taken one giant leap to experiencing the ultimate relationship."

> Treat each other in the present like you did at the start and there will never be an end.

I don't think I'll ever experience fulfillment again. I botched it. Emma knew Titus linked only pain – massive pain – to her now. Her shoulders sagged, and she looked at her shoes while taking a deep breath.

"Can you give us some practical examples?" Isabella stepped around a small orange trampoline placed next to three nearly natural silk fiscus trees. During her question, Titus walked past Blue toward the gate and pulled himself up for a better view.

Blue watched him for a moment, then turned with his white cane twirling in hand. "That's what this room is about. We're going to teach you how to turn even the most menial and mundane marriage tasks into pleasure-based activities so you feel excited about the day-to-day relationship. The magic of marital fulfillment, you see, is in the routines. Forget this and you're doomed."

"No disrespect, but I'm not sure if I buy that." Isabella put one foot on the trampoline, like she wanted to jump on it but feared what others would think.

Blue's eyes glistened, like he held some secret knowledge. "You will. We'll show you how to condition new neural patterns for yourselves, ones that link massive pleasure to your relationship. But more on that later."

"That sounds a little weird." Oliver crossed his arms and eyeballed Blue.

Blue pinched his nose. "If conditioning sounds weird, it's only because you haven't experienced it before. People only think something's weird when they haven't tried it."

"Hey, I didn't mean to be disrespectful. This is your place, so whatever you say goes." Oliver shrugged halfheartedly.

"The real question is . . ." Blue's eyes landed on each person. "How much do each of you enjoy your relationship? I mean, really can't-wait-to-see-each-other enjoyment."

Emma watched Titus leaning over the gate. *Ha! Maybe when we first started dating. Over the past three years, a slow painful path to nothingness.* Maybe that was why they drifted. They stopped doing things together that were enjoyable, and the routines became mundane until finally all the pizzazz left the relationship.

Red held her hands loosely behind her tall slender body. "The most efficient way to improve your pleasure and enjoyment with each other is through conditioning. Most couples rely on willpower to make their relationship work, but that never lasts. Those couples get tired of trying. If, on the other hand, you focus on forming new neural pleasure patterns, you won't have to willpower your way to a sexy, passionate relationship every morning because your neurology will automatically pull you along into playful pleasure experiences—even lighting up the routines. You'll become energy-rich for each other, and you'll not only enjoy your partner more often, but you'll also want to engage each other on a level you never dreamed possible."

"I understood about half of what you just said. So uh, what does all this have to do with hugging?" Oliver scratched his head.

Red hugged Blue while tilting the front of her head toward the group. "When you hold someone for five seconds or longer, it conditions your limbic system to believe the person you're holding is a source of pleasure. Research shows that at the five-second mark, oxytocin is released throughout the body, causing both to feel pleasure, and as a side note, touching each other more often creates an even stronger bond. So the question is, do you want to feel sexy and alive to each other again? If so, hug more often, and playfully extend the length of your hugs. So simple of a strategy, but how often do you hug each other? I mean, *really* hug each other. You don't because you take each other for granted until you feel more pain than pleasure. Since this room is all about playfulness and associating your relationship with pleasure, we stipulate that entry to the Playful Pleasure Room begin with something that produces pleasure, namely, a five-second hug."

It started to sink in for Emma. "So what you're saying is that we shouldn't wait to feel good before we hug . . . We hug to feel good." She glanced at Titus, who'd come back from the fence, but still didn't look eager to embrace the one who smashed his heart into a thousand pieces.

"Correct, Emma." Red gave Blue a final squeeze, then let go.

"Okay, let the hugs begin." Blue chuckled.

Everyone stepped toward their partners, but what was Emma supposed to do? Titus wouldn't even look her way.

Red cleared her throat. "*Everyone* must participate in order to enter the room."

Great, now they're all probably looking at us. Well, he's not going to initiate—and how can I blame him—so what's there to lose?

Titus didn't push Emma away. But neither did he hold her close or show any kind of affection. It was like holding a cold statue. What if this was her last time in his arms?

"All right, break it up, all you love birds." Blue bounced lightly in place. "Now c'mon. Let's go in." He raised the lock and opened the white gate.

When they entered the room, welcoming lights flashed in their direction. It was even better on this side of the gate. Way better. Emma felt like a Hollywood star walking the red carpet. The glitz and glamour seemed to extend forever in every direction like some sort of optical illusion.

"This is the coolest room I've ever seen." Zeb did a slow 360 to soak it all in.

Stations divided the room, with a huge sign above each that read PLAYFUL PLEASURE, along with a number, indicating there were at least 101 stations. Each offered a specific joy for couples to share. On the left side, Zeb pointed out exciting stations to Isabella, including a room with small round tables with stools around the perimeter, hot-tub area, how-to-help-the-homeless center, virtual-reality stations, arts and crafts, cuisine tasting, and a compassion-international area.

Wow, this makes our local theme park and contribution centers feel like peanuts. It's packed with possibilities.

Emma's eyes were drawn to the ballroom-dancing station. If only she and Titus could dance together again, maybe he'd remember what they had. "Look, Titus. A ballroom." In her enthusiasm to renew her relationship with the love of her life, she set her treasure chest on a side table and ran over to the station.

* * *

Olivia knew her husband would be the first to jump on the trampoline. He was back near the gate, midair, calling out, "This place is like Christmas morning for grown-ups!" She shook her head with slight embarrassment.

Olivia was tempted to leave him back by himself but decided to motion for him to catch up to the rest of them where they stood encircled by the stations. When he caught up, she leaned over and quietly asked him, "It's amazing, but don't you think it's a little *too* much pleasure?"

He whispered back, "What are you talking about, O? This is the greatest room ever." His eyes were blinking rapidly, followed with craning his neck in different directions and open staring. The well-lit room was magnetizing. Great music played in the background and pleasure stations just waiting for them to explore.

"I know, but I'm not sure we deserve it." She scratched her cheek and felt a tightness in her chest.

"How much *do* you deserve in life?" Red cupped an elbow with one hand while tapping the lips with the other.

A sinking feeling hit Olivia. *Crap, she heard me.* Olivia tried to stand tall and straighten her shoulders. "I don't know. It just feels . . . selfish, all this pleasure. Especially when there are so many people with so little. Most live on less than $2 per day, and look at *all* this."

Red gave an understanding nod. "I see. Should we give it to those people?"

"I don't know, maybe." Olivia felt like she might need to sit down and reflect.

Red looked directly at her. "It's either a 'yes' or a 'no.'"

"I guess." She put her hands in the air, palms up.

"Not, 'I guess.' It's either 'yes' or 'no.'"

Olivia was taken aback with Red's directness. To counter, she put her hands on her hips and arched her head. "Yes then."

"To whom shall we give it?" asked the tall slender woman with the diamond brooch.

Olivia shrugged. "I don't know. The people in Africa."

"We can make that happen," she answered, unflappable.

Oh! She tilted her head and studied Red. "Really?"

"Of course. There's enough to go around for everyone."

Okay then. They ought to help those less fortunate. Who were they to enjoy all this? Speaking of everyone, it appeared the rest of the couples were now standing there watching the conversation. Olivia pushed her bangs over her right ear and felt a sense of victory. "Okay then."

Red stepped her way, and it caused Olivia to pull her light green blouse out a bit. "Do you believe there's enough . . . for everyone? Including you, Olivia? Do you feel like you deserve happiness and pleasurable experiences to the point where you feel like you might spontaneously combust because of so much pleasure and joy?"

She shifted her weight and thought about the popcorn she could smell nearby. "I don't know. I used to. Maybe when I was a teenager, but

I matured—not to sound condescending. But now I know there are so many people in need. If you have money for all this, then we can help them. We can give them these experiences and show them the way to eternal life. I'm not sure what I'd do with some of this anyway."

"You long for eternal life, but you don't know how to enjoy something on a Saturday afternoon," Red replied, cutting through the veneer. "Perhaps that's partly why you feel so worn out all the time. You never take time for yourself."

You long for the pleasure of eternal life, but you don't know how to enjoy the company of your spouse or yourself. The only person you'll forever be with is you, so you might want to do some consistent self-care. You'll be better and it'll improve your relationship.

Seriously? She's just going to call me out like that in front of everyone? Olivia's rapid blinking turned into a wide-eyed look. "Well, just so you know, I do enjoy some stuff."

When Red leaned in, Olivia put her focus on the half dozen colorful balloons that were tethered to a poll behind Red. The air compressor must've kicked on because the balloons were bouncing off one another. She sensed the rest of the group was watching their conversation like an audience at a prize fight.

"I know you do, Olivia, but it's more of a mind-set shift you need than anything else. Pleasure can be experienced in a myriad of ways. Take challenging yourself, for example, or getting out of your comfort zone, like some of the stations in here offer. Time under tension hurts in a challenge, but ultimately it brings pleasure. Even in the simple pleasures, for example, don't you enjoy a vanilla soy latte every now and then?"

Her head flinched back. "How did you know that?"

Red maintained eye contact. "And don't you take an annual summer vacation, buy new clothes every fall, and purchase a new car every three years?"

"Uh yes. I guess so." She gave a sidelong glance to Oliver.

"You also like to watch good movies on cable and play on your smart phone every day. You do these things in your air-conditioned and heated house, with indoor plumbing."

Olivia stared at her like a mouse caught in a trap. If this were a prizefight, she'd have been stumbling against the ropes.

Red moved into her personal space like a caring mother who knew what was best for her daughter. "I'm only saying that you do enjoy some things, but you're still exhausted. Why is that? You kinda, sorta enjoy things that much of the world has no access to, but you kinda, sorta feel guilty about it. A mind-set shift needs to happen for you to *fully*—not just kinda, sorta—enjoy life. For only then does your marriage have a shot at becoming a masterpiece. This isn't hedonism. Living under guilt and self-doubt about pleasure is not how God created you to live."

Olivia felt her knees giving out. She couldn't recall the last time she really enjoyed a day, where she took in each present moment with her full senses. She was too busy keeping up with the Joneses and feeling overwhelmed at home. Maybe if Red lived with someone who didn't help her clean up around the house; if she paid all the bills; if she cleaned, clothed, and bathed the children every night . . . She probably hadn't ever even babysat before. She didn't look like she had much to do but lecture. Honestly.

Oliver spoke up in her defense. "Hey, give her a break, all right?"

Red stepped back but ignored him and pressed on. "Is it possible to do both, Olivia?"

She fought back the water in her eyes and held her head high. "Both what?"

Red tilted her head to the side. "For you to enjoy life to the fullest with all kinds of wild experiences *and* massively contribute back to humanity? Both bring people pleasure, and we offer both kinds in this room."

She looked around, embarrassed of the spotlight. "Maybe."

Red looked at her like the question called for a "yes" or "no."

"Sure. Yes. But it's selfish to enjoy things while others suffer." If Red was going to be bold enough to knock her out, she'd muster the courage to defend herself in front of the others.

Red's eyes narrowed, her eyebrows pulling down in concentration. "And yet you suffer. And why is it selfish to enjoy things? Who told you that?"

Olivia shrugged. "God. My preacher. The Bible. I don't know."

Oliver tried to break the tension. "Hey, isn't the Bible like the number one most shoplifted book of all time?"

Seriously, Oliver. I could use some empathy here. She quickly swiped a tear from her eye before anyone could see.

Red motioned to the surrounding stations. "I thought God was full of riches, love, joy, peace, and the desire for his people to live life abundantly. Didn't God create from his good pleasure? And wasn't God's very first command for couples to have sex? Isn't that pleasurable?"

Oliver threw his hands in the air. "Finally! Someone's making sense around here."

They wouldn't laugh at Oliver's jokes if they knew how little he did around the house.

Olivia shot eye darts at her husband then turned back to face the music with Red. "That's true, but you're also tying health and wealth gospel stuff to it—and besides, others are suffering. You know that, right?"

Red nodded empathetically. "Ahh, now we're getting somewhere. It sounds like you believe in the law of scarcity. That's definitely one view of divine providence and the world. Have you considered that there also exists the law of abundance and that if you shifted to it, you might not feel so overwhelmed back home?"

Olivia stared blankly at her.

Red switched to a gentle tone. "The former says there's not enough to go around—whether it's water, food, wealth, enjoyment, love, joy, etc.—that we shouldn't enjoy what there is to enjoy because others are suffering, while the latter states that there's always enough to go around. In fact, there's more than enough, and whoever wants to enjoy it all can enjoy it all. The former creates animosity, competitiveness, and comparative unhappiness, while the latter creates giving, community, and marital happiness so that you can enjoy and contribute back. Which do you think comes from your God, the law of scarcity or the law of abundance?"

"Abundance, but . . ."

Red approached her like a counselor with helpful advice. "Right now," Red whispered in her ear, "you're exhausted. But, Olivia, the couples who have fun together, love staying together. Willfully denying yourself the opportunity to live in full enjoyment every day because someone else isn't pulling his weight puts the final stamp of destruction on the marriage. Don't blame him for your unhappiness. You can always choose to have a happier marriage than your spouse. Abundance, whether emotional or financial, exists all around you, but right now, you're operating from a state of emotional poverty."

Don't blame your spouse for your unhappiness. It disempowers you, plus you can always choose to have a happier marriage than your spouse. Make it a game each day to see who can experience the happier marriage in your marriage.

She thinks she knows, but she doesn't know.

Red stayed near her ear. "When you blame someone else for your life results, you give away your power to be happy. Conversely, if you enjoy the moment, despite your partner's behavior, it'll lift you both—and the behaviors will improve. We can help you make your relationship a masterpiece. Would you like that, Olivia?"

Zeb and Oliver both watched her. It felt so strange having two men she loved in one lifetime standing in the same room.

She lowered her chin and pulled it back against her neck. "Sounds like a pipedream, but yes, of course." After taking a deep breath, she wiped a tear from her eye and smiled.

"Sorry to interrupt this philosophical discussion," Oliver said, hands in his pockets.

"Theological." Olivia swiped at more tears that coursed down her cheeks. Her mascara must be all over her face. Zeb probably thought she was an emotional, ugly woman. *But why do I care what he thinks?*

"Okay, theological," Oliver muttered, "philosophical," under his breath. "Either way, there's a really cool bungee-jumping station over there that I'd like to try."

There he goes again, brushing her feelings aside. Olivia's forehead bulged, and she could feel her fingernails slowly bite into her palms. When she saw the other couples looking at her, she opted to block out the frustration. Perhaps if she attempted to take Red's advice and enjoy a station or two, things would naturally improve.

It had been a long time since she'd allowed herself to really enjoy life, much less take responsibility for it. And now Zeb was here, dredging up memories of the past—the joy and the heartbreak and questions left unanswered. She shook her head and focused her gaze and her mind on her husband. *Never mind Zeb. Go have some fun, Olivia. You deserve it. I think.*

Blue adjusted his blue top hat, looked at Red for approval, and said, "Let me explain how this works . . ."

*   *   *

Blue pointed to certain stations with his cane. "Each station is designed to give you a depth of pleasure you've yet to encounter in life. We believe joy is part of God's purpose for your life, and in that sense, it goes as deep as you're willing to go."

Zeb looked forward to a well-earned rest. *Finally, a place where I can have fun and not have to worry about who's paying for it.*

Blue kept pointing to stations. "See the bowling station over there? Or the Shakespeare festival on the other side of the balloons? When you enter, make it a goal to get to a level nine pleasure, then notice how you feel about your relationship. Pretty passionate, I suspect. That's because when you're smiling together, laughing with each other, and experiencing joy in each other's company, you like each other. Do those things at a level nine and you'll like each other a lot!"

Zeb looked around as if Santa Claus himself might come flying through on his sleigh. He'd never seen anything like this, and he couldn't wait to get started. "Blue, thank you for the opportunity, although, I must say, this whole room's a bit strange, in a good way, of course."

Blue winked at him. "Maybe so, but your world contains strangeness too. Someday future archaeologists will dig up Disney World and think there was a strange mouse-worshipping kingdom."

"Did he just say *your world*?" Zeb whispered to Isabella.

"The rooms are designed for you to spend time enjoying each other's company again, to have fun and leave behind the stresses of parenting, work, chores, and paying bills." Blue appeared to know what he was talking about.

I like the sound of that.

"Couples who enjoy life together stay together because they like being around each other. The more enjoyable experiences, the more their overall satisfaction improves. That's why at the end of your time in this room, we want you to ask your partner, 'On a scale of one to ten, how would you rate how much you enjoy spending time with me back home? If it's not at a ten, what would it take to make it to a ten back home?'" Blue held up his hand.

"Are you saying we can get our relationship to your 'consistent nine' by the end of this room?" Zeb looked flushed.

"Yes and no. No, because there's more to getting your relationship to a *consistent* nine. You'll need what's in the rest of the rooms for that, especially room 7. Yes, because you can't get there without shared enjoyable experiences." Blue paused in case they had questions.

Ask this every Sunday: On a scale of one to ten, how would we rate how much we enjoy spending time with one another? If it's not a ten, how could we make it a 10?

Zeb studied Isabella's face; the way her nose crinkled reminded him of their first few dates together when she would get all excited about an idea. She was a good thinker and loved a good conversation over coffee. They used to find each other sexy and fun. But with all the responsibilities that came with a blended family—the mixed parenting procedures, the cost of paying for more people, and the sheer exhaustion of dealing with day-to-day upkeep, not to mention the pain she carried into the relationship—it just hindered them from enjoying, really enjoying, each other's company. *If I could just make more money* . . .

Red's kind eyes shifted to Zeb. "It's not so much about the stations but how you share the experiences together in the stations. Our hope is the experiences mold your emotional patterns so that you link massive pleasure to each other. Once through the rooms, you'll realize you don't need to settle for mediocrity in your relationship ever again. Some couples settle for mediocrity when they are so caught up in the trap of getting more. In that rat race, they never learn to enjoy what they have, thereby settling into a marriage of mediocrity even while surrounded by abundance. One of the secrets to happily-ever-after is a shift toward experiencing massive pleasure with each other in the now, not just in the honeymoon or some future 'more' stage, but consistently throughout your relationship no matter the economics."

If only . . . Maybe if Zeb didn't have to concern himself with bringing in such a big income from a job he didn't enjoy, this might seem more realistic.

"You'll discover all kinds of strategies to make this true for your relationship. For example, recall what the limo driver said about reconditioning your brain to ask better questions." Blue looked like he just drank three cups of espressos. "Asking the right questions can move you in the direction of the ultimate relationship experience."

I'd bet the farm he has some example questions. "What are those questions?" Zeb scratched his jaw. He couldn't believe he just asked that question. He was ready to get on with it to experience the room's pleasures.

Blue was all too willing to provide the questions. "Here are three we recommend to all our couples—one for whenever you're thinking about your past, another for whenever you're talking about the present, and the third for when you're planning your future."

I knew it. Zeb felt thirsty and thought about walking over to the drinking fountain again. But he knew the others were already looking sulky since he had asked a question, so he thought he better stick around and not leave them to hear the answers to the question he himself asked.

Blue leaned on his cane and stroked his throat. "The question for your past, whether ten years ago or just earlier in the day: What did we love about our relationship then, and how does that make us feel?"

There was a lot of good in Zeb and Isabella's past. This shouldn't be too hard.

"Question two, the one for your present: What's fun or pleasurable about our relationship right now, and how does *that* make us feel?"

He sighed. *These days? Honestly, not much, but that's because there are so many demands on us.*

"The final question, the one pertaining to all your tomorrows: What are we excited about, and how does that make us feel?"

At the moment, their future was pretty uncertain. If Zeb enjoyed his job more and made twice his current income, he'd feel free to enjoy home life more.

Red stood near Emma and Titus. "Now just think, if this couple talked through these three questions every day, do you believe they'd be where they are right now?"

Wow, she just called them out. Everyone knew how frosty their relationship was. Titus looked stunned. When Zeb recalled that she'd also called out Olivia, he decided to avoid making eye contact with Red.

"Each person in a relationship needs to feel certainty that he or she will receive more pleasure than pain. The moment there's more pain in the relationship—arguing over money, an affair, or taking out the trash—is when drifting occurs, like two paths moving in different emotional directions. Most couples experience a mixture of pleasure and pain, causing a mix of feelings for each other. Your goal should be to feel massive pleasure for your partner every day. Asking the three questions points your brain daily in that direction." Red beamed like she was unwrapping hidden treasure for them.

> Couples drift because they experience a mixture of pleasure and pain for each other. To experience the ultimate relationship, generate daily feelings of certainty and emotional pleasure for one another.

Zeb felt a shiver, and his eyes widened. While looking at the ground, he thought about what could bring their talking to a close. He said, "Those are helpful questions. Thank you. That's probably the extent of your success strategies to help us enjoy the different stations in this room, yes?"

Red took a deep breath, savoring the moment. "What's the rush? Pleasure is had in savoring the moment, Zeb. The more moments you can enjoy, the better your marriage will get. In fact, we'll have you write down one hundred things you enjoy doing before you leave this room, then circle the ones you enjoy doing *together* so that when you get home, you can keep the momentum going. You'll begin to link pleasure to each other while you're here, but we are more interested in helping you keep that going when you get back home."

"What if there's only, like, three things we enjoy doing together?" Oliver's mouth twitched.

Ouch! Zeb couldn't help but notice Olivia grit her teeth and step away from Oliver. Not that Zeb could really judge. He didn't exactly have his act together. But there was one thing he could make right tonight. He just needed to find a way to talk to Olivia. He owed her an explanation.

*   *   *

Chapter 5

7:15 am

"That's an astute question, Oliver." Red stroked her chin. "And here's why: Couples drift apart precisely at the point when they stop enjoying each other's company. Your relationship begins with massive pleasure, then over time it devolves into moderate pleasure. Then after a while, through the monotonous daily routines, they convince themselves they have nothing in common anymore. A little flirting with someone else, and they think they've finally found a perfect match. What really happened is they linked more pleasure to the new person than their current partner."

Emma rubbed her chest as if pained. "So how can we prevent that from happening?" She looked up and blinked rapidly because her eyes swam with tears.

"*Ahhh*. Now there's the secret." Blue unexpectedly pulled Emma in for a side hug. He was so kind and thoughtful. "It's what this room is all about. Here's the solution: Attach massive pleasure to your relationship's routines because that's where most of the action is." Blue released Emma and walked back near Red who was standing in front of the massage parlor station.

"But . . . what if a couple, hypothetically speaking, has seen their passion wane over the years?" Emma felt a lump in her throat when she swallowed.

Blue adjusted his hat. "That's an inherently false question. You don't 'have' or 'not have' pleasure for each other. You generate pleasure. It's entirely your responsibility, 100 percent of the time. A quote often attributed to one of your former presidents says, 'Most folks are about as happy as they make up their minds to be.'"

"Sure, but some couples have way different interests." Emma rubbed absently at her arms.

Blue gave her an understanding nod. "No matter what state your marriage is currently in, you can choose to enjoy anything with your spouse. If you doubt this, then think about when you first started dating. *Everything* you did together seemed enjoyable—even when you didn't share each other's interests. The idea is that you don't *have* enjoyment, you *generate* it. Like a power company generates electricity, you generate the sparks that lead to the ultimate marriage."

Like a power company generates electricity, you can consistently generate the chemistry and kindness that leads to the ultimate relationship.

"Okay, we generate fun, but—and I'm just being honest—it seems like a lot of work." Zeb stole a glance at Olivia.

That's odd. Why'd he look at Olivia rather than Isabella? That's the second time I've seen him do that.

"Isn't anything worth having also worth the work?" Blue held his hands behind his back, gripping his own wrist. "And haven't you noticed in life that the more you work on something that produces results, the greater overall pleasure you experience?"

"True." Isabella cut her eyes at Zeb and sighed. "But Zeb's right. When we first started dating, everything was easier. Now, and not to be disrespectful to anyone else's circumstances, but with our blended family and new responsibilities, *everything* feels like a challenge."

Blue pulled his white glasses down and looked over the rims. "Everything?"

Isabella shifted her balance and rolled her eyes. "Okay, most things."

"Most?"

"A lot. You understand what I'm saying. I guess my question is, uh, how can we make experiencing pleasure easier to do?" Isabella exhaled.

A long pause filled the room.

"Habit." Red appeared relaxed, her hand casually anchored on her hip. "By making your habits pleasurable."

Habit? Seriously? I need more than a habit to win Titus back.

Red assumed a pose that drew their attention to her best attributes. "Your relationships feel like a yawn at times because you pay no attention to improving your habits. When you first met and began courting each other, your relationship wasn't built on shared habits but rather pleasurable thoughts and experiences. That's why it felt so romantic."

So there is a rhyme and reason to romance. It's in our control.

"But during this time, and unbeknownst to your new partner, you also lived out your own habits when you weren't spending time together, like belching and gossiping and watching too much reality TV. When you went on dates, you checked those habits at the door and went out of your way to impress the other—stimulating pleasure in her brain about you. But at the end of the night, you situated right back into your habits like a comfortable shoe, habits your new partner had no idea about."

Emma kept her mouth shut for fear they'd spotlight one of her bad habits. They seemed to know everything else about her.

Red continued to scrutinize the couples. "After a few months of dating, guess what happened? You started noticing each other's habits, like when he wouldn't put the toilet seat down or when she left dirty dishes on the counter. This is an explanatory cause of why things go sour: The pleasure waned. Those habits were always there, but you didn't see them clearly."

Like Titus's habit of shutting me out when we found out he couldn't have children.

Red widened her eyes when she leaned in toward the couples. "This is so important to understand if you want to make your relationship a masterpiece. You bring all your individualized habits—and you each have hundreds of habits, in fact, over 90 percent of your life is habit—into the relationship. And when two very different sets of habits move into the same house, conflict ensues because you disagree with each other's habits on some level."

Emma couldn't argue with that. "So what do you suggest we do?"

Red surveyed the couples with a pleased smile. "Attach massive pleasure to your habits. The rest will fall into place because that's what habit is—you just naturally do them."

A movie started playing on the huge ceiling—a larger-than-life montage of each of the couples. Scenes from their past highlighting moments when they felt great in each other's company.

Oh, that's embarrassing. Titus held Emma's toothbrush like a microphone, and she wrapped him up with the blow dryer cord. Dancing again. That was when they enjoyed each other the most, when they danced. Definitely embarrassing, but she couldn't deny how happy they looked together.

Red licked her lip with cautious hope. "Most couples treat pleasure as an escape from the stresses of life, sometimes even as a form of hedonism, then they come right back into their daily lives filled with habits. The secret of world-class couples, however—those who rate their overall satisfaction at a consistent nine—is to identify shared habits and attach massive relationship pleasure to them. Do this and you'll find yourselves really excited about spending time together again."

"That's not always true," Emma protested kindly. "See there in the movie, we had shared habits, but we don't do those things anymore. If we enjoyed them so much, we would have continued them."

Red nodded. "The key is to make the enjoyable habits stick so you can feel the passion for each other most of the time, and wouldn't you know it, there's a powerful way to do just that." Red went over to a picnic table where a stack of booklets and pens lay. She handed one to each couple. "Here. Take one of these."

On the first ten pages or so were a bunch of blanks numbered 1 through 100, and after that, there was a letter.

"Before you're allowed to move on to room 2, here are your instructions." Red picked some lint off her dress. "Follow these, and you'll be free to move on. First, read this together. When you finish, fill out your one hundred fun list—one hundred things you have fun doing, whether that's entertainment, giving, and/or contributing back by helping with the Special Olympics, and then circle the ones you have fun doing *together*. Take both home with you. After reading the note and making your list, room 1 is yours to explore. Find pleasure in your days, in your relationship. Experiment and have a blast! Associate each other with pleasure. All couples could use some more fun in their relationships. When you're ready, make your way to the guest rooms we've incorporated down here. Get some sleep, shower, and eat the food we provided. Once you finish breakfast, and no earlier than 7:00 a.m., you may move on to room 2."

Okay, Titus, let's see how far we get on this. They say it'll work for any couple. If it works for us, then I'll believe.

*   *   *

Once they filled out their one hundred fun list, each couple opened their booklets to read the following:

> Dear Couple,
>
> You don't pick what kind of marriage you're going to have. You pick your habits and then those habits give you the kind of marriage you have. More than 90 percent of your relationship is habit. More than 90 percent! Habits are why you feel the way you do in your relationship. Over time they condition your feelings for each other. You're overwhelmed, suffering, and stressed—not because your relationship is broken, but because your habits are broken. Here's the excellent news: If you're dissatisfied with your relationship in any way, just change your habits in the relationship— because when you improve your habits, you improve your relationship.

To help, we're now going to give you the strategies to remove destructive habits and replace them with energizing and exciting habits. It doesn't require any more time to learn and apply new habits. We know you're busy. You just have to replace the old habits with new ones. It may not sound sexy, but if you don't do this, there's little hope for you in any relationship. So stop blaming each other and start taking responsibility for your habits. Of all the amazing ways to improve your relationship, this is the surest and fastest way to create quantum leaps of success in shaping the ultimate relationship.

We're not asking you to overhaul your whole life. We're suggesting you make the small changes that affect everything else. Like a farmer in a tractor driving up and down the field row, if her steering is off just by two inches, she'll veer way off course. In the same way, if you have the wrong habits, over time your relationship will drift.

> You don't pick what kind of relationship you're going to experience. You pick your habits and then those habits give you the kind of relationship you experience.

You may feel like your habits don't affect your marriage that much, but think of it this way: If the next time you watched another TV series (habit!) instead of talking to your spouse and they cheated on you, chances are you might not reach for the remote. If the next time you didn't forgive your spouse (bad habit!) and it instantly mutated your face into the disgruntled spirit you're becoming on the inside, odds are you'd forgive. If one more critical comment to your spouse (bad habit!) caused your daughter to date some thug who's only interested in her body, you'd only speak with kindness to your spouse. If not helping clean up (bad habit!) around the house immediately tractor-beamed you into divorce court, where you'd lose your spouse and kids and half your income, you'd gladly help out around the house. If eating more pie (bad habit!) instantly put fifty pounds on your frame, you'd say "no, thanks." These bad habits *don't seem* to affect your relationship too much, but they do.

The problem is that you've attached so much pleasure to your bad habits that you're blind to the long-term consequences they're having on your relationship. In the moment, those bad habits don't seem to have any negative consequences at all. But like the farmer above, your small repeated bad habits veer you way off course from happily-ever-after. It's why the divorce rate stays above 50 percent and another 40 percent aren't happy living together anymore. Couples wake up one day and ask, "What happened to us? We're not happy." It's the habits, whether thought habits, emotional habits, or any other kind of habits, that make or break your marriage.

The good news is the slightest adjustments to your habits will alter the outcomes to your relationship. Again, we're not asking you to make major overhauls here. It's the routines of life that make all the difference to the quality of your relationship. If you want your relationship satisfaction to be at a nine out of ten with consistency, switch your bad habits for good ones. These habits will multiply your levels of love, romance, joy, and fulfillment, ultimately making your marriage divorce-proof.

So here's how: Make a list of habits that hurt your relationship, and then dump them. Don't hesitate. Toss them. Do it before it's too late! Stop messing around. Then make a list of habits that will create the ultimate relationship experience, and do those. Simple, right? The secret is to go a step further by attaching so much pleasure to the great habits that they stick. An example might be adding $5 to your dream-vacation fund every time you perform the helpful habit for one week.

Let's flesh this out so you really get it because, remember, habits are more than 90 percent of your relationship. Did we mention 90 percent yet? Making your marriage a masterpiece then is not an act or a destination but a habit. Because the power of habit influences everything about your relationship, we will now show you how to leverage that power to make the horrible habits disappear forever and the helpful habits stick so that you experience massive pleasure with your partner.

Just reminding yourself daily about the power of habit keeps you alert to why things are going the way they are in your relationship.

Habits are so powerful that they are the differentiator between world-class couples who rate their marital happiness at a consistent nine and struggling couples who settle at a fluctuating two to seven. The former recognize the power of habit and take action. Massive action is the secret to success here. Take massive action with the right habits and you'll find yourself experiencing the ultimate relationship. World-class couples are simply couples who took massive action with world-class habits.

The psychologist and philosopher, William James, emphasizes the power of habit in his short treatise titled *Habit*. He demonstrates how habits shape one's character and personality. This means your habits will determine your relationship identity. Your identity—that's everything.

James labels human beings bundles of habits and calls habits the enormous flywheel of society. This holds true for couples and families. Couples are bundles of habits, and habits are the flywheel of the family – affecting your kids and generations.

A habit is simply a behavior pattern that becomes your natural reflex. Practically, your habits shaped your relationship into what it's become today. Your individualized and separate habits then need to find harmony with each other like a beautiful symphony. Otherwise, the habits you shaped in your individuality will wield swords on each other in your relationship until you want to kill each other. Fights! It's perfectly fine to have your own habits—you should. Just be aware that these little bundles of energy are acting and reacting to your partner's bundles of energy and vice versa *at all times*. This can lead to conflict or chemistry, depending on what you decide to do after this letter. If you don't make any decision, then like most couples, your separate bundles of energy will lead to conflict, then destruction. Be different. Don't be average. Be special. Create hot, passionate bundles of energy for each other.

Why, because your habits habituate you to inhabit your emotional states, self-told stories, and whole worldviews. That means over time your habits have conditioned how you feel about each other, how you talk to yourself about your partner, and how you see each other. It all flows from your habits.

Once you've found the love of your life, your relationship becomes your daily routines or habits, meaning you're so comfortable with them that you can't imagine life without them—even if they're harmful habits. You might not like it when he's rude, acts like a jerk, yells, and tolerates living life at less than a nine, but you've become so accustomed to it that you can't imagine a relationship any other way, which keeps you stuck in mediocrity. You'll think that's just the way marriage is supposed to be. When you do experience the occasional nine, you'll self-sabotage your relationship because your habits pull you back to a five. That's what identity does. All behavior flows from identity, and your relationship identity is shaped by your habits.

It can be no other way. You start seeing and experiencing the world through these habits, and they become your natural reflex toward your partner. Charles Noble was right: "First we make our habits, and then our habits make us."

Focus right now on developing amazing habits with the switcheroo method:

← THE SWITCHEROO →

Switch 5 horrible habits	For 5 pleasurable habits
1.	1.
2.	2.
3.	3.
4.	4.
5.	5.

Here are a couple of strategies to help you choose sexy, hot, great habits and make them stick so that you can find the love of your life and experience the ultimate relationship. If you're already married, these strategies will make your marriage a masterpiece.

NO. 1: WHEN YOU GO THROUGH THE ROOM (and life), PICK THE STATIONS THAT ENERGIZE YOUR RELATIONSHIP, AND TURN THOSE INTO HABITS.

Here are some helpful habits that will bring pleasure to your relationship. Consider adopting them:

- Set aside time every Sunday evening to prepare, project, and plan the week. This puts you on the same page entering every week. Make sure to do this in a pleasurable state, like while eating ice cream or giving each other a massage. Massages, baby!
- At bedtime, ask each other, "What did you enjoy about our relationship today?" This ends your day thinking positively about your spouse.
- At least once a week, make time to physically interact in a romantic way. Not only does this bond you together, but also science shows all kinds of physical benefits, like boosting hormones and opening up capillaries to help blood and oxygen flow, not to mention the romantic connection. Guys: remember that most females like cuddling.
- Find a cause that you both help with, like ending human trafficking.
- Read a book together once a month. Take turns picking the book.
- Pick a dream, desire, or goal that you'd like to achieve together. Examples include learning salsa dancing, taking a painting class, and running a half marathon together.

Those are some energy boosting habits to get you started. Now walk around the Playful Pleasure Room and add others you'd like to incorporate into your relationship. Identify what causes you to attach pleasure to each other and make those your habits. Choose wisely because once you select habits, they'll shape your relationship.

NO. 2: PICK HABITS THAT YOU *REALLY WANT* AND THAT YOU BELIEVE WILL GIVE YOU THE ULTIMATE RELATIONSHIP EXPERIENCE.

This sounds like a big *duh!* But we here at the Couples' Castle coach so many couples who live according to other people's dreams, desires, and expectations—especially their in-laws'. Forget that. It's not their relationship. *You* guys, together, pick what *you* want—habits that bring pleasure and satisfaction to both of you.

This dramatically improves the odds of making the habits stick. Here are some examples of habits that have helped other couples, a starter list for you to consider and customize:

- Whenever there's drama, immediately focus on forgiveness. You'll feel better about each other. Drama creates pain. Forgiveness feels painful but brings pleasure.
- Instead of judging your partner, vow to only talk about the best in your partner. You have no time to love him if you're also judging. You'll feel great about each other.
- Surround your relationship with positive couples. Much like smoking is outlawed in the public sphere, outlaw negativity in your private sphere. Spending time with couples in strong, healthy relationships reinforces and strengthens your own marriage. Pleasure!
- Family dance parties! Crank up the music and dance with each other in the middle of the living room. Fun habits produce fun relationships!
- Take turns placing your hands on each other's hearts at bedtime and ask three empowering questions: *Who loves you? Who believes in you? Who thinks you're beautiful?* Of the man, you might ask, *Who believes in you? Who admires you? Who is my hero?* Do this every night. You'll feel the power of habit transforming your relationship and skyrocketing your marital satisfaction to nine in a hurry.

These were just examples. Good ones. The idea is to consciously choose your habits before they begin shaping your relationship unconsciously. So, again, pick five fun, energizing habits right now, ones that make you feel fully alive when spending time with your partner.

What should you do if one or both of you have already formed a bad habit, i.e., your nervous system has already set into a daily pattern of automatically going through the motions of the bad habit and it's difficult to stop?

William James claims that "in most of us, by the age of thirty, the character has set like plaster, and will never soften again."

We believe, on the contrary, that it's possible—no matter the age—to replace harmful habits with exceptional habits that'll boost the satisfaction in your relationship.

How?

Not with willpower, but by conditioning your nervous system. Your nervous system operates in natural reflex mode all the time. This means whatever habits you set up in your life—harmful or helpful—your central nervous system operates accordingly. Your brain automatically assumes that's what you're supposed to do—even if the habit is harmful.

You want to make your nervous system your ally instead of your enemy. No amount of willpower can change your nervous system's mind because it's a natural reflex. The only way to make it your ally is to condition it over time with new habits. Then you'll automatically act and react with helpful habits toward your partner.

Willpower is akin to pushing a big boulder up a mountain. That's partly why you feel so worn out in your marriage. Conditioning is like pulling a sled on flat land. There's still work to do, but you'd rather pull than push, especially when the "pull" is from something greater than yourself—like experiencing the ultimate relationship and making your marriage a masterpiece.

Making the pleasurable habits stick is easier than you think. It's what Aristotle hinted at, Freud asserted, Jeremy Bentham outlined, and Anthony Robbins popularized. **Apply the pleasure-pain principle.**

This principle refers to the human tendency to choose behaviors that either avoid pain or gain pleasure. You can leverage this principle to quash harmful habits in your relationship and replace them with helpful habits.

The pleasure-pain principle is not the only influencer of your relationship, but it's the biggest reason you treat each other the way you do. That should inspire you to implement this strategy. It can change your lives."

Here are two ways to use the pleasure-pain principle to get rid of horrible habits, form loving ones, and make them stick for your long-term relationship success:

NO. 1: USE A SCALE OF ONE TO TEN TO LINK PAIN TO THE HARMFUL HABIT.

If one is no pain and ten is the worst kind of emotional or psychological pain, make *not* getting rid of the harmful habit so painful and emotionally intense that you must terminate the behavior immediately. Like now! Conversely, make not developing the helpful habit so excruciating that you must form it right now.

For example, list some of the harmful habits in your relationship. Here's a starter list:

1. Criticizing each other
2. Not putting the toilet seat down
3. Complaining and being negative
4. Not hugging each other good night
5. Letting a day go by where you don't think of your partner as loving and sexy

Next, decide how long it'll take to get rid of the harmful habit. There are lots of opinions regarding how long it takes to get rid of habits and form new ones. Dr. Maxwell Maltz published his findings on habits in his blockbuster book *Pscyho-Cybernetics*, in which he said it takes a minimum of twenty-one days to form a new habit. Many believe it takes even longer.

Both positions are nonsense.

How long it takes to form your new habit isn't nearly as important as starting day one. Change doesn't take long at all. It always occurs in one moment. When you decide that you *have* to change something in the relationship, that's what begins the habit formation.

Third, create an intense painful thought about the habit in the brain so that the neuro-associations shift. Associate that habit with massive pain. This is the process of conditioning instead of willpower. Once you do this, your brain will automatically want to get rid of that bad habit. It screams, "Too much pain! Too much pain!" Get rid of it!

You want your heart to associate horrible habits with pain, not pleasure, because it's your habits that habituate you to inhabit your relational experience. Your habits shape your relationship, and the harmful habits methodically erode it. And by the way, horrible habits are any habits that are not helpful. There's no neutral habit. And average habits over time erode the passion.

Changing your habit is not about a lack of capability. You *can* change your habits.

Think about it. If someone threatened your life, would you change your relationship's harmful habits?

Of course!

So find a way to link pain to *not* squashing the harmful habit before it wreaks havoc in your relationship, keeping you from the ultimate relationship experience. Create a sense of urgency to change it so you're compelled to take action immediately. Make it happen. Now!

In considering how you can create this emotional pain, ponder these questions:

- What will this harmful habit cost our relationship if we continue this behavior?
- What will happen to our love life?
- How is this bad habit affecting our kids?
- How is it affecting the way we spend time together?
- What's at stake?

The idea is to recognize the power of habit and create a sense of urgency to dump the harmful habits. On the flip side . . .

NO. 2: USE A SCALE OF ONE TO TEN TO LINK ENOUGH PLEASURE TO THE HELPFUL (HOT!) HABITS FOR THE

PURPOSE OF CREATING THE ULTIMATE MARRIAGE EXPERIENCE.

If one is no pleasure and ten equals the best kind of emotional or psychological pleasure, make forming this new world-class habit so pleasurable that you must take immediate action. Make it so that you don't want to do anything else until you make this your habit. This should be your next main step to make your marriage a masterpiece.

In considering how you can create this emotional pleasure, find answers with positive and passionate feelings to these questions:

- How can this helpful habit make us feel passionate about each other?
- How will it help us make our marriage a masterpiece?
- How much more hotness will we experience?
- What will the typical day look like? Do we get excited about it?
- What will this new habit do for us over the next five years?

The key is to *feel* your relationship satisfaction number rising. This isn't just about attempting another idea but about emotionalizing it. When you emotionalize it, habit takes over. This isn't just talk or another good idea to nod at. You gotta feel it. Do you feel it? You need to. Otherwise it won't work.

If you do not *feel* the pleasure to the point where you'll take action *right now*, your number's not high enough. There should be no hesitation, no flinching, just doing—because you want to feel fully alive with each other. That's when it'll become sticky.

In sum, link so much pleasure or so much pain to the habit that you must take consistent action because you want to. How would you do that with dinners, taking out the trash, and hugs? Remember, you are bundles of habits shaping each other, so choose helpful, world-class habits and link the right amount of pain or pleasure to make them stick. About 90 percent of your relationship is habit—your future is at stake! Again, you don't choose your marriage. You choose your habits, then those habits design your marriage.

At the end of the day, whether you're picking a pleasure experience in the room, writing out your one hundred fun activities, or forming helpful habits, the Playful Pleasure Room's aim is to improve your relationship satisfaction so high that you think of each other as the love of your life, experience the ultimate relationship, and make your marriage a masterpiece.

Finally, sit down with your partner every Sunday to ask

1. Are we creating more pleasure or pain in our interactions with each other?
2. In what ways am I a source of massive pleasure or pain in the butt to you?
3. When I think about my future with my partner, do I feel more pleasure or pain?

Of course, even when your relationship doesn't feel like heaven, you should walk through hell for each other because that's what world-class couples do. The point remains, however: Your relationship success significantly depends upon playful pleasure, enjoying thinking about each other, enjoying what you do together, and enjoying how you do it. Have more fun! Get passionate! Be the couple at 90 who still feel butterflies for each other. Go crazy! Become a source of pleasure, instead of a pain in the butt, to each other. The easiest, most effective way is to create habits full of pleasure.

Here's to consistent playful pleasure for your relationship.

Sincerely,
Your relationship coaches at the Couples' Castle

*   *   *

Wow, that's kind of a lot to take in. Emma set the document down and looked at Titus. *I wonder what he's thinking.*

When the three couples finished reading, they were given extra sets of clothes and encouraged to explore the surrounding stations.

These included a bowling alley, Shakespeare festival, bingo center, board game area, library, instrument room, how-to-help-the-homeless room, massage parlor, virtual-reality area, mini golf, a photography class, a cooking class, an aquarium, exercise facility, a painting class, hammocks, spa, and a counseling center where Titus and Emma stayed for several hours.

They enjoyed the Playful Pleasure Room for the majority of the day and decided to crash early given they'd stayed up all night the previous evening. Zeb and Isabella were the first to make their way to the guest room and rest, while the others followed soon thereafter. After they woke up, showered, and ate fresh fruit together, they met up in the middle of the Playful Pleasure Room promptly at 6:45 a.m.

"Where's Red and Blue? We need to get going. We've already spent a day here and still have five rooms to get our model treasure chests initialed before we can even think about entering room 7. We can't be late. Did you guys hear me? We can't be late." Isabella motioned anxiously while Zeb moved in and put his arm around her waist to calm her down.

"Yes, the clock's ticking. They said, 'finish or fail!' So ominous. I don't know, maybe they moved on to the next room. And they did say we can enter the next room at 7:00 a.m. I say we go." Olivia pointed to the yellow door marked Room No. 2: POSITIVE PROJECTION. "Everyone ready?"

They all made their way through the snack bar and lemonade stand over to the door. As they approached, Oliver grabbed a patch of blue cotton candy and stuffed it in his mouth. The group stepped into the next room, and the door closed firmly behind them.

I can't see.

Chapter 6

Room 2

"It's p-pitch-black in here." Titus's clammy hands felt along the walls.

The air was cool and crisp, around sixty degrees. Titus couldn't see anyone.

"Helloooooo? Anyone in here!" Oliver's voice echoed.

The room's thick darkness looked like a rainbow compared to the searing dark pain in Titus's heart. A vice gripped his chest, and he struggled to catch his breath.

"Titus?" Emma said, panic in her voice.

"Someone find a light switch, quick!" Emma shouted. "Something's wrong with Titus."

Everyone shuffled around, bumping into one another. The vice tightened, constricting his lungs.

Voices mumbled, "I can't see a thing in here."

"I can't find a switch on these walls."

"These don't feel like walls," someone said.

Whatever they were, they were closing in. Titus yanked on his collar. *Breathe. Just breathe.*

"It's some sort of pattern," a male voice responded softly.

"Maybe we ought to go back to the Playful Pleasure Room."

"We can't, remember? One of rules stipulated we can stay in the rooms indefinitely, but once we leave the room, there's no reentering"

"Ouch!"

Was that Oliver? I don't know. Just b-breathe. Catch your breath, Titus. Be strong and don't let them see weakness. Come on.

"What is it?" Olivia hollered.

The dark room mocked Titus with flashes of Emma's infidelity. *Aren't they seeing this?* Pictures of Emma on top of Larry raced through his mind. He shook his head, trying to block it out, but the darkness was too thick, too heavy—like a death grip.

"Nothing," Oliver responded. "I just walked into a door, that's all."

"Hey, I found a door handle!"

"Where's it lead to?"

"It's locked."

"Someone help us!" Emma screamed. She put her hand on Titus's shoulder, and he jerked away, pressing his fists to the sides of his head. Her touch sent him into a downward spiral.

"Pound that door, and the rest of us will scream for help."

"Help! Help!"

Oliver kept pounding.

Titus couldn't stop the flashes. His nostrils flared, and he began wheezing. *Am I dying?*

"Help! Help!"

The entire room lit up like a Friday-night high-school football game. Titus shielded his eyes. The images lost, his breathing slowed.

"What the?" Oliver pivoted 360 degrees.

Hundreds of televisions hooked into the walls, floors, and ceilings, displaying a black-and-white random dot-pixel pattern of static. *Pitch-black again. Stay c-calm, Titus. Slow, quiet, deep breaths.*

Titus grabbed for something, anything, to lean on—it didn't matter what. His hand landed on Emma's shoulder.

The lights flickered back on, and he jerked his hand away, flexing his fingers.

Silent movies played on the screens, a different movie on each television.

"Hey, *The Notebook.*" Olivia pointed behind Titus. She seemed to have his best interest at heart in distracting everyone to the TV.

There were different movies on different TVs, many they'd watched together: *Titanic, Love Actually, When Harry Met Sally, A Walk to Remember, Casablanca, Dirty Dancing, Eternal Sunshine of the Spotless Mind, You've Got Mail, Gone with the Wind,* and other love stories.

"Love stories," someone whispered.

Titus's breath calmed and he couldn't help notice one TV in particular. "Wait, they're flickering, changing into . . . highlight reels of our relationships? That's Emma and I dancing together . . ." He said it softly, but everyone could hear the pain in his voice.

*   *   *

"Look, Olivia, that's the summer we went camping at Mackinaw Island. Remember the ferry ride over to the main island when you almost fell overboard? What year was that?" Oliver skimmed his fingertips over his jawline.

About two years after my summer with Zeb. My heart was still broken, and I needed that trip to rejuvenate myself and figure out what I was doing with my life. Why was he back in her life? Why now?

Oliver threaded his fingers through hers. "Remember, that's the campfire where you smeared marshmallow on my face. Oh, there it is!"

They looked so happy, him chasing her around the campsite, wrapping her up in a big bear hug. *What happened to us, Oliver?* Had they just gotten too busy and distracted with life?

An adjacent television showed them driving in their wedding car, drinking a glass of chardonnay. A third television, up above and to the right, pictured them holding hands and climbing a flight of steps into the local movie theater—laughing, casting change to a nearby homeless man on their way through the doors.

When's the last time we felt fully alive together like that? Life's gone by so fast, and we're not clicking the way we used to. We're just not.

The other couples watched their own highlight reels on other screens, full of wedding vows, walks in the park, four-wheeler rides, foot massages, and yard work in the spring time. In the latter, Isabella sneaked up behind Zeb with the garden hose, surprising him with a cold outdoor shower. He chased her around the front yard, while their neighbors rocked in their chairs from across the street. *That could've been me in another life.* Olivia's face muscles tightened, and she felt a burning sensation in her chest.

"Good evening," a soothing voice said.

They all turned, but nobody was there.

"We'd like to bring you a special report on the secrets to experiencing the ultimate relationship, finding the love of your life, and making your marriage a masterpiece."

"It's the woman on that center TV. A show host it appears," Isabella pointed, her black hair resting on her purple blouse.

Yes, of course, it is. Olivia couldn't believe the jealous feelings that surfaced. She sized Isabella up and realized it's not her fault. It's not anyone's fault. She'd just never fully dealt with these feelings. Suddenly, the air felt a bit chilly in the room.

The host sat in a brown leather Charlie chair with armrests. Looking straight through the television screen, she motioned to her left. "We now welcome our special guests, Titus and Emma."

What kind of magic was this? Emma and Titus were still standing right next to them. So either this was filmed earlier, or those were their doppelgangers on the TV screen.

Onto the stage strolled Emma and Titus. The host motioned for them to sit. "Thank you for being here."

Emma adjusted her dress, which was different from the black slacks she was wearing at the castle.

The host rested her head on her hand and leaned forward. "It's so nice the two of you agreed to be here, you know, given your situation several years ago."

Titus shifted in his chair on stage.

"You know, since the divorce," she said it with such a straight face.

Divorce? So . . . not filmed earlier. Did that mean this was their . . . future? Olivia glanced over at the real Emma. She was biting her lower lip, tears glistening in her eyes.

"What is this? What's going on?" real Emma asked. Her face had gone pale, and she gave a slow shake of the head.

I don't know, honey, but I bet you're not going to like whatever this is. Olivia turned back toward the TV.

"Yes, no problem. We're happy to help in any way possible." Titus still looked the same, perhaps a few pounds lighter and with some gray in his hair.

"So you both have kids now?" The host raised her eyebrows and nodded.

"Yes, we both remarried. Emma has two kids, and Jan and I adopted three beautiful children." He sat back and smiled.

Oh my. I think real Emma's about to spontaneously combust.

"As you know," the host said, "this is an episode devoted to helping individuals find the love of their life and experience the ultimate relationship." The camera panned the audience full of young, naive individuals and couples.

"Yes," Emma replied. "And after the divorce, we've both come to terms with what happened."

"Oh?" The host sat up straight, relaxed.

"First off," Emma offered a wave to the camera, "we have to thank our life coach who helped us understand how neuroscience affected—"

The host interrupted. "Your what?"

"Our life coach," Emma said with a wide grin. "We first went to counseling, but it really only helped us reinterpret the past. The life coach, on the other hand, told us about the fundamental brain triggers within every human being, one of which is not surprising."

"What is it?" the host woman's eyes darted to Titus.

He crossed his legs and interlocked his fingers. "Well, inside every human being is an intrinsic need, coded into his nervous system, that cries out for a strong emotional connection with another human being. Call it love, a bond, sparks of closeness, the need to feel cherished or cared for—we all have it, and it's more real than the chair you're sitting in. It's that feeling you get with that special someone." Titus softly slapped the chair to emphasize the point. "A connection."

Olivia twisted the wedding band on her left hand. *Ours feels like it's on a tightrope, and I don't know what to do about it.* She'd tried communicating with Oliver about how overwhelmed she was with doing the majority of the work around the house all these years, plus going to work, plus the children, plus, plus, plus . . . But nothing was getting through to him. She was also tired of always thinking about it.

Titus continued. "Every human being *needs* this feeling of connection. There's no way around it. It's so strong that humans will find a way to get it, no matter the cost. Even if you feel strongly connected to your spouse, you still want connection when you leave the house everyday because that same need to feel connected will lead you to connect with others outside the home. It's a constant human need that is always looking to satisfy itself. That's why the connection with your spouse must be handled all the time."

"Not knowing this cost us a lot." Emma held a deep sadness in her soul.

"How so?"

"The affair," Emma said, scrubbing a hand over her face and taking in a deep breath through her nostrils.

Is that what's next for us? That's not what I want. Olivia tilted her head toward Oliver in hopes he'd look back at her. He didn't.

TV Emma let out her breath while saying, "People love to feel connected but they don't really understand the cost an affair brings with it. You lose a lot."

The host lifted her hands, palms up. "We asked you to bring in a list of costs. Do you have that?"

Emma hesitated, rubbed her ear, and then looked at Titus for approval. "Yes, I do. Some of it we learned from our virtual mentor Michael Hyatt and others from our own experience."

"Well, may we hear it?"

Yes, that's something I'd like to hear.

"Okay, it may not be relevant for every couple, but we think it's probably pretty close." She rubbed her blouse down, pulled out a card that contained the list, and shared.

The Damage of an Affair

1. You'll probably lose your family. Most affairs lead to a marriage breakup, and the ones that survive go through years of counseling, repentance, and healing. Add kids in the mix, and the betrayal undermines all moral high ground and trust. They also carry an unfair burden.

2. You'll lose money. Having an affair is expensive. Secrecy, strategies, and cover-ups lead into the thousands of dollars. Then you have divorce lawyers, court, alimony, and child support.

3. You'll lose time. The time spent in the affair, cover-ups, and endless worry could've been devoted to becoming a productive powerhouse. Most people these days are looking for ways to get more time in their lives, but an affair wastes months, if not years, of one's life.

4. You could lose your job. Many affairs occur with colleagues. Company policy typically dictates you get canned for an affair, particularly if it's with a subordinate. If you work for a moral organization, like a nonprofit or ministry, bank on losing your job.

5. You'll lose years of mental focus. The betrayal, cover-ups, and constant hiding creates sideways energy that could've otherwise been spent moving the needle for your dreams.

6. You'll lose friends and the support of family. Typically, your friends are your ex-spouse's friends too. Now it's just awkward. Knowing you betrayed your spouse's trust undermines the trust with your friends. They slowly pull away.

7. You'll lose confidence in yourself. The difference between successful people and others includes confidence. Successful people generally have 95 percent confidence, while others experience a fluctuating confidence. Those who engage in an affair are more prone to a fluctuating confidence, especially

when they feel everyone's eyes staring down on them. Without confidence, it's difficult to make significant progress in life.

8. You lose emotional health, which often leads to physical sickness. The affair brings a surge of exciting emotions, but after a few months of the adrenaline rush, your emotions feel the effect of hurting people, guilt, self-loathing, and sadness. According to the Center for Disease Control and Prevention many sicknesses are related to one's emotions.

9. You'll lose your reputation. It's interesting how there's such disagreement in our culture about morality, except for infidelity. People are forgiving, but it's challenging for others to swallow an affair. Everyone believes this is wrong. And now they associate you with what's wrong.

10. You'll lose your positive life story. What story do you want to tell your kids and grandkids about your life? Will you be proud or want to skip over some major indiscretions? What kind of role model will you be?

11. You'll lose the respect of colleagues, customers, and future employers. People are longing for leaders and role models, and having an affair leaves a negative after effect.

"There's joy, love, and hope after the affair, but it's a painful process to get there, and you lose a lot of things you may never get back." Emma stared down at her hands.

The host shifted in her chair before clearing her throat. "Thank you for sharing."

Titus made strong eye contact with the host. "If I can add something, there was something persisting behind many of our negative interactions."

Olivia huffed. *Like not getting the kind of support one needs at home? Titus is so right. Wait a minute, I don't hear the Titus on TV stuttering at all.*

The host nodded.

"All actions are tied to how someone wants to feel. Don't make the mistake of thinking emotions are just shallow ways of thinking. Emotions are everything for both females and males, and they lead to every single action someone takes." Titus rolled his neck to find relief from a memory.

"Okay." The host arched her eyebrows.

Titus raised his own eyebrows, then leaned forward. "So that includes affairs."

"Oh. I see."

"People need to be honest with themselves. When one of their friends or someone they know is having an affair, they're like, 'What are you thinking? Why would you do that? Hello!' But it's much more challenging to be honest with oneself, and it's all because one is trying to satisfy an emotion."

"Go on." The host squinted.

Titus rubbed his nose. "Well, take a marriage partner who is lonely, angry, or frustrated with her partner. She feels the need to satisfy the feeling of connection and it's so strong she feels compelled to do so."

The host cut him off. "Yes, that happens everywhere."

"Of course, but before one considers an affair a live option, he should ask a couple of questions like, 'What feeling in me is causing me to consider this and how can I satisfy it in other ways?' and 'Who am I, besides myself, putting at risk with this idea of an affair?'" Before the host could interrupt him again, he answered his own question, "Those you love and those who love you, that's who."

The host eyeballed the audience, then looked back at Titus. "So you're saying we all want connection and that it's a powerful desire."

"It's the *need* to feel close with someone. Life's about relationships, and we all want an intimate one. I want to emphasize: it's a need. We *need* to feel connected with others, especially a special someone. The need is real, and when we didn't get it, we acted out in negative ways toward each other and, worse, sought connection elsewhere."

The host squished her eyebrows together. "That's interesting. But how does one learn to recognize that's what's causing the behavior?"

Titus leaned in, hand on one knee. "Just knowing the information goes a long way. Know that your partner always needs, on a neurological level, to feel close and to do so *in his own way.* If you practice making each other feel close, it'll become part of the nervous system's subconscious—automatizing the process. That's a fancy way of saying that you can get those feelings of ongoing closeness to become part and parcel of your relational psyche instead of feeling like marriage is all work, exhausting even."

Emma was still looking down, picking at her fingers. "It's why most people fantasize about being with other people. They're meeting their own need of feeling connected with someone. What they don't realize is that when those fantasies come true, they turn into dark nightmares."

"If we'd just known . . ." Titus leaned back, crossed his arms in front of his chest, and sighed.

"If you'd known what?" the host prompted.

"If I'd known that what Emma wanted was also really a need, this fundamental biological need, to feel connected . . . I was the one that was supposed to meet that need for her. It led to our breakup. Breakups happen when couples don't treat each other the way they did at first. There would never be a last if we kept treating each other like we did at first. It still kills me that she had to go looking for it somewhere else. I should've . . . I could've if I'd been asking the right questions."

Emma sat up. "Since then, our life coach taught us one of those right questions to ask each other, *On a scale of one to ten, how connected do we feel to each other today? And if the number is below a ten, what can I do to help get it to a ten?*"

Olivia had told Oliver a thousand times that she didn't feel close when she was so overwhelmed—and he still came after her for sex in those times. He just didn't connect the dots. Maybe this question would help him finally get it.

"That question is why we're sitting here today," Titus added. "We want everyone listening to know that routinely asking each other this question goes a long way toward building the ultimate relationship experience. The chemistry and closeness you're longing for is found in the answer to this question." Titus sat up, radiating with a renewed energy.

> On a scale of one to ten, how connected do we feel to each other today? If it's not a ten, how can we make it a 10?

"But you filed for divorce with Emma?" The host tilted her head.

Titus bit his bottom lip and nodded. "Yes. I wish I'd known then what I know now—about the biological needs that weren't being met and about that question. Sometimes I wonder if it would have saved us." Titus seemed unfazed by the host's antagonistic tone. "I was so hurt and focused on my own feelings I just couldn't give anything to Emma anymore. I've since realized that suffering comes when you focus on your own pain. I didn't stop to think that I had responsibility to bear. I take responsibility for that now. Most couples fail to realize that each person in the relationship must take 100% responsibility for the relationship's success and stop waiting for the other person to do something to improve it." He looked over at Emma who had a tear sliding down her cheek.

So did the real Emma. A fat tear slid down her cheek as she stared at her doppelganger on TV.

I bet she's wondering if a mental replay is running through TV Emma's mind. Maybe her replay includes the Couples' Castle.

Either way, the real Emma looked desperate for real reconciliation.

"We were so caught up in keeping score that we missed the whole point of feeling connected." TV Emma clasped her hands together in her lap.

Keeping score—that was the issue, wasn't it? Olivia had a lead so big Oliver had no hope of ever catching up. She was fine with doing her fair share and then some, if he would just acknowledge it every now and then.

"Keeping score?" the host asked.

Emma bent her neck slightly forward. "Yes. All couples do it at some point in their relationship. You know, 'I'm cleaning the house, doing more than my share of the dishes, and paying the bills, and he does what exactly?' While he's thinking, 'I'm paying down the mortgage, bought her a diamond ring, and work at a job I don't even like while she just does the little things around the house.' Sounds a bit sexist, but that's generally how it goes."

Titus appeared relaxed now, nothing like the Titus standing in this room. "Yes, John Grey, in *Men Are from Mars and Women Are from Venus*, highlights this. He talks about how men and women keep score differently. Men believe that if they do big things, like work a lot and buy the house or ring, that it scores a lot of points, and they believe the woman is really impressed and feels loved in proportion to his big deeds. So in his mind, one regular deed should cover her emotional bandwidth for an entire month, and a big action, like the ring, could bring feelings of love for a year. He thinks she feels connected all those months based on his one big action."

You can either keep score or feel connected, but you can't do both simultaneously. And only one of them will help you experience the ultimate relationship with the love of your life.

Are you serious?

"The woman, on the other hand"—Emma shifted in her seat, now more relaxed—"believes every act of love, no matter the size or scope, scores equally, that every act of love scores one and only one point."

Did Oliver hear that? He seemed to be paying attention, but that didn't always mean it registered. He needed to know how she scored points.

"Both men and women think it's crazy that the other sex could believe differently about points, but it's true." Emma gave a side glance toward the audience.

TV Titus reached for a sip of water. "One more thing on this note, keeping score is the sure path to going crazy in a relationship. We kept score on both a subconscious and conscious level, and it destroyed our marriage. Relationships are sacred and deserve more than keeping score."

Then what were they supposed to do? Just ask the one-through-ten-connection question every day? Olivia was starting to think she didn't understand men at all. First, she'd lost Zeb—no explanation, no nothing. And now she might lose Oliver too. Olivia rubbed her forearm while thinking about her own shortcomings. She was the common denominator after all.

*   *   *

"Do you think they're hearing what the room's trying to communicate?" The short pudgy man in the light blue top hat asked the tall slender woman in red. They watched the couples on a video monitor.

"You know how this works." Red sighed.

Blue rolled his neck. "Yes, yes, I do. They're not even close to ready for what awaits them in room 7."

Chapter 7

Friday

"Let's take a few questions from our audience." The host raised her chin and looked down over her nose.

"Sure." TV Titus straightened the wrinkles in his blue jeans.

He looks so confident again. How did I ever let us get to this point? There had to be a way to reconcile before it was too late. Just because their doppelgangers were divorced didn't mean their future was sealed. Why else would they be invited to the Couples' Castle? There had to be a way.

"Hi, yes, you over there in the white 'I Love NY' sweatshirt," the host said.

An older woman, maybe in her late sixties, stood, and the bald technician walked the mic over. "Um yes. Thank you. My question is um . . . I'm sure the way one experiences connection at a level of nine or ten is different for everyone, yes, but would you be willing to share one of the best ways you've found in connecting? Personally, you know? Okay. Thank you."

Emma smiled. "Sure. In all relationships, there's always the temptation to hope for a magical ride but hoping just leads to a mediocre rut. Certain triggers like taking out the trash, paying the bills, working a stressful job—just the routines of one's day—squeeze the sexiness out of the relationship until it becomes more of a toleration than a dream come true. But with the right strategy you can overcome those triggers and experience the ultimate relationship"

We definitely settled—into what, I don't know, but it definitely became mediocre. Maybe if he'd just opened up to her more—or at all—about not being able to have children . . . She needed that connection. She looked over at Titus, standing beside her yet miles away. *I can't take all the blame for this.*

"So you're claiming any couple can perpetuate the chemistry stage forever?" The host coughed, pretending her drink went down wrong.

Titus and Emma waited for her to regain her composure. The host excused herself and asked, "Let's get back to the audience member's question about your best way to connect. How would you respond?"

Emma's face lit up. "Positive projection."

"Positive projection?" The host's eyebrows squished together.

"Yes," Titus responded. "It's something we first heard from a Brendon Burchard video. We would've never divorced had we known."

The host flinched. "Even once you found out about the affair?"

"There would've been no affair," they both answered simultaneously.

TV Emma leaned forward in her chair. "I mean it. If a couple wants their relationship satisfaction to remain at a consistent nine, then they should practice positive projection. They could take baby steps at first, like taking the fifteen-day positive projection challenge—where you only say and think positive things to your spouse. One mess up, and you begin again, even if the mess up's at day fourteen."

"Okay, but what does 'positive projection' actually mean?" the host asked.

Emma didn't seem to care what others thought about the smile that she couldn't contain. "Positive projection is intentionally exuding positive energy toward your partner. After you've been in a relationship for a long time, it's easy to think the relationship has lost its magic to the monotonous and mundane. Kinda like a Monday morning commute to a dreary job, the surroundings become familiar and listless. The key is to switch on your positive projection, which means you intentionally become fascinated with your spouse. It's really easy and a much more enjoyable way to live with someone."

She was on a roll, and TV Titus admired her for it. "So when your partner's talking, listen while thinking thoughts of positivity toward her like 'I want the best for her. She's amazing. She deserves my attention. She's fascinating. I want her to feel the way she wants to feel.' Think these things as if you're filling her with invisible pockets of positive energy. Do this intermittently throughout the day, including when you're both in the same room doing your own thing."

Emma had never done that. Or maybe she had, when they first started dating.

TV Emma was talking fast now. "You can also sit on the couch with your spouse and ask about her desires, fears, dreams, interests, and what she values most. Just, you know, become extraordinarily curious about her. Let your face shine, like you're on a first date. Remember your first date? Like that. Be her champion, and remember—and this is so amazing—that in showing incredible interest *for* her, you become incredibly interesting *to* her." Emma breathed out a long breath and picked up her knee with her hands while smiling.

"We learned that when you positively project on each other"—Titus closed his eyes momentarily to savor an experience—"it stimulates the love hormone, oxytocin, and that's when the mundane becomes magical, the routines of life become pleasurable, and the to-dos of your day become truly transformative. I know it sounds a bit"—he moved his head back and forth—"different. But it really works."

"What about if your partner doesn't want you to be so 'positive'? Maybe she's having a bad day and just wants to vent. What would you say to that?" The host tugged at her blouse.

"You're right, sometimes your spouse just needs to talk through things," Emma replied, "so she can resolve her feelings through emotional cleansing. No need for the man to take it personally. Just be careful about doing this in the heat of the moment because the data via, um, what was his name?" She looked at Titus. "Oh ya, Dr. John Gottman. He's professor at the University of Washington, and in his book *The Seven Principles of Making Marriage Work*, he shows that airing your grievances when you're upset doesn't work. Even more, he demonstrates how he can predict a separation/divorce with 90 percent accuracy based on this."

"Oh really, how so?" The host's body posture perked up.

Titus's smile disappeared. "Well, we were guilty of this, weren't we, Emma?"

Her voice dropped. "Yes, unfortunately."

"So . . ." The host studied them. "What is it?"

Titus placed his hands on his knees and leaned forward. "In all his research, he found that couples who tried to fix everything in the heat of the moment experienced 'flooding,' which is a physiological response that leaves both parties' hearts pounding and their focus shot. The couples get more and more fed up with each other, seeing their problems in a permanent and personal way. When couples do this, one gets labeled the winner and the other the loser, and this ends with a 90 percent chance that both lose."

"So what's the alternative?" The host sat on the edge of her chair now.

Titus scratched the back of his head. "Well, you can choose between positive projection and pounding. The latter refers to one partner not letting things go. Instead, he verbally and emotionally pounds the other until flooding takes place. And we know where that leads." He pinched the bridge of his nose and closed his eyes.

"With positive projection, the arguments roll off your back, if they even start to begin with," Emma added. "It contains the attitude that 'this too shall pass.' It's a process, you know? Learn to let things go and instead access more beautiful emotional states via positive projection. You learn that problems are not permanent. They're opportunities to grow virtues like empathy and joy. This means that just because one partner picks a fight, like we all do from time to time, it doesn't mean you have to accept the invitation. There's no need to attend every fight you're invited to. Life's too short for that nonsense. We're talking about a commitment to create a beautiful world-class relationship."

Olivia folded her arms and whispered, "Commitment. Now there's a word we should revisit, Oliver."

"Hey, I know what commitment means." Oliver showcased a grin that conveyed secret knowledge. "It's opening an ice cream container and throwing out the lid."

She whispered back, "Yes, but so is taking out the trash that you threw the lid into." Olivia shifted her weight, then shook her head before looking back up at the TV.

"Also"—Titus uncrossed his legs and leaned in—"and this is really important. Just like you can project positivity, you can project negativity. Whenever your partner projects negative emotions, beware of mirroring any bad energy."

"Mirroring?" The host looked over to her side, probably at a teleprompter.

Titus crossed his legs to match the host's seated position. "Mirroring is where your neurons mimic your partner's moods, feelings, and actions. So if you positively project on your partner, she'll positively project on to you—it works the same with negative projection. Because energy, negative or positive, is contagious, when your partner negatively projects, you have to attempt to transcend it so you don't mirror it."

"How?" The host had shifted from casual conversation to pointed questions.

Titus clasped his hands under the chin. "Positively project on to your partner while letting her be whoever she chooses to be. Even in the swirl of her negative projection, her mirror neurons will pick up the good vibes from you, and this will help her naturally change course. See, neutral energy doesn't exist." He put his hands out like he was measuring the air. "All energy is either positive or negative—either moving your relationship toward the ultimate relationship experience or to brutal heartache."

"It's so important to stay positive in your thoughts toward each other." Emma nodded, smiling. "You'll never reach a consistent nine if you don't. Whenever you see your spouse, wish him happiness, health, love, respect, and peace. He won't hear you say these things out loud, but he'll feel the energy coming from you," she said with her hand on her heart, "and this will make him feel great about the relationship. His satisfaction surges to a nine. The more you wish each other good experiences and feelings, the more attractive you'll find each other and the more your marriage becomes a masterpiece."

The host arched a pencil-thin eyebrow. "So just be happy-go-lucky all the time?"

"Focus on the positive the majority of the time." Emma attempted to swivel in her chair toward the audience but forgot it didn't turn. "But by positive, we don't mean happy-go-lucky. Weeds do exist in your backyard garden. By *positive*, we mean holding a firm belief that things are always getting better—it's a mentality—regardless of any weeds that crop up. Even when there are problems in the relationship, and there are problems," she said, shaking her head, "focus on the good in every situation because the problem is never really the problem but rather your marital *response* to the problem. The problem is the attitude and perspective about the problem. And you can always control that." Emma seemed calm and relaxed, in control of her thoughts and emotions.

Positive projection means you fill your partner with pockets of positivity throughout the day. You'll feel good about your spouse, find that problems are not permanent, and flourish in a relationship that's always getting better.

"Here's why that's so important." Titus' eyes glistened, and he leaned forward. "And it's something I read in a self-help book. What you focus on . . . grows. Where your attention goes, your energy flows, and where your energy flows, your outcomes show. It's really that simple—and profound. What's wrong and right about the relationship is always available for you to focus on, and which do you think focusing on—negative or positive—moves you toward finding the love of your life, experiencing the ultimate relationship, and making your marriage a masterpiece? The quality of your relationship is always in direct proportion to your emotional state. So it's imperative to focus on the positive emotions like joy, happiness, love, and gratitude. When both of you do that, you amplify the emotional experience, which makes your marriage a masterpiece."

Emma stood in room 2 with a strong sensation of being flooded with warmth. She could feel her own heartbeat and a shiver that brought her pleasure at the thought of Titus seeing the two of them on TV getting along. More than anything, she wanted to touch him, but she trusted that his gaze on the TV meant he was considering his options. Maybe one of those options was reconciling. Or maybe he was thinking about who he's married to on the TV and how relaxed he looks. *That's not good!*

TV Emma tilted her head in a side-to-side rhythm. "Most couples throw their arms up in response to their negative circumstances—like we did when I was, um, unfaithful to Titus—but world-class couples understand successful relationships start with their thoughts, not their circumstances. They replace all negative thoughts with positive thoughts because thoughts generate feelings, feelings generate actions, and actions generate the relationship's results. Negative thoughts lead to negative emotions, actions, and circumstances between the couple. Conversely, positive thoughts lead to feeling good about each other, which creates better circumstances. It's not a denial of reality but a transformation of it. In this manner, positive projection upgrades your relationship from negative to positive, from a low number to a ten."

Positive projection isn't a denial of your relational reality but a beautiful transformation of it.

The host turned to the camera. "Wow, food for thought. We need to take a break. They've saved the best for last, so we'll be back for the best details to experience the ultimate relationship right after this commercial break."

*   *   *

Zeb stood in the corner of room 2, leaning against the wall with the first sense of calm he'd felt in years. So if he just took control of his thoughts, he wouldn't feel so stressed out about work and the mixed parenting procedures between him and Isabella? If he projected positivity on to her, it would reciprocate back to him? Sounded easy enough. He looked over at Isabella who was staring at the TV with an unfocused gaze. *Isabella, you're the best. Isabella, you're beautiful. Isabella, you have brilliant ideas about raising the kids. Olivia, you still look beautiful.*

TV Titus pulled a card from his front pocket. "Since the separation, I now carry around a couple of quotes that remind me of positive projection. The first is by Harvard psychologist William James: 'The greatest discovery of my generation is that a human being can alter his life by altering his attitudes of mind.' How powerful is that? And the second one is 'You are today where your thoughts have brought you; you will be tomorrow where your thoughts take you.' James Allen said that."

The host looked at Titus, then Emma. "And, Emma, where are you in all this?"

TV Emma smoothed the front of her shirt and gave a deep, gratifying sigh. "The way I see it is the temperature of your relationship is nothing more than a reflection of the temperature of your thoughts about your relationship. That's why nothing can stop a couple from the ultimate relationship experience when they generate the right mental attitude. And unfortunately, nothing in the universe can help the couple with the wrong attitude."

Emma in room 2 felt the warmth spread through her body. She felt proud of what she saw on the TV. She sounded smarter, wiser than she thought she'd ever be, and hoped this communicated something positive to Titus. Her lips twitched, and she bounced lightly on her toes. The room started to warm up a bit.

> The temperature of your relationship is nothing more than a reflection of the temperature of your thoughts about the relationship.

The host raised her eyebrows. "So you're saying there are 'weeds' in a relationship and we can talk about them with our partner?"

"Negative thoughts are like weeds"—Emma picked at her pant leg—"while positive thoughts about your relationship are like planting seeds in the ground. Each positive projection on to your partner is like watering your relationship. Keep it free from weeds, negative thoughts, and it's just a matter of time before your relationship gets better."

"There are storms in life, to be sure," Titus added, gesturing with his hands. "We know firsthand. But what we've learned since the split, and what we wish we'd known before the court proceedings, is when storms approach your relationship, it doesn't mean you need to let the storms *inside* your relationship."

Zeb scratched his jaw. Some ominous clouds were approaching *their* relationship, and unless they did something, the storms would hit hard.

"The happiness in happily-ever-after," Emma added, "then depends on the quality of your thoughts. *The way* the partners choose to view their relationship creates the relationship they experience. No counselor too good or enemy so cruel can affect you—either positively or negatively—like the thoughts you consistently hold about your relationship. Blah thoughts equal a blah relationship, negative thoughts translate into a negative relationship, positive thoughts reap a positive relationship, and exciting thoughts generate an exciting relationship."

Except Zeb and Isabella's weeds were the financial issues. So if he just thought positive and projected positivity on to Isabella, it would solve the weed issues? *What a bunch of feel good BS.* A dark cloud hung over their marriage, mainly because Isabella still blamed herself for the tragic death of her child on October 19th almost eight years ago. When she missed picking up her son from little league practice by a mere ten minutes because her appointment ran over, he got a ride from one of his friend's parents. There was a car accident, with no survivors. Zeb looked over at Isabella and didn't think any amount of positive projection would help. She would always be heartbroken. The only hope might be whatever's inside the red treasure chest in room 7.

Titus was full of fresh energy. "So the point to all this is you can use positive projection to find the love of your life, experience the ultimate relationship, and live an authentic happily-ever-after. Because when you positively project on others, they reciprocate it. And that turns into chemistry and connection." Titus sat up straight and alert, holding his arms out wide with vigor. "Because, look, all of it—your vows, paychecks, houses, cars, ups and downs, joys, bedroom activity, exercise routines, stories, and habits—they're all a result of your thinking. So one awesome exercise is to ask 'What are five thoughts I continuously have about my partner?'

1.
2.
3.
4.
5.

"Now substitute those with five passionate or romantic thoughts that would help create the ultimate relationship experience and ruminate on those everyday. Go ahead, list them out. We'll wait.

1.
2.
3.
4.
5.

"See, it's like carrying around a mental camera. Focus on what moves your relationship up to a consistent nine, and capture the really fun and good times, and if some things aren't working out, just take another shot. Turn that list of 5 thoughts into a card, take a picture of it and look at it often because you get the kind of marriage you focus on."

The host nodded to something she was hearing in her earpiece. "We have to take a commercial break, but when we return, we're all—including our audience—going to experiment with positive projection on one another. Maybe someone will even find their soul mate through this exercise. Does that work for you, guys?"

People in the audience immediately began texting, probably to their loved ones about the interactive exercise that'd soon air on live television.

"Sure! Sounds fun!" Emma beamed at the camera.

This ought to be good. Zeb glanced at Isabella who comforted Emma with a side-hug, knowing full well the relentless pain she carried just beneath her compassion and confidence. As the commercial ended, Zeb tucked his hands behind his elbows and wished for a drink of water for his suddenly dry throat.

After the break, the host instructed members of the audience to find a partner—spouse with spouse, friend with friend, colleague with colleague—didn't matter, just so everyone partnered up. She even had Titus and Emma face each other. Once everyone located a partner, the host directed, "Let's begin. Project positive thoughts on to your partner."

The audience members faced each other to test out the theory, which looked awkward and uncomfortable at first. After sixty seconds, the host said, "Thanks, everyone. You can stop now. Wasn't that wonderful?"

So maybe this positive projection was able to change energy and thoughts and moods, and from there, they could come up with new ideas and plans for how to take care of the weeds.

The host turned to Titus and Emma—only to find they were still staring into each other's eyes, radiating positivity on to each other, oblivious that the audience had stopped.

Half the front row placed their hands over their mouths.

Emma and Titus still had feelings for each other.

On TV at least.

Back in the Positive Projection Room, Emma turned to Titus. His eyes remained fixated on the TV.

Zeb couldn't help but notice. *Wow, this is awkward.* She looked ready to reconcile, but did she deserve it? What's Titus thinking?

Titus stood like a statue, frozen with resentment.

Maybe if they made it to room 7 with their key and found what's inside the treasure chest, they'd figure out how to make it work. Who knows what they can do at this point?

Emma looked around frantically. "My key! Where's my key?"

*   *   *

Oh boy, she's in full freak-out mode. Olivia nudged Oliver. "C'mon, let's help look for her key."

"Where's my treasure chest and key?" Emma grabbed fistfuls of her hair and ran from person to person with an emotion-choked voice.

She looked like a a bird flapping it's wings over a chick that fell on the ground. And Titus, he appeared spooked, haunted by TV Titus and Emma. *He looks like he's seen a ghost.*

"I must've left it in room 1!" She pounded on the door with a fury of desperation.

She must really believe the key will save her marriage. Olivia gripped hers a little tighter.

"Open up, someone open up! *Please!*" Emma slumped against the door, her banging steadily slowing, hopeless.

Olivia could identify with that kind of bone weariness. *I wonder if her affair began with similar feelings of overwhelm and under appreciation at home that I feel. Is that how it begins?* She turned to Oliver.

Oliver crossed his arms over his chest, then rubbed his nose. "What?"

Should I tell him about Zebediah now? Footsteps behind her made Olivia turn around. Emma walked toward Titus with a sense of purpose. *Oh boy. This ought to be interesting.*

She positioned herself right in front of him. "Titus, honey," she said, holding herself tight.

I don't think I've ever heard Titus say more than a few sentences at one time.

He lowered his gaze to match Emma's, and she searched his empty, lifeless eyes.

"Titus, honey." Emma's shoulders were curling with a bent spine.

No one moved. The future Parkers on TV were still playing, but for some reason, it had gone silent. The other TVs continued to play silent flashbacks. *Someone must be watching us.*

"Please, Titus," Emma begged.

Her words bounced off him like a hard rain. He was too bruised and broken.

"What can I say? What can I do, baby?" She moaned and rocked in place.

At the word "baby," Titus shifted back a step.

Emma reached for his hands, and he didn't pull away. "I made a mistake—a very big mistake, and I'm so sorry. Please forgive me, baby. Please, Titus." She broke into uneven sobs.

Olivia tried to look away, but she couldn't. *Are his eyes watering?*

Emma wiped the tears from her face and took a deep breath. "When I first saw you, I knew it was meant to be. When you picked me to dance with at the Halloween festival after they awarded you best costume, I went home and told Mom, and she said, 'Keep that young man.'"

Emma's head fell briefly. She searched for the right words. "Titus, you're the one for me, and even though you have every right to walk away from this marriage, I won't let you give up on us." She pointed to TV Titus and Emma. "Did you hear them? They said they wouldn't have gotten divorced if they'd known about this room, about this . . . whatever this Couples' Castle is showing us. That means there's hope for us. Right, babe?" She didn't seem to care who heard her at this point.

Small tears dotted his cheeks and a look that could have been regret or resentment flashed across his face. Emma looked . . . terrified.

She talked faster now, like a psych patient in the emergency room without her meds. "Look what we might miss, baby. Aren't we worth it?" She rocked in place and grabbed a fistful of her blonde hair and pulled. "I'll do anything. I'm so sorry, Titus! I never meant to hurt us. I love you."

He dropped his hands, her words sailing right past him as he turned and walked away.

Emma just stood there, alone for the first time in her life, without her key—without her husband.

Chapter 8

Room 3

The north wall of TVs creaked and cranked until it unexpectedly transformed into double doors opening in the middle.

The sunrays warmed Emma's skin while the sound of the great outdoors behind the colossal castle whistled around her. There were waves of green grass and lilac bushes. God couldn't have picked a better time for fresh air. With her key lost, she stood hugging herself thinking about what to do next. She stepped out into the unknown.

The couples cautiously followed.

Pink butterflies cheerfully flitted from flower to flower, infusing Emma with fresh hope. But one was caught in a spiderweb, flapping for its life. She found a stick on the ground and freed the butterfly from its captor. Even though it was now free, it couldn't lift itself from the ground because one of its wings was broken. *I can relate, little one.*

The sky's purple hues indicated it was early morning. A soft breeze blew through Emma's hair, drying the tears on her face. Moments later, the broken and battered butterfly from the web fluttered toward her, folding its wings gently upward until it landed safely on her shoulder. *Hey, little one. Maybe there's redemption for us after all.*

"We made it out of room 2 faster than I thought we would. I think we're making up some time." Isabella inhaled and brushed her hand over a line of yellow and white Charlotte roses.

Oliver and Olivia were just on the other side of the rose bushes when he said, "Well, at least they'll have an amicable separation."

Olivia lowered her voice. "I've seen more improbable comebacks in my life."

I think they're talking about me. Whatever.

Oliver cocked his head back like a doubtful ostrich. "I don't know. He looks pretty cadaver-like to me. Remember the ninety-nine-year-old man who divorced his ninety-six-year-old wife after seventy-seven years of marriage because he discovered she'd had an affair when they were in their twenties? Stuff's real man. Titus has totally moved on, babe, and besides, the crazy whatever that was we just saw, futuristic TV doppelgangers, reinforced it. At least they find happiness on their own. I just hope we don't have to witness any more meltdowns or crazy relationship drama while we're here. Know what I mean?"

Emma felt naked, like she was on display for the world's judgment. She just wanted to hide somewhere and curl up in a ball. A stiffness settled in her jaw, and her blood pressure rose. *Like you guys are perfect. I'm sure something's wrong with your relationship and when it surfaces we'll all see what kind of judgment you have for others then.*

"Yeah," Olivia said, while rubbing the back of her neck and quickly eyeballing Zeb. "I know what you mean."

The couples walked further in the botanical gardens toward an arboretum on the northwest end, filled with colorful flowers of every kind and displaying some kind of native and indigenous plants. Emma's eyes widened. She couldn't believe this place was local anymore. They had to be in a faraway land. She studied the others to see if they were experiencing the same amazement.

Up ahead, a tree line edged the property and the sound of rushing water told Emma a river flowed somewhere on the other side. She turned to take in another panoramic view of the breathtaking scenery. *Surreal.* A blaze of colorful royal gardens led back up to the Couples' Castle. She surveyed the first section full of flowers growing like trophies triumphantly displayed. Their purity lay in stark contrast to the stain she felt on her life. Beyond it was a genius display of attractive flowerbeds, bamboos, orchids, and roses. The smell triggered memories of wearing a corsage to her senior prom with Titus.

"Look." She pointed to a big brown wooden sign nailed to a massive oak tree with big bold yellow letters painted on it.

The couples spun in the direction of Emma's voice.

"What does that sign say?"

"I don't know. Let's go find out." Oliver ran ahead.

They picked up their pace, walking past the last of the flowerbeds until they made it to the sign. They stood on a mowed line between the end of the gardens and the entrance of the tall proud forest that seemed to whisper ancient secrets of life's purposes. Whatever was in there, all the living creatures, the trees especially, seemed to play a continuous enchanting symphony to direct their relationship.

The sign marked the spot where five separate paths bordered with plants and trees diverged into the deep woods. Hoofprints and footprints disappeared down the dirt paths, each marked with a number, from left to right, path 1 to path 5.

The sign read, ROOM 3: PURPOSEFUL PARTNERS. Under it, in small letters, it said, *Enjoy your own couple's path. Take all the time you need. Then meet at the waterfall.*

"Room?" Oliver looked around. "This is a dagum forest. Any of you ever been in a forest before?"

Not me, but I already feel lost. Maybe Emma would find something worth living for in there.

"Well, I'm up for an adventure, babe." Oliver turned to Olivia. "Which path would you like to take?"

"Um . . ." She surveyed her options. "Path 4."

Titus didn't even turn around or make eye contact with her. He just disappeared down path 1. Maybe if Emma followed, they'd get some alone time to work this out.

"Well, which path?" Isabella wrapped her arm around Zeb's bicep. "We never get any time alone anymore, so I'm fine with any of them as long as we go together."

"How about path 3?"

Off they went, each couple walking their chosen path into the deep, thick woods.

*   *   *

"This is something, isn't it?" Oliver shuffled his feet through the autumn leaves.

Olivia felt like a kid again, swinging their hands together. "Yes. Who would've ever thought a place like this existed? It's magical, something only kids would believe in."

Oliver pinched her arm.

"Ouch! What was that for?"

"It's real, like that pinch."

"Oh, you think so, huh? Well, wait till I pinch you."

"You have to catch me first."

Oliver took off down the path, and she chased after him. The wind in her hair felt like freedom.

Up ahead, Oliver pretended to trip, and she seized the opportunity to catch up and jump on top of him.

Oliver laughed. "Let's just lay here for a while, like two grade-schoolers on the playground."

This feels nice.

Two bluebirds perched up on the nearest oak tree, serenading them. Oliver wrapped his arms around Olivia and swept the hair out of her face. "I miss this."

"Miss what?"

"This. Us. Looking into each other's eyes like we used to. Don't you just want to stay right here under the swaying trees and soak it all in?"

She nodded. "I miss it too." She looked away, deep in thought.

Oliver squirmed to an upright position. "I feel like we're continents apart these days. Is there something going on that I should know about?"

Maybe this was the time to tell him about Zeb. Honesty was the best approach. *I mean, what the heck is Zeb doing here?*

"O?" Oliver's brows furrowed.

Olivia sat up. "Do you feel happy, Oliver?"

"What?"

"I mean, do you feel happy . . . with us?"

"I always feel happy until someone wonders if I'm happy." He closed his eyes and rolled his neck back and forth.

"Seriously, Oliver. Do you?" Her fingers gripped the key.

He scooted close to her. "You're my whole world, O. I would collect all the stars in the universe if you asked me to. I love you."

At the mention of stars, Zeb's voice rang in her ears. *I love you to the stars and back, Olivia.*

Zeb knew her so well that summer. Their souls just . . . clicked. Olivia sat there, feigning a smile, assailed with memories of the magical night of fireworks when she convinced herself that Zeb was her soul mate.

"Do you believe in soul mates?" She pinched the bottom of her lip.

"I don't know." He chuckled. "But look at that tree over there. It looks like some lovers carved their names in it. Why do you think so many people are carrying knives on dates?"

Olivia stood to her feet, thankful she wore tennis shoes. "Oliver, can you take me serious for once?"

Oliver jumped up, his eyebrows squished together. With his arms raised up, he said, "Where's this coming from?"

She leaned in to place her hands on his sides. "Do you?"

He raised both hands in surrender. "I don't think there exists one and only one person for everyone, if that's what you mean."

"You don't?" She looked away, her fingers touched her parted lips.

"No. I think it's more about becoming someone than it is finding the someone." He tilted his head to make eye contact.

"What do you mean?" Olivia had a sinking feeling in her stomach.

"I mean with every thought in my head, every standard I set, and every action I take, I'm becoming a certain kind of person that will repel some and attract others." Oliver shrugged.

She weighed the pros and cons of his idea. "And?"

"So if I want to find, uh, what the castle referred to as an irresistibly attractive person . . ." He waggled his eyebrows at her. "I should probably become a person who is irresistibly attractive."

Her head flinched back slightly. "So you don't think we're destined for each other?"

"Not in a traditional *soul mate* sense. More like, you know, becoming the person that the person you're looking for is looking for. They will connect. They're drawn to each other like soul mates. And hey, we love each other, right?" He playfully nudged her on the shoulder.

"Yes, of course." Her breathing slowed as a memory took over.

Oliver slid his hands into his pockets and shuffled his feet through the fallen orange leaves. "Well, the more two people love each other, the more their souls become one. That's how I see it anyway. In that sense, I guess, we *become* soul mates."

Olivia looked at the ground and felt dizzy.

"You all right?" He paused, then combed his fingers through her hair.

"Ya . . . ya, fine." She swallowed hard and pressed her hands to her temples, then mirrored his eyes. "So you don't think there's a person out there for all of us that we just, you know, click with?"

He tilted his head and smelled her hair. Moving back, he lifted her chin with his fingers. "I think we can click with a lot of people, but the temptation is to believe there's only one someone who will always make us feel like we click with him or her. But think about it this way, O: Anyone—and I mean anyone—you think is a perfect match for you also has people in his life who think, *I'm so tired of his BS.* Right? I mean, hey, I know you get tired of me."

She smiled and squeezed his arm. "So you think you can attract whomever you want if you just send out the right intentions?" She slowly shook her head and softly kicked at the ground.

Oliver grabbed her hand, pulling her along on the path, playfully swinging her arm. "I think it's much more than sending out an intention about who you want. Most everyone does that from time to time. I don't think you attract who you want in a sustainable way, but you attract who you *are*. That right there cuts out the majority of possible connections. At the end of the day, babe, I think the goal is to become the kind of person you want to attract into your life so that you attract the kind of person you become. That's my basic understanding to your question about soul mates."

She struggled to find the right words while she navigated the uneven path. "I wonder if that idea applies to married couples too since we're always in the process of becoming. So if I grow into the right kind of person, it'll cause you to run away from me or grow into who I'm becoming and vice-versa. We still each carry our own individuality but do so within an unbreakable bond—a unity without uniformity. What do you think?"

"Totally. You are the winner with that answer." He dropped her hand so that he could raise his arms in a victory V.

> You attract who you are. So become the person in your marriage that the person you're looking for your spouse to become is looking for you to become.

After a brief smile, Olivia rubbed her ear and pondered the pros and cons of whether to tell him about Zeb. It'd be good to clear the air, if nothing else.

"You sure you're okay?" He gave her a sidelong glance.

"Yeah. This place just causes me to think more than usual." She just couldn't find the courage to bring it up. She feigned another smile, and a tightness formed in her stomach.

He grabbed her hand again. "Don't think too much. Remember the old saying, 'If you stay in your head, you're dead.' That's the route of depression. C'mon. Let's pick up our pace so we can see where this path leads."

They walked in silence for five minutes, listening to the birds chirp and watching the squirrels dart and dash their way across the path and up the tree trunks.

"I love you, Oliver. I really do."

"I love you too, O." He looked at her sideways with a big grin.

The powerful rays of the sun beamed through the thick trees, illuminating a sign thirty feet ahead. It read *Purpose-Driven Relationships* in yellow letters, with an arrow pointing straight ahead.

Olivia chuckled. "Well, that seems too coincidental. That's what I've said about us needing—some sense of direction for our relationship."

Something rustled deeper in the woods, to the right of the path, followed by what sounded like a man's laugh.

"Who's there?" Oliver craned his neck forward and squinted.

A man with an LA Dodgers ball cap, dark skin, crazy eyes, and a small crooked nose came sauntering out to the path with a shovel in his left hand and a bouquet of flowers in his right.

Oliver's head jerked back. "Hello. My name's Oliver, and this is Olivia. Who are you? Are you with the Couples' Castle? And if you don't mind my asking, what's with the shovel?"

The man stepped out of the woods and reached out his hand. "Well, I'm Clive. This here shovel's for my work."

"Nice to meet you, Clive. What's your work?"

"I'm a grave digger."

Well, I certainly didn't expect to meet a grave digger today.

Olivia swallowed hard. "A what?"

Clive chuckled. "I'm a grave digger, and I work right over there." He pointed straight through the woods, to a shortcut off the path into a cemetery.

"What were you laughing about?" Olivia asked.

"Nothing." Clive couldn't contain his grin.

"Oh. I thought I heard a laugh." Olivia pointed in the direction from where he came.

"Well . . ." He motioned for them to follow him toward the cemetery. "I heard what you said about waiting for a sense of direction for your relationship."

"And why's that funny?" She had her hand on her hip and lifted her eyebrows.

"Because you find your purpose by living on purpose, that's all. If you wait for it to fall out of the sky, well, you'll be waiting a long time." He looked up into the sky like he was waiting for something to fall out of it.

"Oh, so you're a philosopher?" Olivia nodded.

"No, no, just a simple man who's figured out the purpose of my life and the purpose of my marriage." He tipped his hat in humility, and she noticed for the first time he was missing a pinky finger.

"Oh, so you're married. We are too. Is your wife here at the castle?" Olivia scanned the woods behind him.

"She's right over here." He motioned up the path. "Would you like to meet her?"

"Yes." Olivia imagined what she might look like and if they'd get along.

He guided them up the path and through the south gate of the cemetery, where two silver lamplights stood like guardians of the dead. The dew from the grass seeped into Olivia's shoes.

Oliver planted the shovel in the ground. "Whelp, here she is."

"Where?" Olivia looked all around.

"Right there." He pointed to one of the tombstones.

Oh no. "I'm so sorry." She thought about placing her hand on his shoulder for comfort.

"Thank you, but it's fine. We're good." His face was etched with a deep sadness, and his fingers played with the cross hanging around his neck.

As he laid the flowers on her grave, it was like he was closing the distance between him and her, the living and the dead. Was it possible to love someone so much that the love crosses the invisible boundaries of life and death?

Clyde closed his eyes, drew a deep calming breath, then looked up toward the sky, as if his wife was whispering sweet nothings from the other side.

Olivia privately prayed for Clyde and was uncertain about what to say. She was like those flowers, both alive and dead, pulled from their roots but seemingly fine on the outside. Though rootless and worn out at home, this place was reenergizing her. Would it just be the same again when they got back home? If so, she'd wither away.

And Zeb. She thought she'd completely moved on from him. *But now I have these feelings resurfacing. How do I unfeel them?* Maybe Emma was right. Maybe the answers to the ultimate relationship experience were really hidden inside the real treasure chest in room 7.

"So how'd you become a . . . you know . . ." Oliver fumbled over his words.

"A grave digger?" There was a light in his eye.

"Yeah." Oliver bit his thumbnail.

Clyde stood up. "Well, I used to be a trader on Wall Street, making millions, but I was losing my marriage and family in the process. When a friend told me to visit a cemetery for clarity about what to do next, I did, and it worked. So I started making it part of my routine whenever I needed clarity about anything. I even started volunteering at local cemeteries, mowing mainly. Eventually, I walked away from Wall Street into living my purpose and passion of writing books and speaking my message of love all over the world. It was awesome because my wife and kids traveled the world with me."

"And you still volunteer at cemeteries?"

"Just for the Couples' Castle. I owe this place my life. The rooms saved my marriage." He looked beyond the tree line toward the castle.

"What about the rooms helped?" Oliver had moved on to the other fingernails.

Clyde tipped his head back for a moment and closed his eyes. "Most couples are just busy making false progress toward little that is truly significant. My marriage was on that path until the Couples' Castle helped us design our marriage with an annual purpose, which enabled us to make significant progress toward what mattered most to us."

"An annual purpose?"

Clyde's eyes were open again and they were still crazy looking, creepy even, especially here in the cemetery. "Yep. Very few couples have one. But then again, very few couples are truly happy year in and year out." He knelt on one knee in front of his wife's headstone. "If you want to *outdo* the current trajectory of your relationship, which I hear is 'frustration,' you need a purpose that helps you *out-believe* your limiting thoughts about your relationship, *reprioritize* how you spend your time, and *raise* your current standards. Know what I mean?"

Olivia looked at Oliver for permission to say something vulnerable, then back at Clyde. "I don't want to feel worn out anymore. Are you claiming that a purpose can help with that?"

Clyde spoke with an easygoing manner. "You feel overwhelmed because you don't have a structured purpose for your marriage. Without it, your relationship is like a ship without a rudder. A structured purpose that's felt in your heart will catapult you beyond your current level of living, command your energy, and shape your circumstances rather than vice versa. Most couples become slaves to their experiences and circumstances and, consequently, their environment dictates their potential. Your purpose, on the other hand, will push you to higher levels of spirituality, economics, and happiness. When your relationship is infused with purpose, it's fire, so to speak. You become the thermostat that warms the room rather than the thermometer. The latter takes its cues from life's circumstances, while the former determines the temperature of the room. Your purpose will function like an invisible guiding force to elevate you into a relationship that matters most to you. That's the kind of relationship you want."

A shared purpose will help your relationship become the thermostat rather than the thermometer.

Olivia was so taken with his words she began staring off into the distance trying to process it all. She barely even noticed Oliver's nudge to her rib.

Clyde held his arms out as if to hug the world. "Now pay attention because this here's important: Your purpose becomes your relationship's identity. You should really care about that because human beings are wired so that their actions will match their identity every time."

Olivia looked around at the crooked headstones where time had worn away the messages they bore. "So everything we do in our relationship is a result of how we perceive ourselves—our identity?"

He paused to size them up. "Yes. Your entire relationship is the culmination of your thoughts about what your relationship is. Your relationship identity leads to your actions and results, and it's your purpose that transforms your identity to produce better results beyond your circumstances and environment. Would you like better results?"

"Yes. Of course. That's why we're here." Olivia rocked on her heels, pretending to study a tombstone. "We've tried a number of things, Clyde, including counseling and setting new goals, but we're still worn out. At least I am. And Oliver, he's probably worn out with me being worn out."

Clyde tilted his head to draw eye contact with Olivia. "Couples who go to counseling and set goals still often fail. Both are helpful, but neither is part of the couple's identity. The goal is 'out there' to achieve, while your purpose exists within. You need a burning desire deep within – your purpose. Set goals, yes, but just remember that your actions and behaviors will always match your identity sooner or later. That's why so many couples never achieve their goals. They self-sabotage their progress because their goals are beyond their identity, that is who they think they're supposed to be, and sooner or later, your identity brings you back to the same level on that scale of one to ten."

She felt her shoes sinking into the grass. "So you're saying we need to change our identity and that having a purpose is the most effective way to do that?"

Clyde paused long enough to lean over and brush dirt off his wife's headstone. "Yes, because a purpose helps you transcend your experiences and circumstances that would otherwise trap your thinking. See, when you change your relationship identity, then your actions, behaviors, and goals will trend in the right direction because what you think about your relationship is who you'll become. What you think of your relationship, you will get more of. There's a reason couples who think they are a couple with problems (identity!) always have more problems. A strong, healthy purpose can change all that. A robust purpose doesn't just strengthen your identity, it's the DNA of your identity. So if you don't like the way you are now, that is your identity, then creating a robust purpose is the way out and up to a better relationship."

"Speaking of identity"—Oliver scanned the cemetery—"who do all these other tombstones belong to?"

Clyde remained at the side of his wife's tombstone. "That, my friends, is not for you to know." The tick of dead leaves tumbled along a stone pathway.

Oliver gave a close-lipped smile. "Okay, sorry. I was just going to say that, that, uh, I think cemeteries would be way more interesting if they'd put the cause of death on the headstone, you know?"

Clyde smiled, then pushed up his sleeves. "How they died isn't important. It's how they lived that made the difference. Many couples go to their graves with unfulfilled dreams and unrealized passion for each other. They allow the twists and turns, the ups and downs, to throw them off course—because they don't have a purpose to keep them on course."

Olivia's chin lowered to her chest. For all the berating she dished out at Oliver, Olivia felt worthless for having no idea in how to come up with a shared purpose.

Clyde raised his hands wide. "A couple's purpose gets them through the inevitable ups and downs on the path to becoming a world-class couple. It's why Mark Twain said, 'The two most important days in your life are the day you are born and the day you find out why.' The same is true for your marriage."

Oliver tapped his lips. "Hey, if you think about it, being born is the first time I did something for the last time, and dying will be the last time I do something for the first time."

Clyde's crazy eyes glimmered when he smiled. "If you're asking me your relationship definitely needs a shared purpose."

"You're probably right, Clyde. Olivia has been on our case about this for awhile now." Oliver stole a glance at O.

Clyde leaned on his shovel. "Did you think it was a coincidence that your path led to me? From what I've been told, Olivia, you, especially, are always preparing for a purpose, preparing to live but never really living, like you're waiting for something . . . or someone."

I'm not waiting on anyone, unless he's thinking about Zeb, but how would he know about that? And I'm not waiting for him anymore. I just want to slap him.

"What do you mean?" Olivia felt heat rising behind her eyelids.

Clyde feigned a smile and nodded. "Couples aren't designed for the purpose of preparing to live, but that's how they talk to themselves all the time. They say things like 'When we get a house, then we'll be happy. When we have kids, then we'll be happy. When, when, when.' The fact is you're both living right now—this is your life—and you don't wait for happiness, you generate your happiness by what you repeatedly think and do. If you're the total sum of your actions and not just your intentions, which you are, then you need to *live* on purpose to get better results."

Clyde pulled the shovel out of the ground and tapped at the surface. "My challenge to you today is to figure out why you're married and to etch that purpose on your hearts so that you live it. I mean, what's your vision for the ultimate relationship? I'd ask that whether you're single or married—you gotta ask yourself what kind of person you're looking to marry or live with from here on out. Here, let me give you the steps to purpose your way above and beyond your current circumstances and into the ultimate relationship experience:

1. Answer 'Why do I want to be married?' or 'Why are we married?'
2. Answer 'What's my/our vision for the ultimate relationship?'
3. Write down all the characteristics of the person it would take to experience the ultimate relationship with. Start with fifty characteristics.
4. Answer 'Am I worthy of the relationship I expect to have with this person?'

5. Become a similar kind of person so that you'll attract that person into your life—even if it's your current spouse, he'll transform.

"Now if you just treat this as some silly exercise, you'll never take action. And without action, you get no results. You stay in a mediocre marriage. But if your vision and purpose is etched on your heart, then the sky's the limit. Like I said, most couples will never do this. If we're honest, they're just too lazy and prefer to complain and point fingers. If you want to have a world-class relationship go through the five steps right now. Otherwise you're deceiving yourselves."

"That's great. But how do we come up with a purpose phrase or sentence to summarize it all, you know? Does that make sense?" Olivia shrugged.

Clyde's eyes ping-ponged between Oliver and Olivia. "Once you've gone through the five steps, and if you really think you're ready to go to the next level of happily-ever-after, here's the process of purpose that transformed Shaniqua and my relationship:

Step 1: Pick three words that you want to describe your relationship this year. The three words can change from year to year, but these words will glue your paths together. They'll become your personal standards and form a new identity for your relationship. Remember, actions always follow identity, so pick empowering words that you want to live out. Place them throughout the house and on your phones.

Step 2: Pick this year's relationship purpose by asking 'What would double our happiness this year?' This too can change from year to year. It keeps things fresh."

Clyde then raised a third finger.

Step 3: Add in the look-back-one-year-from-now exercise. Imagine a year from today you're looking back over the year with a huge smile on your face because it was the best year of your relationship ever. What does that year look like, and what would you have to do to make it come true? Your answer will shape your purpose."

Olivia opened her mouth to say something and then closed it. Clyde was patient in the stillness. When she didn't say anything, Clyde moved on. "Now take the answers to those questions and flesh it out into the three common elements of a purpose statement that you can hang on your fridge or home wall. What do we want to *be* and *do, so that* . . . ?"

The steps felt a bit overwhelming but Olivia didn't want to say she felt overwhelmed ever again. She also felt odd standing here in the cemetery, knowing someday she would never leave again. She wanted to find her marriage's purpose long before that happened. "Can you give us an example?"

Clyde spoke in excitable tones, almost like he knew Shaniqua was listening in. "Yes. Let's say you agree with each other that the way to double your happiness this year, which was step two, is to become the most positive couple you know. Now you just flesh that out. Here's an example: Our marriage's purpose this year is to *be* the most positive couple we know, *fill* each other with pockets of positive energy three times a day, *so that* we experience more of what matters most to us this year. Then you just add step one, which were your three words. They could be 'positive,' 'fun,' and 'love.' You can include the three words in the sentence or place them around the sentence. Step three would be to ask if the sentence and words would lead to your best year ever. If not, add some personal pizzazz to the sentence.

Clyde forced himself to be quiet so that it could sink in. He then raised his fingers. "Let's say the positive example isn't your thing. Here's a second example: You may agree with each other that the way to double your happiness and fulfillment this year is to get your relationship satisfaction to an eight or higher. To flesh that out, you'd say, 'Our marriage's purpose this year is to *be* a consistent eight and *apply* the rooms' strategies from the Couples' Castle every day *so that* we always remain the love of each other's lives and experience the ultimate relationship in an authentic happily-ever-after together."

"Nice, that's helpful." Oliver put his hands in his pockets, nodding and smiling at the same time.

Clyde looked him in the eyes. "That might be enough for you. But to take it up another notch, you still need steps 4 through 6. Here's step 4: Connect your relationship to one metaphor."

"What?" Oliver's eyebrows squished together.

Clyde leaned on his shovel while he talked. "For example, you could use a movie metaphor. Ask yourselves, 'If our relationship becomes a movie this year, what kind of genre do we want it to be? A drama? Action? Romance or suspense? Or perhaps a comedy? And what kind of role would each of us play in the movie?' Again, it can change from year to year."

Has he been working too long digging graves?

"Stay with me. After that, there are two steps that'll bring it all together. I promise.

"Step 5: Pick a time marker and ask, 'What are we willing to do to make this happen?' In other words, you could say, 'By December 31, we'd like our relationship to be _____ (the most positive relationship we know or a consistent eight), and we are willing to _____ (meet every Sunday night to review our progress). We want this because _____ (positivity brings joy and resources that otherwise would remain distant or life is short).

"Step 6: Set the *purpose tone* with what we called the breakfast-bed method. Each morning at breakfast and every night before bed talk about your purpose, even if only for a minute or two because what stays on your mental dashboard becomes the trajectory of your relationship."

Zeb and I used to talk about stuff that really mattered on my front porch until the wee hours of the morning. Maybe that's why we felt so connected.

Oliver laid his hand on Clyde's shoulder. "Okay, I'm intrigued by all this, Clyde. It feels like a lot, but I think some of this could work. I'm glad I met you."

Clyde gave a hearty laugh. "I'm glad I met you too, Oliver. But it's for no good if you don't take action. The secret to your success is in taking massive action consistently. About 97 percent of couples I talk to will never do what I've just shared, but you should run away from the 97 percent—become the 3 percent who flourish in happily-ever-after. Transform your identity with a passionate purpose because, remember, your actions flow from your identity. You're more prone to take actions if you connect your emotions to your purpose. Get radical about it with creative action steps because your purpose will pull you to the top, keep you from feeling overwhelmed, enable you to say 'no' to good—but not ultimately fulfilling—options, and lead to the best year of your relationship and to the best rest of your relationship."

Oliver grabbed his jaw. "Wait, there've been other couples who've come to the Couples' Castle?"

Clyde nodded. "Yes, and now it's your turn to decide whether you'll put more joy in your relationship. Everyone wants more happiness and joy, but not everyone's willing to go through the steps I just outlined. As such, they remain an amalgamation of everyone else's expectations and desires. They become average, mediocre, and stale. They live in the same house together, but they're strangers. They argue. They divorce. They want to kill each other. They blame each other. Be different. Be remarkable. Be great. Be unified. Be fulfilled. The way to do that is to live with purpose. Your purpose focuses your relationship, and focus is everything because where your focus goes, so goes your relationship. Think about it. Putting together a shared purpose will only take one day or just a few hours, and it will completely transform your relationship to elite levels."

> Without a shared purpose, your marriage becomes an amalgamation of everyone else's expectations and desires. You'll go through life feeling the tug and pull of mediocrity until you finally die inside.

Oliver considered his options. "So does the Couples' Castle have a purpose statement?"

"They sure do. It's hanging up in room 7." His eyes glowed when he said room 7.

"Well, what is it?" Oliver's eyebrows furrowed, then released.

Olivia noted that Oliver seemed more interested in talking about purpose now than he has their entire marriage. She suddenly felt the unfulfilled lives of the deceased calling out from beyond the grave—songs left unsung, books left unwritten, and marriages gone sour. She gave a quick glance Oliver's way to express her gratitude for his desire for more purpose.

Clyde's eyes sparkled. "The purpose of the Couples' Castle is *to be* a community for individuals who want to find the love of their lives and for couples *to experience* the ultimate relationship and make their marriage a masterpiece *so that* they flourish in an authentic happily-ever-after."

"Hmm, that makes sense. I'm down with that. What say you O?" Oliver bounced lightly and had his hands tucked in his armpits, thumbs visible.

"What?" She felt a light breeze go through her hair. *I must've been daydreaming.*

"Did you hear what he said?" Oliver pointed at Clyde.

"Uh yes. I think so." She gave a sidelong glance while keeping her head still.

"Well . . . what do you think babe?"

She lifted her chin to look confident. "I think it's probably time to go hun. We've been out here for a while and I think we're all supposed to meet at the waterfall."

Clyde eyed her like he knew her better than she knew herself. "The forest pays no attention to clocks or calendars. Appointments and meetings are inconsequential here. Couples convince themselves that they're so short on time these days, but that's only because their life rhythm is busyness rather than purpose. Everyone gets the same amount of time in the day—from the president of the United States to a poor old grave digger like me. The difference between world-class couples and other couples is how they spend their twenty-four hours each day. The former have hearts set on fire with purpose."

He's got an answer for everything. I wish he was my uncle and lived in my neighborhood. Of course, the locals might be weirded out by his crazy eyes. But wait until they hear him talk.

Clyde stared off into the distance. "Out here in the deep woods, birth and rebirth echo in daily triumph. The birds' songs and the trees' applause celebrate the sun's warmth, the moon's majesty, and the stars' nightly shows. The deep roots ground us in humility, while the butterflies' fluttering calibrate our inner compass."

Olivia raised her eyebrows. *So much for making sense.* "What are you talking about?"

Olivia couldn't get over how white Clyde's teeth were. Must be some great dental plan at the Couples' Castle. "You just have to listen. Open your eyes. Be mindful—feel your surroundings. It'll root you into what matters most. You're too up here." Clyde pointed to his head.

Okay, I'm outta here. I really don't need someone pointing at his head to indicate that I'm out of touch. "Oliver, I'm going to go sit at the entrance of the gate and wait for you there. I need some time to think about these astute points Clyde's making."

"You're too up here. You're too up here," Clyde repeated, like a senile nursing-home resident.

Is he from another planet?

He put his hand up. "Before you go, please allow me to give you one more exercise on finding your purpose that moves it from just a good idea in the head to an I-must-do-this in the heart so you really feel it in a way that will pull you through anything—propelling your relationship to a stratospheric level. Life coaches and marriage counselors use this exercise and it'll create massive momentum and sustained success in your relationship. If you no longer just want the years to eek by; if you no longer want to settle; if you want to fill that empty dead space; if you want a passionate, magnificent love, you have to do what I'm about to tell you."

*   *   *

Chapter 9

Mediocre or Masterpiece

Oliver tilted his head slightly. "Really? What's it called?"

"Seven Levels Deep—Joe Stump originated the idea, and Dean Grazioi helped popularize it. Let's see what happens when we apply it to your relationship." His feet were spread wide, his arms loose at his sides.

Olivia looked at Oliver, who was rolling her neck from side to side, for confirmation. "Okay, let's do it."

Clyde studied their faces. "It involves asking seven progressive 'why' questions to dig deeper until you discover your purpose. Each question is basically the same with the intent to draw a deeper answer each time. The first four responses draw out rational, heady answers, while the final three unearth your soul and heart responses. Those final three will form your relationship purpose this year. You'll want to do this exercise once a year, and the answers can change. So who wants to go first?"

"She does." Oliver pointed at O.

Olivia looked at Oliver, crossed and uncrossed her arms, and then cleared her throat.

Oliver put his hands out. "What?" With hushed tones, he whispered, "*You're* the one who's been talking about living with purpose." He shrugged.

"All right, you have a point." Olivia batted her eyes, folded her arms, and leaned back on one heel. She felt thirsty.

Oliver rubbed his hands together and said, "Okay, Clyde, ask away. She's ready."

Clyde's eyes landed directly on O's eyes. *"Number seven:* Why is it important to you to be married this year?"

Olivia scratched her cheek and stole a glance at Oliver. "Well, just because. Because we *are* married. What do you mean 'why is it important for you to be married *this year?*'"

Clyde nodded. "It's the perfect question with which to begin because it wakes couples out of their marital sleepwalking and starts them on the journey of relational purpose that will get them results. So again, why is it important for you to be married *this year?*"

A moment of awkward silence filled the space. She coughed to buy some time. Oliver gently touched her on the shoulder and rubbed it until she relaxed.

"Um, because we've always just stayed married each year." *Well, that didn't sound very romantic, Olivia.*

Clyde's face revealed no judgment. *"Number six:* Why is it important to you just to stay married each year?"

"Because we made a commitment on our wedding day to stay married?" Oliver removed his hand from Olivia's shoulder and drew a deep breath. *Great, now Oliver's discouraged. Hello, Olivia. You can do better than this.*

Clyde's shoulders were back, his chest out, and his crazy eyes remained focused on Olivia. *"Number five:* Why's it important to you to stay true to your commitment?"

Olivia forced herself to make eye contact with Clyde. "I guess, I guess we've been questioning that ourselves lately you know? What do you say, Oliver?"

Oliver leaned back and waved her off. "He's asking you, babe."

Olivia shifted her weight to the right and opened her mouth to criticize Oliver, then stopped short. Instead, she gathered her thoughts and answered Clyde, "Because without following through with commitment, there'd be no trust." *There that sounded better.*

"Number four: And why is it important to you to keep trust?"

No pause for appreciation or reflection? He's relentless. "Um, because without trust, there's no relationship. And without that, we have nothing, just two strangers living under the same roof. Maybe that's what they refer to when people talk about empty nesters. They have no purpose holding them together anymore. Plus, our kids will become skeptical of relationships, jaded even. It could wreck not just our future but theirs as well."

Clyde may have shown a small smile before continuing. *"Number three:* And why is it important to you to keep your relationship?"

"Okay. Well, if I'm honest"—she looked over at Oliver then back at Clyde—"because I don't want to live and die alone." She rubbed her nose and looked down at her feet.

> Marriage is magnificent because emotions, when combined with another, are amplified. So some love becomes deep love, some romance becomes ravishing romance, some joy becomes abiding joy, and so on.

Clyde lowered his voice. *"Number two:* And why is it important to you not to live and die alone?"

She fidgeted and drew a deep breath. "Because I'm afraid, and life's most rewarding moments are the ones you share with someone you love. Having a soul mate, or someone you do life with via marriage, holds the strongest capacity for love, I believe."

Clyde stepped closer. *"Number one:* And why is it important to you to avoid being afraid and, instead, experience the strongest capacity for love and joy?"

She hooked her hand in Oliver's belt. "Because emotions, when combined with another, are amplified. So some love becomes deep love, some joy becomes abundant joy, and that's where I can experience the most happiness in my short time on earth."

Clyde stretched out his hands. "Ah okay. Well done, Olivia. See how we progressively moved from the head to your heart?" He sprayed his hand over his heart. "Write your answers out and hang them up so that they're visible—they'll energize you when you see them. You should practice this exercise on each other, once per year minimum. You might have different answers, and that's the point. The key is to hold no judgment toward your partner's responses because when you find *your big why*, especially the top three, it has the capacity to pull you through anything the relationship encounters during the year. When you get a big enough 'why,' it'll sink into your emotions, and that will carry your relationship to the height of fulfillment."

Olivia's smile had a genuine build until it lit up her face. "Thank you, Clyde. That just might help improve our future." She leaned forward to hug him and didn't let go.

Clyde patted her on the head, stepped back, and tipped his cap to her. "Your marriage will either become mediocre or a masterpiece. Think about it this way: picture two wavey lines and inside the lines are everything that will make your marriage a masterpiece while everything outside the lines will make your marriage mundane. Decide what goes in the lines and then do those things." Clyde reached into his pocket and pulled out a folded piece of paper and handed it to Olivia. "This is the paper my wife and I used, with our wavey lines."

Complain – criticize – blame – shame – dumb conversations – too much T.V. – pity party

100 playful pleasure list – daily positive projection – visualize our purpose & goals –
Pray together – tuck her in at night – ask better questions – retreat every 90 days –
cuddle time – make feel appreciated & important – peace of mind – open doors for her
– compliment him in front of others – ask 1-10 questions on Sunday – make love – build

wealth – contribute to cause – date night – flirt together – workout – have role models

No goals – no purpose – lazy – unhealthy – bad friends – broke – bad habits – negative

Olivia looked up. "Wow, Clyde, this is really helpful." She attempted to hand it back to him.

"Keep it. I no longer have use for it. Clyde took in a deep breath and smiled. "And modify it according to what matters most to you guys. Just remember, on the outside put activities and thoughts that lead to a mundane marriage while on the inside put that which leads to your marriage masterpiece. We used to put our purpose and wavey lines up on our fridge. You can have any kind of marriage you like, but you have to be purpose driven about it to experience it."

Olivia turned to Oliver. "Oliver, can I talk to you for a second?"

Oliver squished his eyebrows together. "Sure, babe. What is it?" They scooted back from Clyde.

She was biting her nails. "I know were supposed to stay together, but would you mind if I went up ahead to the waterfall while you stayed here and finished up with Clyde. If you don't want me to, I understand."

Oliver's head flinched back slightly, and his eyelids blinked rapidly. "I don't understand. Why? Plus, the woods. We don't know if it's safe or dangerous out there."

She pinched her lips together and shrugged. "I know, I know. It's just my answers to his questions gave me clarity for the first time in a long time, and some alone time on a walk will help me process it. I can wait until later hun, but I just thought now, since you know, I'm still feeling clarity of purpose." Olivia felt a floating sensation, like some of her burdens had finally been removed.

Oliver grabbed her hands. "Okay, honey. If that's what you want. Just go straight to the waterfall, okay? And please be careful."

"I will. Thank you." She kissed his cheek and walked away.

*   *   *

Emma froze. *It'd be embarrassing if they see me without Titus. Maybe if I stand really still, they won't notice I'm over here.*

Zeb read the sign aloud to Isabella: "Answer to make a triple checker jump for your relationship: *On a scale of one to ten, how would you rate the quality of your relationship's purpose? If the answer is less than a ten, what would it take to make it a ten?* Please answer these questions on your way to the waterfall."

Isabella pressed her lips tight, then frowned. She stood there pondering her marriage before saying, "Well, we both know it's not a ten, and it might take a while to get even close."

Apparently, Emma and Titus weren't the only ones with problems here. But Zeb and Isabella shouldn't give up just because of the time it would take. The time would pass anyway. And at least they had a chance. Emma stepped softly to her left, and a twig cracked under her foot.

"Someone's out here." Isabella looked all around before her eyes landed on Emma. A flush crept across Emma's face while her thoughts searched in vain for an excuse for the perceived eavesdropping. "Hello, it looks like our paths are intersecting."

Isabella craned her neck up. "How long have you been standing there and where's Titus?"

Say anything but the truth. "Oh, he wanted to meander through the woods in search for mushrooms, an old pastime he shared with his dad, you know." *Not sure if they're buying it, but whatever.* "Because I didn't want to get dirty, he said he'd meet me at the waterfall."

"Well, you can join us. We're taking this path around that corner up there." Isabella motioned for her to walk their way.

Emma tipped her head back a moment and let out a thankful breath. When she took her first step in their direction she felt the thick tension leave her body.

The three of them walked on the path and around the corner while talking about the castle's mysteries. Emma felt an immediate bond with

Isabella when the latter opened up about her own problems back home. That turned into laughing about needing to pee out in the middle of the woods. She took a deep breath, thankful to finally have a friend in this place.

As they made their way around the corner, Zeb pointed ahead of them. "Is that Oliver talking to someone with a shovel?"

Isabella squinted. "I think so."

"Let's go check it out." Zeb grabbed Isabella's hand with Emma next to her.

Oliver spotted them approaching. "Hey, guys, good to see you. This here's my buddy Clyde. The smartest guy I've ever met."

Clyde waved off the compliment, placed the shovel in his left hand, and then stretched out his hand with the missing pinky to greet them.

*   *   *

As they engaged in conversation about living on purpose, Zeb noted Olivia's conspicuous absence. Assuming she was on her way to the waterfall, he nudged Isabella and said, "I'm going to head over to the waterfall and see if I can find Titus on the way. Maybe I can talk to him and perhaps I'll see Olivia too. I don't see either of them here." He motioned sympathetically toward Emma so that Isabella would glance at her. She turned back to Zeb and gave an understanding nod. At that, Zeb headed out of the cemetery and back on to the path.

Zeb quickened his pace and kept his eyes peeled for Titus, but his main interest lay in finding Olivia. About twenty minutes of walking past mossy rocks, sidestepping branches hanging out into the path, avoiding broken spiderwebs, and stepping over tree roots that crisscrossed the uneven trail, he spotted Olivia sitting just up ahead on a cold stone. As he neared, she looked up, immediately petting her own hair with one hand.

Zeb stopped five feet in front of her. "Hey there, old friend."

She dropped the leaf she'd been twirling in her other hand and jumped to her feet. "What are you doing here? Where's your wife?" She searched over his shoulder and seemed almost scared.

He nodded back toward the cemetery. "She's back there talking to some man with a shovel. We saw Oliver there too." The distant sound of a waterfall could be heard in the background.

"Ah yes, Clyde." She pushed her hair up over her ear.

"Who?"

"The man with the shovel. His name is Clyde." She clamped her lips together.

"Ah. I see." He nodded and slipped his hands into his back pockets, rocking lightly on his feet. "So uh, I told Isabella that I would meet her up at the waterfall. I was, uh, kinda hoping to see you there. I thought maybe we could talk, you know. This is all so strange that we're here together and all."

She hesitated and then made eye contact. "Ya. Okay."

They took a few steps down the path before he stopped. "I know it's been a long time, but I owe you an apology." He drew in a quiet breath. "I'm sorry, Olivia."

She waved it off. "Don't. It's not that big of a deal."

He flinched. "Oh. Okay."

She looked frozen, like she was waiting on him to do something.

He motioned with his hands. "Well, I just thought since . . ."

"Honestly, Zeb, I don't know whether to hug or slap you." She shook her head softly.

"How about a friend hug? It's been, like, forever." His breath temporarily bottled up in his chest.

She stepped forward tentatively and wrapped her arms around his waist.

Her skin is softer than I remember.

She leaned back and looked up into his eyes. "Where have you been? I don't understand." She was back to smoothing her hair while studying his face.

He bit the inside of his cheek. "I will tell you everything, Olivia. To give us ample time before the others arrive, perhaps we can take a shortcut to the waterfall and talk there?" When he didn't get a response, he continued. "I think if we take a shortcut through the trees, we'll gain time. We just gotta avoid getting slapped by those tree branches."

"Ya, okay." She twisted her neck as if sore. "I'll lead."

He leaned away and glanced around uneasily. And off she went, with him having to play catch-up. They dashed through the timelessness of the ancient trees, jumped over slippery rocks, and dodged past brier brushes and snapped branches. Zeb was glad he'd started losing weight and jogging again. She was in shape.

Surveying the widening path to their right, she veered left where the ground was damp and the trees dark green. They ran through the wet and rocky terrain. They leaped over a fallen tree and found their way into a muddy brook, the roar of the waterfall not too far ahead. The moist ground and air soaked Zeb's shoes and clothes. Olivia brushed her hair back around her ear, probably wondering what he'd say when they arrived.

The tops of the trees swayed, allowing rays of the morning sunrise to breakthrough. The forest's animals were waking up, stretching, and calling out warning cries about the human intruders. Olivia and Zeb veered right, following the sound of the meandering river, and slowed when they neared the edge of the tree line.

They stopped, finding themselves opposite the base of a magical waterfall that welcomed them with nature's songs. The perfectly large stream of clear blue water dovetailed over a rocky bed. The signs of deer prints in the soft banks gave them a sense of privacy from other humans.

Zeb bent over to catch his breath. When he looked up, he saw majestic trees beyond the waterfall high-fiving the clouds with their sprawling branches, alive with birds chirping and nestling within their strength. The ancient beings surrounded them, holding a sacredness that flooded them with appreciation for God's creation. Zeb breathed in an air that brought with it the smell of woodland at the beginning of a fresh rain.

When he realized just how alone they were, guilt crept up his spine. Maybe they shouldn't have run off that way. In fact, if Isabella did something like this, it wouldn't sit well with him at all. This felt different, however. Why in the world were they brought to the Couples' Castle at the same time? This was no accident, and he needed to explain what happened anyway. Olivia may not like it, but she deserved to know.

Olivia looked up at him, the same guilt clear on her face. "Okay, Zeb. What is it you want to say?"

Her eyes were filled with purity, just like he remembered them on their last night together, before she fell asleep in his arms.

He opened his mouth and then closed it, searching for the right way to say it. Behind her, a continuous curtain of white water poured over the top of the falls into the blue river. The cove seemed like the perfect hiding place for squirrels, swans, and secrets.

Zeb nodded toward the side of the falls. Olivia followed his stare straight to the entry behind the waterfall. To get there, they'd have to walk in the opposite direction, where the water turned into a lazy stream, and cross over from there. She nodded back. They made their way down and crossed over on slippery rocks, then picked up their pace toward the back entrance of the falls.

The noise increased steadily until he could no longer hear her footsteps. Now behind the curtain of the waterfall, the mist sprayed their skin, while the thunderous noise of the falls aroused powerful emotions. The place felt sacred, wrong, and needed.

She abruptly stopped. "Okay, where are we going? Just get to it. Where have you been, Zeb?"

The falls were deafening, and he didn't want to shout over them.

Eyeing a cave-like entry behind her, he gently guided Olivia into it so they could hear each other better.

He dodged her question. "You look happy."

"Cut to the chase, Zeb." She sat back, guarding her personal space.

He took a deep breath, his eyes filling with tears.

Her defensiveness relaxed. "Zeb?"

"I didn't leave because of you. I left *for* you." He exhaled deeply.

She shook her head. "I don't need an intimate explanation. Maybe back then, but we're both married now, with children."

"Then let me explain for my sake." He studied a rock next to his shoe before looking back at her.

"Okay." She sat straight up and uncrossed her arms, hands falling gently on her lap.

His throat felt dry and he wetted his lips. "I left because I had a brain tumor."

"What? '*Had?*' Are you all right?" Olivia's face grew with concern.

"Yes, but not at the time."

She leaned forward. "You should've told me, Zeb. I would've supported you."

He twisted the ring on his finger. "I know you would've, and that was the point. I didn't want to put you through that when you had your whole life ahead of you."

"So did you." She gave him a long pained look and then broke eye contact.

He shrugged. "I didn't know that. There are over a hundred types of brain cancer, plus different grades of each cancer, and we didn't know exactly what I had yet. Prior to visiting Mom, I started having headaches and nausea, so I finally went to the doctor. That's why I came out to spend the summer with Mom."

Olivia looked up and to the left, trying to recall any details. "Is that why she put her house up for sale?"

He raised his eyebrows and sat back. "You knew about that?"

Her eyes widened. "You left so abruptly that I drove over to your mom's to see if she knew anything. But all I found was a *for sale* sign in the front yard and an empty house."

He nodded. "Yes, she put the house up for sale to help pay for my cancer treatments. She moved out East with me to help throughout the craziness."

"That's so sweet." A smiled broke the tension on her face.

"Yes, that's Mom. And uh, during that last week you and I spent together, I had a seizure. That's when we made an appointment to get a second opinion."

Her eyebrows squished together. "So you didn't believe the first doctor's diagnosis?"

He shook his head. "I guess I was in denial. I was alone and wanted to spend some time with Mom. That's why I flew out to visit."

"So what did the second doctor say?"

"The MRI scan confirmed the first one. I had a pineal tumor."

Olivia exhaled. "I'm so sorry." Her hand massaged her chin.

"Thanks." Zeb tipped his head back for a moment and closed his eyes. After opening them, he said, "It's the kind of brain cancer than can be slow- or fast-growing, and we didn't know which one at the time."

She stood up. "You mentioned something about grades."

"Of the four grades, I fit in grade two." He stood and slipped his hands into his pockets.

"What does that mean?" She tilted her head slightly.

"It meant that the tumor was growing slowly, but it could spread into nearby tissue or recur." Zeb curled his mouth in a sour expression.

"So what'd you do?"

"The new doctor said it required surgery but not just any surgery. Because the pineal region is in the center of the brain, it required a superior level of surgical expertise to remove the tumor." Images of possible death flashed through his mind, and he looked up to fight the tears. "I opted to start with radiation therapy, and they agreed, but later, when it regrew, we had to consider chemotherapy or surgery. We chose surgery."

"So did they get it all?" She raised her eyebrows.

"So far, so good."

They stood there for a moment only inches apart now, contemplating their past.

She slapped him.

He jumped back, stunned, and rubbed his cheek. "Ouch, what'd you do that for?"

"You should've told me, Zebediah!"

"It wouldn't have been fair to you, Olivia. There were too many unknowns." He was still rubbing his soar cheek.

"Well, I thought we had something. But maybe we didn't." She crossed her arms and waited for a response.

His sense of deep calm and relaxed breaths put her back at ease. He looked her in the eyes. "We did. Like I said, it wasn't you. I'm sorry. Please forgive me."

Her eyes fell to the wet rocks. "How long did the whole thing take, from the MRI to radiation and then surgery?"

Zeb dropped his hands to his sides. "A while. Plus, they put me through oncology rehabilitation that included different therapies to rebuild my strength and endurance afterward. When I did feel better, I looked you up, but you'd just gotten married, and I didn't want to step into that. I still care for . . . Well, your happiness meant more to me."

She unconsciously parted her lips. "Well, I'm glad you're better."

"Me too." He shifted his weight, searching for words to keep the conversation going.

"We have good memories, Zeb, and that's something." Olivia bit her bottom lip while she played with her hair.

"Yes, we do." Zeb nodded, feeling his breath bottle up in his chest. "Meilleurs amis pendant la vie?"

"I see you've stayed up on your French. *Très certainement.*"

She smiled. "We better head down to the base of the falls. They'll be here soon."

"Yes. Let's do that." After a few steps, Zeb stopped and turned. "I just wish I knew why we were both invited to the castle at the same time. Do you have any ideas?"

Before she could say anything, they heard a loud shout from the other side of the falls' curtain. "Olivia!"

She froze. "They're here."

Chapter 10

Room 4

"Oliviaaaaaaa!" This time a boat horn followed.

Olivia took a deep breath and looked at Zeb. "I'll walk from behind the waterfall first. You follow."

"Hi, honey, up here!" She waved and offered a nonchalant smile. Zeb stood behind her.

Oliver and the other two women were all standing on a white speedboat near the base of the falls.

Oliver pointed. "There she is!"

"It looks like Zeb's up there too." Isabella craned her neck and squinted.

After they joined them on the boat, Oliver asked, "What were you guys doing up there, Olivia?"

Say something. "Exploring." *He looks unsatisfied, say more?* "We got here before everyone else and saw a trail that led up to the falls. We thought we'd just go see what it's like. Sure enough, it led to an entrance behind the water's curtain." Why did she just lie? *Because this is getting more awkward by the moment.*

"Where'd the boat come from?" Zeb asked, changing the subject.

"Clyde showed us, and he gave us some food too. Here, grab a sandwich and apple." Oliver held out his hand with a bag of snacks.

"Thanks, I'm hungry. What time is it? It's gotta be past noon." Olivia grabbed an apple and bit into it.

Emma cast a worried glance around the cove. "Where's Titus? I thought he'd meet us here."

"I don't know. I didn't see him on the trail, and neither of us saw him here." Zeb turned when he heard the engine rev.

"What?" Emma put her hands in her armpits, hugging herself, and looked all around.

Uh oh, here she goes again. Total basket case—not that I blame her.

For the next hour, only one word echoed through the woods: "Titus!" They walked in ever-expanding circles around the glade calling out for him. They even split up and followed each trail back to the trail head. When there was no sign of him, they reconvened back at the boat.

"Should we check to see if he went into the next room?" Oliver glanced at his wrist like he was wearing a watch.

"No, no, no, no, no, no, no," Emma muttered. She was pacing now, her teeth biting down on her upper lip. "I know the clock's ticking, but what if he's lost out here somewhere or, worse, injured and can't move?"

The boat went up and down the river for another two hours, sometimes docking to let them search in the thick of the woods. Olivia couldn't help but wonder if he'd just went home. For all the stuff she and Oliver were going through, she didn't want to trade places with them. Just thinking about separating from Oliver gave her an empty feeling in the pit of her stomach.

Emma sat down and sobbed until Isabella went over and placed a hand on her shoulder. Emma blew her nose and said, "Just so you guys know, I used to be a very happy person." She blew her nose again. "Maybe he just went home. I think I broke his heart. He's just ready to move on without me, and I can't blame him. I'm such a horrible person."

It grew silent, and they could hear a turtle plopping into the water. After a couple of minutes, Emma wiped the tears from her cheeks and turned to the captain. "Go ahead," she said with slumped shoulders. "We need to keep moving. Clyde did initial your chests, and I don't want to hold us up any longer. The next room. It's time." She swallowed hard.

"Are you sure?" Isabella pulled her close.

Emma scrubbed her hands over her face. "It's okay. Let's go. If he wants to be found, we'll find him. I don't want us to miss room 7 and finding out what's in the treasure chest."

When they docked, Isabella and Olivia stepped off the boat first while fiddling with their keys. Their husbands walked next to them, with Emma following close behind. There was only an hour or so of sunlight left.

Just ahead stood a dilapidated wooden sign that read *Room 4*, with an arrow pointing straight ahead. They walked toward another sign that pointed to their right, so they turned right and walked for another hundred yards on an uneven trail before stopping at the foot of a large hill—at the top of which sat a greenhouse. Oliver pointed out some bottled waters sitting out on a tray on top of a concrete block. As they climbed the hill, they downed the waters.

Once they made it to the top, Emma shouted, "Titus? Titus? Titus, are you here?"

On the left side of the greenhouse, near the coiled water hoses, was an entryway with a sign that read *Room 4: Progress Patterns*.

"Progress patterns? What the heck is that supposed to mean?" Oliver gave a long side glance to the group.

"My guess is, well, since this is a greenhouse and we're here to improve our relationships, the greenhouse is a symbol for the perfect growing environment." Zeb scratched his head, and Isabella looked at him with a new sense of respect.

After entering the greenhouse, Olivia stopped to admire the organization of the room. It was divided into colorful sections. The one on their immediate left grew vegetables and fruits. There were tomatoes, leafy greens, cucumbers, citrus trees, and there were baskets full of bright red strawberries and cherry tomatoes hanging.

The section on their right, thirty feet away, introduced a floral section. It was a stunning display of flowerbeds and roses, exuding a sweet fragrance. The petals were precious works of art, and the dashing carpet of every hue of the color orange inspired Oliver to pick three roses for Olivia. "Surely they won't mind if we pick just a few, given we're here to improve our relationships."

He's such a sweetheart when he wants to be.

Olivia walked to the side of the greenhouse and into an arboretum filled with more colorful flowers and native and indigenous plants with green vines crawling up the sides of statue displays. She had a wandering gaze, taking in random things, and noted the tags sticking out of pots to identify seedlings. Suddenly, she felt a lessened need for worldly goods.

She walked around the arboretum and let her hand glide over the fresh, fragrant blooms that grew in the stunning Mediterranean gardens filled with olive trees, green spires of cypress, giant water lilies, and rose gardens all around. A group of picnic tables sat in an orchard between the greenhouse and the backside of the Couples' Castle. A covered balcony overlooking the gardens looked like the perfect place to sit privately in the sun with Oliver.

Oliver plucked a low-hanging pear from a tree as he walked past. "I've always thought cities should plant fruit trees in their public parks to help feed the homeless."

"That's a great idea." Zeb leaned back on the wall next to a handheld broom and dustpan hanging off a peg, at ease and in control.

A sense of pride warmed Olivia's face. Maybe feeling overwhelmed at home wasn't so much about what Oliver did or didn't contribute. Maybe she bore some of the responsibility for feeling worn out. She'd realized she'd been way too hard on him. He was always making her laugh with his jokes and wit, generating good ideas, and demonstrating his affection for her—like he just did with these flowers. Why was she so unappreciative?

"Did you feel that?" Oliver looked up in the sky.

"Sprinkles." Olivia held out her hand.

When the group walked back into the greenhouse, they flipped on a light switch and looked around for clues about what to do next. Olivia noted the dirt-stained gloves on a wooden tabletop and wondered if someone was near. She found a note there by the gloves that said the couples may help themselves to the food, drinks, and sleeping bags provided in the storage space and that the hosts would be back in the morning after the couples had a chance to eat and rest. Their extra sets of clothes were also sitting there in duffle bags.

"Thank goodness." It was approaching evening, and Olivia was practically starving.

After eating, they walked around the greenhouse and found a restroom with indoor plumbing. Once they all freshened up, they laid out their sleeping bags and reflected on their experiences. While they talked, Olivia found herself dozing off in her thick, warm red sleeping bag.

She could've slept for days if it hadn't been for the rain tapping against the roof and walls. It must've been around 8:00 a.m. when she rubbed her eyes and sat up and heard faint voices on the other side of the greenhouse. She headed straight to the restroom and did her best to look presentable in her new yellow blouse before moseying on over to the voices. It was the other couples. Emma looked beautiful in her pink top and white slacks, while Isabella still looked the part of a mom who kept forgetting to take care of herself in the midst of attending to everyone else. Her hair looked patted down and her green top suited more for the occasion of lounging around at home. If she'd just tidy up some, she'd shine. Zeb's black button down fit loosely over his belly while Oliver wore his favorite blue jeans and Mickey Mouse shirt from back home. One big happy family.

Oliver was asking if any of them had seen the most recent superhero movie. This engaged the whole group in deciding who the greatest superhero was. Even Emma chimed in, claiming Wonder Woman was the greatest. Zeb went with the Tick. Olivia didn't have one, and Isabella responded with "Hawkgirl!" A collective laugh followed.

"You're all wrong," Oliver petitioned, using exaggerated movements. "It's Spider-Man."

"What? No way." Zeb waved him off.

Oliver bounced from foot to foot in his white sneakers, imitating Spiderman. "No, really. It is. Think about this: What if, instead of shooting web, Spider-Man's power was shooting spiders out of his hands? I bet no one would ever commit another crime again."

Ew!

A voice sailed from across the room. "Have you figured out the purpose of this room yet?" An Asian man bent in front of one of the garden beds, perhaps the garden's curator.

Everyone spun around to see who was speaking.

Emma went beyond a proper greeting and immediately asked if he'd seen Titus, filling out a description of him in the process. The man stayed on bent knee and silently shook his head no.

He seems like a nice man. I bet his grandkids love visiting him.

The group approached the silent man, walking past a section labeled Medicinal Plants.

The man stood with an air of dignity and held out his hand, palm up. In it lay a seed. "What's in my hand?"

"I got this one, guys," Oliver said like he was about to win Double Jeopardy. "It's a seed."

"Try again," a woman replied, entering from the right.

Okay, this is kinda spooky. They're either siblings or married. And possibly killers.

The man welcomed the woman to his side. "This is my wife, Meiying." She bowed with dignity. "My name is Fai." He also bowed.

"Nice to meet you." Zeb attempted a head bow, but it looked more like a curtsy.

After they exchanged pleasantries, Fai said, "This is much more than a seed. It demonstrates the power of a world-class couple, a couple who lives their lives at a consistent level nine."

Okay . . .

They all stood in silence, waiting for him to continue.

The short thin man with glasses looked at the seed in his hand, then back at the group. "Pay close attention because this seed is the beginning of the Chinese bamboo tree—just like each couple has a beginning to their relationship. It can lead either to heartache or a masterpiece—all depending upon whether it takes root and grows."

Then Fai, with the help of his partner, bent down and dug a hole in the ground, placing the seed in it. He turned back to face the couples. "It all begins as a tiny seed. It always does."

Oliver raised his eyebrows. "Are you referring to sex?"

Olivia gave him a slow sideways look, her face flush.

Meiying walked over to one of the geraniums, picked it up, and inhaled deeply. "When one plants the seed of a bamboo tree, one spends an entire year watering and fertilizing it, and do you know what happens?"

She looked each of them in the eye.

"Nothing. There's no evidence whatsoever that anything is working under the ground, but the truth is it's either progressing or regressing. And it's the same with you."

What?

Fai lifted his bamboo coolie hat. "She means you're placed on this planet to grow into a certain kind of person. When you enter into a relationship, you are always either progressing or regressing as a couple—amplifying and maximizing your emotional experiences of joy, love, and happiness or regressing and devolving into a spiral of animosity, pain, and resentment. There's no in-between."

Oliver and I have been regressing for the past two years.

"Most couples"—he tilted his chin down and frowned—"are way too focused on *what* they can do and *what* they can have and *what* they can buy—collecting a bunch of *what*s." He looked up with a face that seemed to shine. "You are not, however, placed on this planet to keep replacing one *what* with another *what* with another *what* with another *what*—whether it's a *what* job, a *what* house, a *what* car, or a *what* spouse."

What in the world was this old man talking about?

"Take his words to heart." Meiying stood in such a relaxed manner. "Couples keep exchanging, trading in, and trading up their *what*s, thinking cars, houses, and clothes will stop their disillusionment and discontentment with each other. But when couples focus on *what*s, a slow decline begins. What they're really doing is distracting themselves from . . . *themselves*. Your relationship isn't sustainable when it's focused on *what*s. The moment your focus goes to *what*s, you regress. The key then is to focus on the *who*s, to grow with each other, to progress, to become a person who is worthy of the relationship you expect to have in your wildest dreams."

Olivia was *trying* to get Oliver to grow. He just didn't listen. If he'd just help out around the house more . . . How hard was that?

Meiying handed each couple a seed and asked, "Who are you becoming? *What*s are fine, but *who* you're becoming is everything. Get that right and what you want becomes clear. Future uncertainty about the *what*s, *why*s, *where*s, and *how*s will vanish when you know who you are in your relationship. Let this seed be a reminder that your fears, anxieties, and pain will fade away when you shift your focus from *what*s to *who* you're becoming in the relationship—you'll find yourself living the ultimate relationship experience."

Fai handed Zeb a pitcher, pointed toward the seed he just planted, and nodded. "Water it."

*　　*　　*

Isabella stood in her oversized green shirt with a stiff posture and an air of readiness. She had been preoccupied with thinking about what could possibly be waiting for them in room 7, but was becoming more intrigued with where Fai and Meiying were going. Maybe it was the way they appeared so calm and in control.

Nothing happened.

"So you're saying the seed will take a while before it grows." Isabella received the pitcher from Zeb and handed it to the gardener.

"You can water that seed for an entire two years and you won't see any results, try as you may." Meiying remained relaxed and had such easy breaths.

"Okay, so what are you wanting us to do with this information?" Isabella fiddled with her treasure chest, now wanting to speed things along so they could move on to room 7. After spending hours looking for Titus and now this, talking about seeds in the ground, she was starting to feel like they were wasting valuable time. Yes, there was good information in this room, but they were ultimately here to find the real red treasure chest and they needed to get there on time, if not before.

Meiying leaned in. "The point is that this seed is a symbol for consistent progress to your own relationship, and that's where you and Zeb will find the ultimate relationship experience. Growth makes you irresistibly attractive to each other. When you make progress, you feel happy, and happy people are more attractive."

"What?" Isabella's head flinched back slightly, and she poked her tongue into the cheek. Irresistibly attractive sounded like a good thing, but she still didn't understand what that had to do with watering seeds, much less room 7 and the real red treasure chest.

Fai pulled his glasses down and looked over the rims. "Our friends in the East call this kaizen. It means constant and never-ending improvement. Most individuals in relationships are trying to improve their partners, but what if, instead"—he scanned the group—"you applied kaizen to yourself in the context of the relationship? What if each person constantly grew in love, kindness, and respect for his partner?"

"Kaizen," Oliver said to Olivia. "It sounds like something I'd put in my cereal."

"Indeed." Fai chuckled. "Kaizen is something you should put into *everything*, especially your relationship. Like you would with the seed, seek to cultivate your relationship—water it and grow it—even when there's no proof of positive results."

Oliver's ears turned red. "I was just saying, you know, that it's a funny word. I didn't mean any offense."

Fai put his hand in the air and smiled. "No offense taken. It's simply about you taking consistent action toward making your marriage a masterpiece."

Isabella was nodding along as he spoke. "*Consistent* action?"

"Yes, like cultivating this seed."

A streak of white light split the sky. As Isabella looked up, an explosion like a sonic boom shook them to the core. The heavens opened up and dropped an ocean of water. The pattering of tiny drops had transformed into bullets.

Isabella felt jolted and experienced a flashback to October 19th when it was also raining. The day she lost her little boy. A truck ran a stop sign in the downpour and smashed into the car carrying her child. She was supposed to pick her up that day from little league practice.

When she arrived to the scene the strobe of police lights, fire truck, ambulance, and tow truck were already there. Policemen with bright flak jackets were redirecting traffic and securing the scene with yellow tape. A rubbernecker held up a phone to record the scene while paramedics carried medical bags and wheeled gurneys.

She ran toward the yellow tape with the single-minded focus to save her little Corbyn. Pushing past the crowd and ducking the tape, she ran past the officers toward the paramedics near the car. When she saw the blood and lifeless body of the little boy that came from her womb, she pressed her fists to the sides of her head and let out a primal scream that tore through the crowd like a great shard of glass. Her scream came again, desperate, terrified... maternal. She took her boy off the gurney and crumpled to the ground with him in her arms. The blood drained from her face and her heart thrashed in her ears while she rocked him back and forth crying, "Baby, come back to me. Corbyn. It's going to be okay, Corbyn. Honey, I'm so sorry I was late. I'm so sorry. Come back to me son. No! No!!"

"Isabella, are you okay?" Zeb had come close and wiped the tear falling down her cheek.

"Oh, yes. I'm sorry." Isabella blinked hard and came back to.

Meiying inhaled the scent of rain. After a couple of minutes, the storm settled into rumbles in the sky. The clouds parted, and the sun's rays shined through.

Meiying picked up where she left off. "If the seed analogy doesn't resonate, maybe the magic penny will. You've heard of it?"

"I don't think so," Isabella said, then looked at Zeb for assurance.

A playful grin grew on Meiying's face. "If someone showed up at your front door and gave you ten seconds to decide between receiving a briefcase full of $3 million in cool cash right then and there or one penny that doubles in value every day for thirty-one days, and which ever you did not choose would go to your neighbor, which would you choose?"

Oliver raised his hand, then blurted out, "The $3 million!"

It's a trick. You probably should've chosen the penny.

"And that would not be a bad choice, Oliver." Meiying spoke like a loving grandmother. "Of course, it might not be the best choice either. Now day one, your neighbor would only have one penny while you're out spending or investing your $3 million. You're parking a nice new car in the driveway next to your neighbor's car. On day seven, your neighbor has only made seventy-four cents. You, you're a millionaire. Half the month goes by and your neighbor, using the principle of kaizen or the compound effect, has only made $163.84. Then with only eleven days left, on day twenty, while you're still out celebrating, your neighbor only has $5,242.88 and feeling like she's made very little progress. But by day thirty-one, she reaps the huge reward of $10,737,418.24—almost $11 million!"

"I guess I should've chosen the penny." Oliver grabbed his throat and cleared it while shifting his weight.

Meiying pushed up her sleeves, continuing to make strong eye contact. "It gets even better. Your relationship is never static. Your relationship is either moving toward mediocrity or toward a masterpiece. With every action (or non action) you take, you are either progressing or regressing. Because relationships regress by default, you must take action to improve. If you don't know how, use the Couples' Castle strategies. One challenge couples have found helpful is to take the 1 percent challenge—that is, pick one thing a month that you'd like your relationship to improve in by 1 percent. Then the next month, add another 1 percent and so on. You can even pick one extra area per month to improve. Over the course of one year, you'll have improved twelve areas. The results of progress are amazing. Plus, remember, progress itself will make you feel happy, so you also get the added benefit of feeling happy on the journey to becoming a masterpiece."

Relationships regress by default. If left on autopilot for too long, you'll find yourself alone. On the other hand, progress equals happiness. If you both improve by one percent each week, you'll find each other irresistibly attractive again and again.

Isabella's breath temporarily bottled up in her chest. When she saw everyone else nodding, she decided to ask a question. It came out like a nervous kid selling cookies door-to-door. "Can kaizen restore a broken relationship?"

"Your growth and progress," Meiying reassured her, "is how you become irresistibly attractive to each other forever. Many couples continue to trade their spouses in for another, but the secret lies in your own relationship's growth, in establishing progress patterns, in creating daily, weekly, and monthly patterns to stimulate individual and relationship growth. As married couples know, you can't just get to the marriage ceremony and think you've 'arrived.' Keep growing, progressing, and you'll make your marriage a masterpiece."

Isabella shifted her feet. "In the beginning of Zeb and my relationship, it was ravishing, a tale that rivaled the beauty of a Shakespearian love story." She noted people's blank stares. "No, seriously. But—and this is my point—creating a thriving relationship after experiencing past loss and within a blended family takes a lot more work than I anticipated."

Meiying gave an understanding nod. "So what patterns of progress can you set for your relationship?"

"What do you mean, 'patterns of progress'? Can you give examples?"

"Sure, here're some options to get you started. What if you

1. Read one book together every month.
2. Attend a marriage seminar, couples retreat, or personal development seminar twice a year. You should be spending a full couple of days together every ninety days.
3. Spend three minutes together in daily prayer or meditation.
4. Give, volunteer, and contribute to a cause or organization together."

"We could do those things." Isabella's muscles relaxed, and she felt a lightness in her chest. The forced smile that formed on her face reflected the cheeriness of Olivia's yellow blouse.

Meiying looked like she wanted to hug Isabella. "Happiness awaits the couple who grows together. Saying 'I do' doesn't bring happily-ever-after. You can't treat the marriage ceremony like pixie dust. If you truly wish for a romantic and sexy marriage, you need to build in progress patterns, growth, and the strategies found within the Couples' Castle."

Fai hitchhiked on his partner's proposal. "Most couples leave much of their relationship unexplored, which creates a stale and stagnant relationship. The secret is growth because it stimulates positivity and attractiveness between individuals year after year. It's why new relationships feel so exciting—they are constantly growing and learning new things about each other. Once you know each other, you need to install patterns of progress to keep yourselves growing and learning together. In the modern world, too many couples are choosing comfort over growth and it's ruining their relationships. You must grow—together."

Isabella could hear the chirping of birds again now that the storm had passed. She and Zeb had never really taken the time to grow. Their new marriage was all so rushed, with the kids and relocation and everything. They felt like they grew during the first few weeks of the dating period and then just assumed "I do" took care of the rest. *It's so obvious now.*

Fai lifted his chin and pushed his glasses up a bit. "Couples get bored with each other because they don't stimulate growth. Think about it. What if the two of you are really good at something but don't know because you've never tried? Try things, experiment with things, always ask what else is possible—and you'll grow. Carrying the kaizen attitude generates amazing feelings toward each other because you'll always be thinking *We haven't even seen the best of us yet!*"

Isabella looked around at the vibrant and fragrant flowers and trees that surrounded them. The smell was refreshing. Honestly, she and Zeb had just tried to get by recently. They'd tiptoed through marriage, hoping to reach the end of each day with minimal bumps and bruises, but their relationship had disappeared in the process. She raised her hand. "So why is it people fall in love and have dreams of the ultimate relationship experience but wind up wanting to kill each other sometimes? I mean, you guys keep talking about making our marriage a masterpiece, but really, we just want to move beyond calling each other a piece of work."

Fai chuckled. "You're right, Isabella. Every couple is either regressing or progressing. And there's one powerful thing that causes both."

Her eyebrows arched. "Oh ya? Well, what's that?"

The Chinese couple stood side by side now, facing the group. They laced their fingers with a warm and calm love radiating around them.

Isabella's eyes ping-ponged between the two of them. *I wish we had what they do.*

Oliver whispered to O, "He would totally win a staring competition with Mount Rushmore."

Fai spoke from the heart. "It's called the law of attraction. It's always working behind the scenes—always. And if you don't use it properly, you'll regress. But use it wisely, and wow! The important thing about the law of attraction isn't sitting around waiting for something to happen to you, but rather the 'action' in 'att*raction*'. This law is about taking action and it means whatever a couple consistently thinks about (action), talks about (action), feels toward each other (action), and believes strongly about each other (action), the couple will manifest in their relationship because it leads them to taking massive action, and massive action leads to results. It can be no other way. Simply put, like attracts like."

Zeb crossed his arms and looked to the group for reassurance. "This is all new to me, and being a church person, I've always heard this was kinda sketchy. I don't know what to believe. I'm trying to be open-minded. So no offense, but could you explain it a bit?"

Fai had a soothing tone when he talked. "Humans are emotional beings. Relationships are made and broken because of emotions. Everything you do is generated from emotions. Thus, you want to put the right energy in motion because you'll attract the same emotions back from those around you. Whatever emotion you feel, that's the energy your life puts into motion. Your partner feels that energy and reciprocates it. It's the explanation for your relationship results."

Meiying talked with the urgency of a volleyball coach during a critical timeout. She said, "Like a radio station, everyone—and everything—is sending out a frequency. The frequency you send out attracts more of the same—similar people, thoughts, and energy.

1. You send out negative energy, that's how your spouse will respond.
2. You act loving, your spouse reciprocates.
3. Couples who carp, complain, and criticize are always confused about why their relationship remains stuck in complaining, carping, and criticizing, but the reason is really quite simple."

"They're manifesting more of the same," Isabella muttered like she just had an epiphany.

Meiying smiled, erasing the wrinkles on her aged skin.

"Couples are generally focused on what they don't want," Meiying added. "The way to an extravagant love affair with your spouse, however, is to give your attention to that which you want to manifest in your relationship because the law of attraction only knows how to say *yes*. So when you think about what you don't want in your relationship, the law of attraction says *yes* and gives you more of what you don't want."

Isabella looked at her shoe and thought about her prior marriage, wondering, if perhaps, focusing on what she didn't want played a part in their divorce. After the loss of Corbyn, they tried everything - counseling, therapy, going to church. The regret was overwhelming and she felt her husband's resentful eyes carve her up every night. The pain was just too much for the marriage to survive. *I wish I'd known this earlier in life.* Now—with Zeb—is what she had, and she didn't want to screw that up too. Isabella raised her head. "Can you give us an example?"

Meiying nodded. "Here are three:

1. If you want more love, think thoughts that make you feel like your partner is the love of your life. It's not the thoughts themselves but rather the thoughts lead to emotions and, if

intense enough, lead to actions. The greater the thought, the greater the emotion and the more action you take. Act as if you're already fully in love at a nine level, which means you're thinking and feeling that way, and you'll attract more of it because your partner will respond in return.

2. If you want more respect, think respectful thoughts toward your partner. Feel feelings of respect, and more respect will flow. The 'action' in 'attraction' follows the thoughts and emotions. But you can also start with action and the emotions will follow too.

3. If you want more sexiness, think thoughts and feel feelings of sexiness. Again, it's because your partner reciprocates the kind of energy you bring to the room.

"Most couples," she continued, "think thoughts and feel feelings from a state of lack because—and this is what most couples don't know—your brain's MO is lack and attack. It operates from a state of fear and leads to fight, flight, or freeze in order to keep you alive. But you can choose a state of faith which leads to freedom, fulfillment, and flourishing in happily-ever-after where you thrive."

Emma raised her hand. She looked so pretty in that pink top and in those perfect fitting white pants.

"Yes?" Meiying nodded to Emma.

"I do think thoughts of love and respect, and it's not being reciprocated. Like is not attracting like in my case." She sighed deeply.

"I see." Meiying rubbed her chin. "One explanation is you are now reaping the results of thinking different thoughts a couple of years ago or, perhaps your roadblock comes from thinking about love in terms of what you don't have. Instead, think and feel love from a state of fullness, like you already have the love reciprocating between the two of you. It sounds strange, but it'll absolutely work better than if you feel from lack. Most couples never improve because they feel from a state of lack, which is what you're doing when you're wishing for more love. It keeps couples stuck, spinning their tires in confusion and pain. You should, instead, think about, talk about, feel, and believe with emotional fullness and intensity what you *do* want, *as if* you're already experiencing it. In this way, instead of waiting for those feelings to come to you, you'll generate them and operate toward your partner from that loving state. This state, in turn, creates a new reality—a consistent nine—for your relationship, family, and future."

"No offense," Zeb said. "This sounds plausible but a little like mumbo jumbo." He reached over to grab some berries off a nearby bush. "Are these okay to eat?"

"Seriously?" Isabella whispered, giving Zeb the motherly look.

"What? Eating is a great way to pass the time between meals." He winked at her before dropping one into his mouth.

Meiying didn't miss a beat. "It's far from mumbo jumbo. There are real neurological channels, like the reticular activating system, which controls what you pay attention to, and real scientific foundations, like bio-entanglement physics, that generate and create the results found from the law of attraction, but if we go there, it'll simply attract more of the same kind of discussion rather than the kind that'll improve your relationship. Would you like to go there?"

"Uh . . . maybe later." Zeb looked around the group. "I think we're probably more interested in how to experience the ultimate relationship, as you claim we can."

Meiying rolled her neck back and forth for a bit. "Okay. Think of it this way: Every human being is a bundle of energy, including you. Just look at any human being through an infrared camera in a dark room and that's what you'll see: energy. Then tell the person you're observing in the camera to think something, anything. Guess what happens? The bundle of energy called you shrinks and grows, depending upon the kinds of thoughts you are thinking. This shrinking and growing is called an energy vibration. Vibration just means everything is in movement and nothing is still. The walls, chairs, and ceilings, they're all vibrating at the atomic level. And so are human beings. Your body is a molecular structure at a very high speed of energy."

Emma raised her hand again.

"Yes?"

"How's this relevant to me winning Titus back?" Her eyes were so desperate.

Meiying nodded. "It's important because you are sending out energy vibrations to Titus, and the law of attraction says Titus will respond in like. This isn't mumbo jumbo new agey stuff, but simple physics. That's why whenever you brought up a problem about him, he pointed out a problem about you. It's why he's placing a dividing wall between you and him, because your past indiscretion placed a dividing wall between him and you. Like attracts like in proportion to the action done. It's why when he says 'I love you,' you do the same. It's why when someone gets you a gift, you feel the desire to get him a gift. Feelings are contagious. The key then is to be intentional about your energy—to become the vibrational match for the kind of feelings and experiences you want to attract into your relationship."

To get the ultimate relationship experience vibrate at a higher frequency because over time your partner will respond in like, which means your relationship will then amplify the kinds of emotional experiences that bring about happily ever after.

"So you're saying the way we generate our energy levels and feelings gets reciprocated back to us?" Isabella was revisiting the hurdles that led to this moment.

"Precisely," Fai said, lowering his head and looking over the top of his glasses.

Zeb cleared his throat. "I don't know. I'm more of a God-and-Bible type of person than this law-of-attraction type of stuff. Again, no offense."

Fai smiled. "None taken. I'm a conservative Christian too. Let me ask you, do you believe in the law of gravity?"

"Of course." Zeb scratched the back of his neck.

"And do you use the knowledge of the law of gravity for your benefit?" Fai raised his eyebrows.

"Ya, I guess."

"Well, in creation, God put lots of laws in play. The law of attraction is just another law that God put into the universe that couples can discover and use for their relationships. Sure different groups use their own language to describe the laws, but that doesn't mean the law doesn't exist. You don't have to get weirded out about it. People think things are weird when they don't try to understand it or know what it is. It's simply emotional energy attracting like emotional energy. Do you have emotions? Of course. Well, your emotions attract like emotions. Feel crappy when you get home? It brings everyone down. Your wife feeling good? It uplifts your spirit. Why? Because your thoughts generate an energy others can feel and that attracts like thoughts, and it's always working, whether you want it to or not. So why not use it to purposefully grow your relationship into the greatest love story ever told?"

Zeb tipped his head from side to side and swallowed hard. His black button down made him look thinner than he really was.

Olivia chimed in. "So what if you're feeling apathetic or angry toward your spouse and you don't feel like growing together?"

Oliver gritted his teeth at her in disbelief and Isabella found some consolation in it.

"Hypothetically speaking," she added.

Ya right.

Fai inhaled deeply through the nose, then exhaled through the mouth. "If you're in the middle of an argument or feeling apathetic toward each other, simply generate a new energy motion, one that makes you *feel like* your marriage is exactly what you want. Whether it is or not is irrelevant. Like you said, you might just think *He's a piece of work!* Just think better thoughts and change your energy because your energy attracts like energy from your partner. If you're stuck on how to do this, remember you can generate better feelings with better questions. Even when you're arguing, you can ask questions to transform the energy, like:

1. How would a couple who's experiencing the ultimate relationship handle this?

2. What can I feel and do right now to make my marriage a masterpiece?

3. How would I talk to him right now if I felt like he was the love of my life?"

Fai studied the couples while they pondered the answers to those questions. "See, you guys keep waiting for something in your outer worlds to get better before you feel better toward each other, but it's about what's going on inside of you that makes you happy or sad. That's why the questions are so helpful. They're not just questions. They're questions to change your inner world, which, when you do that, transforms your outer world.

'Additionally, try doing the following exercise three minutes per day: Whatever answers you get to the three questions I just gave you, make it a point to get in an emotional state that matches those answers so that the law will bring more of it to you. Sit there and think those thoughts and feel those feelings about your partner, and before you know it, you'll be loving your relationship again. You don't need to wait for your partner to make things better again. That disempowers you. You can generate your emotions that'll attract like emotions in just three minutes a day."

Fai and Meiying smiled affectionately at each other. If they weren't so sincere and real, it would've been obnoxious.

It seemed to work for them. Isabella was going to try this. Regardless of circumstances, from now on, she'll feel and act *as if* her marriage was a masterpiece whether the circumstances warranted it or not. She had nothing to lose at this point.

Fai moaned quietly and looked around the greenhouse. "Too many couples spend way too much time talking with each other about their current disappointing realities, but guess what this does—it puts them in a disempowered state and invites more of the same.

"Instead of talking about the way things are"—he inhaled—"the Couples' Castle recommends that you think, talk, feel, and act with certainty that you're growing into the greatest love story ever told. If you want your relationship to be full of love, focus your thoughts on things that bring you love. If you want your relationship to be full of romance, focus your thoughts on romantic ideas. Over time you attract into your life the kind of person you become, the kind of experiences you have a strong passion for, and the kind of relationship you believe in with emotional intensity."

Meiying stepped forward. "The law of attraction is like watering and nurturing the seed of the bamboo tree. You can't see it, but it's working at all times."

"Is it?" Zeb asked incredulously. "Because when I watered it, nothing happened."

Isabella raised her chin. "Ya, and the longer nothing happens, the more time's passing us by. We are on the clock here. I'm not trying to be rude, but that's the castle's rules. Room 7 will only stay open for so long, and that's why we're here—to see what's inside the red treasure chest. We can't be late."

*   *   *

Chapter 11

Saturday, 10:00 am

Fai asked Zeb, "Would you like to water the seed a third time?"

There must be a catch. He raised his hands. "Nah, I'm good."

Fai picked up the water pitcher and offered it to Olivia. "How about you?"

Don't take the bait.

"Okay." She grabbed the pitcher, walked over to the dirt, knelt, and watered the ground where they'd planted the seed.

"In China, we water the bamboo tree for a third year, and guess what happens." Fai grinned.

Nothing.

"Nothing," he revealed.

I was right! "Well then, why are you talking so much about progress, growth, and setting patterns for growth when the seed in your illustration isn't even growing?"

Meiying, giddy like she was about to reveal one of the universe's main mysteries, stepped toward Zeb.

What's she doing? Why is she getting close to me? Okay this is awkward.

She reached out and wrapped Zeb in a big hug.

His body froze in place. "What are you doing?"

"Receive it."

His face and neck felt impossibly hot. *It reminded him of the time in Jr. High when he was with his buddies and a girl approached and asked him to the dance.*

"Just receive it." She continued to hold him and gently tapped him on the shoulder blades.

About ten seconds passed.

I haven't felt this cared for in a while.

"Allow yourself to feel loved."

A single hot tear gathered in the corner of Zeb's eye and trailed down his cheek. He struggled to free his hand and wipe it away before anyone saw.

Meiying turned him to face Isabella and instructed the other couples to face each other as well. Fai placed himself eyeball to eyeball with Emma and said, "Pretend I'm—"

"Titus." Emma's lips quivered.

"Now hug your partner," Meiying directed. "I'm turning on some background music for you to slow dance to. Forget the awkwardness of it all. You'll never be happy if you're in your worries about what others think."

Zeb stepped forward and wrapped his arms around Isabella. Her body was rigid at first, but then melted into his embrace. *I miss this. Isabella and me. I'm not the best husband, but I'm so grateful to have you.*

Meiying circled the couples. "Those who grow together go together."

I really do love my wife.

"Every human being has coded within his nervous system the need to make progress, grow, learn, and expand his capabilities and capacities. It drives individual behaviors within the relationship. One of the secrets to marry the love of your life and experience the ultimate relationship then is to grow *together*."

Isabella pulled Zeb even closer, her nervous laughter transformed into tears that soaked through his shirt and burned into his chest. *Oh, Isabella, I'm so sorry. Please forgive me for my inattentiveness.*

"The more you grow together"—Meiying closed her eyes and smiled like she was thinking of the progress she'd made with Fai over the years—"whether it's spiritually, intellectually, economically, morally, or with new experiences—the more your number will improve. Relationships become stagnant and stale when they stop growing. In fact, they regress. And if one of you is growing while the other is not, a ceiling forms to cap your number. When you both grow together, however, the ceiling disappears, and there's no limit to the love you'll experience . . . because love itself is infinite."

Next to Zeb and Isabella, Emma rested in Fai's arms. He held her like a father comforting his daughter after a high-school breakup.

Zeb just kept holding Isabella, hoping she could feel his love breaking through the barriers that had formed between them. He couldn't recall the last time they danced together.

Your partner naturally wants to grow—whether it's to grow the bank account, grow a garden, grow your understanding about something, grow muscles, or grow your love. The key is to develop patterns that will foster progress and growth in the relationship. The temptation is to settle for comfort. Don't do that. Comfort will not bring happiness. I repeat, comfort will not bring happiness. Comfort fosters inaction and laziness. Most young couples are busying themselves to attain a comfortable life. And while it's true some comforts are great, the mentality of comfort is destructive. Have a growth mindset in your comforts or, ironically, you'll stop growing and spiral toward pain in the midst of all your comforts. Set up patterns, systems, rituals, goals, and conversations for growth."

Many couples plateau or, worse, fail, because they have goals and conversations built around comfort rather than growth.

Zeb sneaked a peek at Olivia and Oliver. Olivia looked really happy, like she loved Oliver. He stroked her head tenderly, like he knew what a precious thing he held in his arms. Zeb looked back down at Isabella, his own precious gift. They'd both done all right—more than all right. Somehow all that heartbreak turned out to be for the best.

At some point before room 7, they'd still need to tell their spouses about their history. That could be awkward or, worse, misinterpreted.

Meiying started circling again. "Keep holding each other."

Zeb wasn't ready to let go anyway. For the first time in a long time, he *felt* like Isabella was the love of his life again. He rested his head on hers and thought about the joy they'd share in growing old together. He pictured them sitting in rocking chairs on their front porch watching the sun set. Just when they'd get all the time in the world to themselves, they'd lose track of time in all their joy.

The rain left it feeling a little stuffy, so Meiying turned on a fan. She leaned against the plastic wall and examined a basket full of red cherries. "Many couples strive for perfection in a spouse, but there's no such thing. Progress is far more important than perfection. In fact, progress equals happiness. You entered the Couples' Castle with your own struggles, and every couple feels like their relationship is stuck in quicksand during different seasons, but we all fall on our face sometimes. If you didn't struggle, it would signal apathy. Struggle is a sign of progress, so enjoy the process of progress and welcome being perfectly incomplete. It's a dance—sometimes you step on each other's toes, but when you know the right steps to take, it feels like magic. That's what we're doing—teaching you the right steps."

Zeb clung even tighter to Isabella. If he never let go, he couldn't lose her. "So here's what you're to do: Think weekly, if not daily, about how you would rate the quality of progress in your relationship on a scale of one to ten – whether toward a specific goal or something else. If the answer is less than a ten, what would it take to make it a ten? Then take 100 percent responsibility for making it happen— no excuses, justifications, rationalizations, or blaming, shaming, and complaining—just give 100 percent to stimulating growth together. It may not sound romantic, but when you do, your number will improve, and that's when it will feel downright sexy, romantic, whatever you want to call it." Zeb loosened his hug and leaned back. When he made eye contact with Isabella, he felt the same floating sensation he had when they first started dating, like all his burdens had been removed.

*   *   *

Fai stopped swaying and gave Emma an encouraging smile. He was kind enough to partner with her, saving her from the embarrassment of standing there alone while the other couples danced. Emma's smile had a genuine build that lit her face.

"Would anyone like to see if the seed grew?" Fai motioned his hand toward he dirt.

Oliver knelt slowly to avoid getting dirt on his white shirt, and after investigating for possible growth he came up shaking his head.

"Maybe it needs to be watered again?" Isabella shrugged.

Zeb and Isabella grabbed the pitcher together. They were feeling a renewed connection. Kneeling, they watered and fertilized the seed again.

Emma waited for something to happen. After everything she'd learned in this place, and after Fai's sweetness, she just wanted something positive to happen with that seed. For her, it symbolized any remaining hope she had for reconciling with Titus. She stared at it and locked her hands together to force stillness while the basket of cherries rocked from Meiying's touch.

Emma noticed a ray of sunlight on her arm. She looked up and saw that the clouds were almost totally gone now. Fai walked over and said, "The Chinese people water and fertilize the seed for an entire fourth year. Again, they reap nothing."

Nothing, that's exactly what Titus probably felt for her—wherever he is.

"Maybe something's holding it back." Olivia shrugged.

Fai squinted at Olivia. "Good insight. Always be alert to what's holding your relationship back. There are emotional poisons all around that can stunt your relational growth."

"Like resentment." Meiying got a little too close for comfort.

Olivia stole a glance at Oliver. Her cheeks were flushed, and she fiddled with her shirt sleeves. Resentment must've been festering underneath their veneer of politeness.

Meiying continued. "You do know that holding resentment in your heart against your spouse is like—what did Mandela say?—drinking poison and expecting the other person to die?"

Olivia was looking anywhere but at Meiying. She was either looking for something missing on the ground or thinking a way out of this conversation.

"One of the dominant reasons couples cap their growth is quite unintentional, but it can be remedied." Meiying put the basket of berries down.

"Oh." Olivia grabbed Oliver's hand.

"Your brain stores memories from the past that were full of emotional intensity. Because negative memories create more emotional intensity, you tend to store more of those than the positive ones. You felt an overwhelming amount of emotional intensity during your arguments, breakups, and stresses, and you ruminated on them for a long time to the point that the brain anchored it in. In the process, neurological connections were formed and cemented so that now you subconsciously poison your present relationships with stored negative memories." She picked up one of the berries, tasted it, and spit it out.

Emma tilted her head to the side and repeated the statement as a question. "If these negative memories are affecting our relationships adversely, what can we do?"

"By letting go." Fai clapped and watched his hands slowly separate.

"Just . . . let it go, like Elsa and Anna?" Oliver's eyebrows furrowed and then released.

Fai walked up to them, one at a time, and looked into their eyes for what seemed like an eternity. "Let it go."

Don't cry again, Emma.

She pushed her emotions back and watched as he approached the last person in the group. Isabella seemed to erect a wall between them, but when he stood in front of her and said, "Let it go. Let the stress from the blended family go." She shook with emotion.

He spoke like a caring professor. "Letting it go causes your body's meridian points to dislodge the negative emotions and energy that's been tangled up for years. It'll set you free."

"Meridian points?" Oliver pressed his lips together and rocked on his heels, pretending to study the floor.

He smiled and approached Oliver. Placing a hand on Oliver's shoulder, he said, "It's why you freeze up when you see an old crush from twenty years ago. You thought you'd moved on, but your emotions got stuck in you. You were told time would heal the pain, but it hurts just the same when you see her again and you're like what the heck? But I can sense that it sounds like hokum to you. That's okay." He took his hand off and gave him some space. "We fear and demonize that which we have not attempted ourselves. I'm just trying to help. The practical point for you to take action on is to let the past go. You'll have to do this again and again until it's emotionally gone." He spoke with an unhurried warm voice and caring tone, one that expressed a greater interest in the happiness of the couples than in trying to prove a point.

"Can what you're talking about help really restore a broken marriage?" Behind Emma's question was a longing so intense she found herself hugging herself.

A glow grew on Fai's face. "Yes, the secret lies in the power of forgiveness."

Emma didn't seem to care what others thought at this point. "What if he won't forgive me?"

Fai walked over to Meiying and put an arm around her waist. "You can only control who *you* can forgive. You can go to all the counseling you want, get therapy, and meditate, but forgiveness—that's one of the most powerful forces in the world. Always find a way to forgive your partner for all that he's done to you. That includes proactively forgiving for everything in your future too. You should make it such a practice that every morning, before getting out of bed, you allow yourself to experience the power of forgiveness all throughout your body. Forgiveness releases the rich growth potential in your relationship. Can you do that? Will you fully forgive each other?"

But Titus would never open up to her about not having kids. And then with what she'd done, how could he ever . . . ? *Try, Emma. At least try. Titus, honey, wherever you are, I forgive you for everything. I bear all kinds of guilt, I know, and I'm asking for your forgiveness too. I can't control that. I leave it to you, but I fully forgive you.*

Meiying walked out from Fai's hold and over to Emma. "Many couples are worried about the affair and what others will think. The key is to know—and believe—that your past doesn't have to poison the present, rumors don't define the couple, and the relationship doesn't have to live within the prison of what others think."

Meiying leaned into Emma's ear and whispered, "And will you forgive *yourself* for your costly mistake?"

That would be the hardest part. She just didn't know if she could. There was a large part of her that wanted to crumple into the corner and hide, even die, but there was another part of her that wanted to step out into the world like a newly forgiven woman and fully live.

Meiying pulled back and bent down to look at the dirt where the seed was planted. "Once you forgive, focus on what's good in the relationship because where your focus goes, your energy flows, and where your energy flows, your results show. Appreciate and acknowledge all that you do well in the relationship. Focus on what *can* work instead of what's not working."

That sounds like a much better plan than hiding in a corner for the rest of my life. Emma felt empowered and emboldened to be herself again, to not let the past define her. *Forgive yourself, Emma. Stop the negative self-judgment. Oh, I wish I could.*

"In other words, create emotional intensity around that which makes you feel fully alive, filled with passion for each other—like you're experiencing the ultimate relationship. Here's a starter list to do just that:

1. Encourage each other twice daily.
2. When your partner arrives home, jump up to greet her.
3. At night ask what two things you did well for your relationship that day.
4. Keep a gratitude journal about your partner.
5. Record your relationship victories and celebrate them."

Meiying hooked her hand in Fai's belt. "Successful couples know that the future can always be better than the present and that they have the power to make it so."

* * *

I want to make it so. Olivia squeezed Oliver's hand.

"Let me water it again." Zeb grabbed the pitcher and poured. Nothing.

"What'd you expect?" Meiying chuckled. "It's a bamboo-tree seed."

"So this is all a joke, and we're the punch line?" Zeb rubbed his brow as if to ward of a headache.

"No, no, not at all. You did very well," Fai said, sage-like.

Olivia studied the wet ground. Then why wasn't it growing . . . or doing anything?

Fai leaned forward and rubbed his hands together. "You all watered the seed five times. Let's say each time represented one year of your relationship. Well, that's how long we water and fertilize a bamboo tree seed without seeing any evidence of growth—five years."

That was some serious dedication. Of course, quantity does always equal quality. The longer Olivia had been with Oliver, the more unsettled she'd become. Only now—in this place—was she feeling a renewed sense of passion and love. She took a quiet deep breath and leaned against Oliver.

Fai's eyes sparkled, and he was unable to stay in one place when he talked now. "Can you see someone walking into the field every day to water the seed? They water the ground for an entire year—365 days—and nothing. Doing the same thing, every day, for a second year. Then a third and a fourth. Nothing. Nothing. Nothing. No results to see. Just watering and cultivating."

"Then . . ." Meiying's eyes widened. "Sometime in the fifth year, the seed grows ninety feet in six weeks!"

"Ninety!" Oliver craned his head and raised his eyebrows. This unnestled Olivia, who looked around while scratching her jaw.

"Yes, but do you think the tree grew like that in six short weeks?" Fai pinched his lips together.

Olivia opened her mouth and then closed it. She raised her hand and said, "No, it was developing a root system all those years so that when the time came, it could handle the exponential growth."

"Yes!" Fai couldn't contain his smile. "Now do you see how this relates to making your marriage a masterpiece?"

Zeb let out a deep, satisfying sigh. "We may not immediately experience the ultimate relationship we want, but when we take the time doing the little things every day to develop a root system and cultivate our relationship, we're preparing ourselves to handle the explosive growth that comes later."

"Yes!" There was a genuine joy Fai and Meiying shared in helping other couples make their relationships remarkable.

Shame burned Olivia's cheeks. She didn't want to ruin the moment, but she also didn't want to miss out on getting real answers for her own relationship. "But we've already been married for more than five years, and we're not seeing those kinds of results." Oliver put his hand on her far shoulder.

"I understand," Meiying replied. "As you probably know, Olivia, it's not about the years but about cultivating your relationship every day. You know this better than most: it's the little things done every day that count the most. When you first dated, I bet you watered your relationship every day—and the result? Your relationship made progress. But over time you gave your attention to other things—and the result? Your relationship drifted. It's time to water again. The longer you water, the better it gets."

Olivia shifted from a casual conversation to a pointed question. "How?"

"That's what the rooms are for. Listen closely to their messages, ask the one-through-ten questions, apply the strategies that are given, and you'll experience massive results." Fai's hands were lifted and spread out, like he was measuring massive results.

They'd already experienced so much. *Time to apply it.*

Meiying stepped over a mound of dirt and approached Olivia. "Information plus application equals transformation. The application is in the consistent watering, the tending and cultivating of your relationship. This creates passion to replace that empty dead space. Too many couples drift and water whenever it's convenient or, worse, water relationships outside of their marriage."

Meiying looked up to the ceiling and sighed, then back to the group. "Flirting with people outside your relationship, playing peekaboo with others, using social media to feel connected to others you're attracted to, and trading in your spouse never gets to the root issue. Those activities give you an endorphin rush, but the fantasies that you're experiencing are not sustainable because you haven't grown yourself." She paused for effect.

"Go on." Oliver looked far more perplexed than the smiling Mickey Mouse on the front of his shirt.

She pressed her pants down and walked over to the workbench and grabbed gloves to slip on. Her face seemed to age well. "Every time you change, exchange, and trade up—which happens when you're focused on the *what* or a *who* outside of your relationship—you stunt your growth. It's like you're digging up the bamboo seed and planting it elsewhere, hoping for something better. But this puts your happiness in the hands of external factors. If you keep digging up the bamboo seed, you'll never see the growth that's needed to experience true marital happiness. If you keep planting it in other places, you'll only start the process all over again." She bent down to a knee and dug three more holes to illustrate her point.

She looked up and squished her lips to the left. Fai nodded her way. "That's why some people who remarry say, 'If I'd treated my first wife the way I treat my second wife, I'd still be married to my first wife.'" Meiying waited to see if his words landed in their hearts. "He watered and cultivated the second relationship and realized that's why he experienced more fulfillment the second time around. But he could've experienced the same level of fulfillment in the first marriage. It's not about the years in marriage or the initial happiness you feel in your 'I-do,' but rather, the daily cultivation and connection that transforms into the ultimate relationship experience."

Fai walked over to help her up. She dusted offer her pants and said, "If you keep wondering about whether you should've planted a different kind of tree, i.e., married someone else, your focus will keep you locked into a disempowered state, meaning your marital satisfaction number will be low. Or worse, you'll live in a state of constant comparison with your neighbor's tree, and comparisons always bring about depression, dissatisfaction, and despair."

Fai's lips twitched, and he bounced slightly on his toes. Olivia knew whatever he'd say next meant the world to him. "What's really important for your relationship is to ask 'On a scale of one to ten, how would you rate the quality of growth for our relationship this week?' Ask it until both of you answer with a nine or ten because then, and only then, will you experience an irresistible attraction for each other—no matter how long you've been together. Couples who feel like they're growing are happy."

Olivia wondered if it were really that simple. Could just asking some questions save their marriage? She inhaled through the nose and asked, "So growth creates an irresistible attraction? And *anyone* can do this, no matter what they've endured?"

> On a scale of one to ten, how would we rate the quality of growth for our relationship this week? If it's not a ten, how can we make it a 10?

A proud grin stretched across Fai's face. "Never, never, never put limits on your relationship. So many couples who pass through here have a disempowered look and feel to their relationship—each complaining that even after they've given it their all, it still remains bleak. Nonsense. The strongest and healthiest couples all know there are no limits to their growth, which is why they're strong and healthy." The way Meiying admired him as he spoke made his words seem all the more plausible.

Fai grabbed a bowl of strawberries and passed it around to the couples. While they were snacking, he poured them cups of water.

Olivia hadn't tasted such a sweet strawberry in all her life. She grabbed another and took the snack time to consider any limitations she'd placed on her relationship with Oliver.

Fai's body was in constant motion. He bobbed and weaved when talking, raising his arms and using his face to make points. "What I'm saying is"—he looked for the right words—"it's like the elephant at the circus."

"How do you mean?" Zeb said with strawberry juice running down his chin.

Fai went right into it. "Well, when circus trainers receive new baby elephants, they tie one of their legs with a rope to a post deep into the ground. The baby elephant tugs at and pulls on the rope, hoping to free itself, but eventually, it stops trying. When the elephant grows up, the trainer can tie it to a smaller post, and yet the elephant—now a behemoth—doesn't even try to break free because of its self-imposed limiting thoughts."

"In the same way," Meiying said, licking her lips in hope, "you have put limitations on your relationship—for a variety of reasons—but here in our room, we want you to know you always hold the power and potential to grow and transform your relationship, to set yourself free from mediocrity to a consistent nine. And when you do that, you'll feel like you're the love of each other's lives and flourish in an authentic happily-ever-after—truly."

Meiying moved closer, almost invading their space. "If you're unaware of your limiting stories, growth won't occur like you want it to. So here's what we want you to do: Name five limiting stories you tell yourself about your relationship."

1.
2.
3.
4.
5.

"Outloud?" Zeb said while eyeing the rest of the strawberries.

Fai chuckled. "Just to yourself. We'll give you some time. Think about those stories, how they limit your relationship. Once you have them, replace them with empowering stories. Then when you talk together about these new, improved, and empowering stories, which you should sprinkle in every day, before long, you'll have grown into those stories. Please don't just treat this as a mental exercise. Your happiness is at stake."

Olivia looked around at the others—Zeb with his arm around Isabella, Oliver doing the same to her. Even Emma looked hopeful. *This place is doing something to us.*

"There's much more to say, but things are taking root in you, so we'll leave it at this: Water every day."

Olivia smiled and nodded. "We will. Thank you for all of your guidance."

Meiying knelt to pick a folder filled with papers. "Now before we initial your model treasure chests to exit our room, you must do two things.

"First, we ask that you sit down with your partner and address the one-through-ten question we gave earlier. Emma, you may sit with us.

"Second"—she began handing out one piece of paper to each person—"the butler who welcomed you into the Couples' Castle handed you the 'Guide to Finding/Keeping the Love of Your Life by Becoming Irresistibly Attractive and a Person Worthy of the Relationship You Expect.' He gave those to us, which is being handed back to you now. Please spread out and reflect on your answers with your partner. When you feel satisfied, take some time on your own to take individual walks throughout the garden with the purpose of When you're finished, return here so we can initial your chest and escort you into room 5."

Around noon, everyone had returned, except Zeb and Olivia.

Chapter 12

Room 5

The castle towered over Zeb and Olivia in the background while they sat within a white garden trellis, overlooking the garden.

"Stay here. I want to pick some of those flowers for Isabella." Zeb walked over to a maze of flowers in the arboretum, dusted off his pants, and then picked all her favorites—mini sunflowers, purple asters, and small white chrysanthemums. The stems were still wet in his hand.

"Those are nice. She'll like those." Olivia's legs rocked back and forth from the bench.

He sniffed the flowers and smiled. "Yeah, I hope so."

While making his way back to the trellis, he asked, "So, uh, have you given any thought to, uh, how you're"—he cleared his throat—"going to tell Oliver about us? It feels like it could get awkward."

Olivia scratched her eyebrow. "We just tell them. Beating around the bush will make it weirder."

Zeb liked the way Olivia thought. She was always straight to the point and offered a unique perspective. He couldn't help himself from stealing glances at her body, especially at her skin where the top of her yellow blouse stopped, and her face was gorgeous in its own right. Her clear thinking just made her the total package. She was definitely more real than any two-dimensional Photoshopped model on a magazine cover, that's for sure. *Zeb, you gotta stop. And you definitely don't need to be alone with her anymore.*

Thankfully, she didn't seem to notice him ogling her. Her gaze remained on the distant river. "Little did I realize that what started at a concert festival in a park would wind up here in a mysterious castle. After all this time, how did we wind up here together? Someone must've known about us."

Zeb looked around to see if anyone from the castle was spying on them while he took a deep but subtle breath to enjoy her smell. "I don't have a clue, Olivia. We received the same key you guys received, and we thought it was worth checking out."

Olivia stood and scratched her jaw. "You ready? Clock's ticking on room 7."

Zeb's head joggled. "Yes, yes. Of course. Ya, let's go tell them."

*   *   *

"Where've you been?" Isabella raised her eyebrows and gave Zeb a glassy stare when he stepped into the greenhouse.

"Taking a walk in the arboretum." *Just play it cool.*

"Have you seen Olivia?" Oliver held his hands behind the back, griping his own wrist.

"Here I am." She entered nonchalantly from the opposite side. "What can I say? I had a lot to learn about myself," she added, waving her guide.

Isabella's eyes squinted and ping-ponged between Olivia and Zeb. She didn't seem satisfied with their answers.

"All right, everybody, time to go." Fai initialed their chests, then walked to the door on the far side, with the group following close behind. The noise from their shoes on the dirt caused a bluebird to flap its wings to take flight.

Zeb stopped and lowered his voice. "Isabella, can we talk for a minute?"

Isabella turned around and gave a slight headshake. "Can it wait? You already took a long time filling out those sheets. We need to get to room 7. And I don't want to risk getting separated from the group. Remember Titus? We don't want to end up like him." She grabbed his hand and picked up her pace.

Zeb looked over at Olivia who was getting similar treatment from Oliver. Looks like both of them would have to wait until the next room. He felt a stress headache coming on.

When they exited the narrow doorway, Zeb stopped to give Fai and Meiying a hug. A warmth glowed from Fai's face when Zeb thanked him. During their final handshake, Fai gave Zeb a light squeeze and whispered something in his ear that gave Zeb an empty feeling in the pit of his stomach.

Before closing the door, Oliver asked, "So which direction down the hill takes us to room 5?"

Fai and Meiying pointed to an ageless oak tree behind them. Wooden planks had been nailed into it, one after another, in ladder style, and at the top there was a deck-like platform with a zip line extending over the gardens back to the roof of the Couples' Castle.

Olivia's face turned white, and she pressed her elbows into the sides, making her body as small as possible. "Seriously? We're to zip-line over there?" Before she could turn around and protest to Fai and Meiying, the greenhouse door had already shut.

*　　*　　*

"Holy smokes! This is awesome!" Oliver skidded to a landing on the roof of the castle. "C'mon, O! I'll catch you!" he yelled back.

Olivia closed her eyes and stepped off the platform. *Awesome* wasn't exactly the word she was thinking. She opened her eyes just in time to see the castle rushing toward her. And Oliver. Standing there at the top, arms outstretched to catch her. She put her feet down and stumbled into him.

He held her until she felt steady on her feet again. "See? Wasn't that fun?"

"Actually, it *was* kind of fun." Her big grin betrayed the "kind of," and she let out a big exhale.

When he tucked a strand of hair behind her ear, guilt gnawed at her gut. She had to tell him. Maybe there would be a place to sit down somewhere in room 5.

"I'm starving." Zeb's voice broke through the adrenaline that kept them on the roof. "It's the middle of the afternoon, and we haven't had lunch. Let's hope this next room, wherever it is, has something to eat."

"We don't want to take too long to eat." Isabella paced as if in a hurry. "We only have a little over twenty-four hours left and still two rooms to go before room 7. Who knows how long it might take to get through those rooms?"

Circling the rooftop, they spotted a door and climbed down a flight of stairs, snaking their way into a long corridor with tall mahogany doors all the way down the hall on either side.

"Hallelujah. I smell food." Zeb patted his belly.

Olivia didn't even want to think about food right now, the nervous pit in her stomach growing by the minute. She massaged the temples on her forehead while they walked the hallway.

"Hey, look!" Oliver pointed to an oversized door. "That door says *Room 5: Paramount Personalities.*"

Emma didn't wait for permission. She turned the knob, and the door swung open without a sound. They stepped on the soft brown flagstone floor and moved toward the impressive medieval banquet table that commanded their attention in the middle of the vast romantic banquet room. Down the table's center was a runner with a royal design in red and gold woven into the fabric.

"Hey, look over there." Zeb pointed to the far side of the room where the window sat ajar to let in the cool breeze and fresh smell of the arboretum. Six midsized mahogany tables, three on each side, looked like doll furniture set up in the gigantic room.

A red bench against the wall reminded Olivia of the royal roses under the sun rays outside. The whole room whispered of the natural world and the stunning trees in the forest next to the waterfall. The crisp gold wallpaper matched the gilded mirrors hanging up near the tables.

On each table stood two empty wine glasses behind polished silver cutlery that shone in the crisp light. Bright red candles burned in tall, silver candelabras in the center of each table, their wax never melting. Next to the plates were perfectly folded napkins to match the candelabra. Olivia wiped her hands on her black slacks, afraid to leave fingerprints on the perfectly placed china.

The two couples walked toward the far side, while Emma stayed behind.

"You can sit with us." Oliver's voice echoed in the immense room.

Olivia offered her a sympathetic smile. Emma had to feel like the odd person out.

"Oh, thank you. But I have a feeling each table is meant for one couple only." Emma quickly replaced her broken voice with false bravado. "I'll be fine over here. Thank you though."

"Are you sure?" Olivia couldn't shake the feeling that they were being watched.

Emma stood tall in her soft pink blouse and returned her smile with one that would make a car salesman proud. "Yes, yes. I have a bellyache anyway. I'll sit over here and wait for whatever's supposed to happen next."

Isabella and Zeb chose the first table. Olivia steered Oliver for the one on the opposite end of the room. Things could get awkward if they told them at the same time. Then again, it would be more awkward if they told them at separate times. *Quit being so melodramatic about it, Olivia. It's not like you did anything wrong.* Oliver pulled out Olivia's chair. Just to the left of the centerpiece was an iPad, a high-quality clear-glass apothecary jar half full of folded notes and a white envelope.

Oliver sat down across her and grabbed the envelope. "Should I open it?"

"Sure." She pressed down on her yellow blouse and waited for him to read it.

"It says,

> *Welcome to the Paramount Personality room, where you'll find out how to make each other feel important and ignite the passion again.*

Behind every behavior in your relationship is a feeling you're hoping to satisfy. All your actions are because you want to feel a certain way, whether you're dating or are married. It's human nature. You've already learned some of the strategies to satisfy those feelings in the four preceding rooms, and you've discovered that the more you satisfy these desires, the more you experience the ultimate relationship.

This is important because if you can identify the feeling behind each behavior, you'll no longer simply respond to behaviors, like most couples do—act and react—but you'll instead help satisfy the desire your partner is looking to fulfill. This creates those amazing feelings you're always looking for in a relationship. When you do that for your partner, she'll boomerang the passion back to you. The more the both of you identify the feeling, the more you make your marriage into a masterpiece.

To ignite the fires of passion, first, stimulate and stroke your partner's desire to feel important, special, or paramount. We designed this banquet room to help you feel just that.

Your personality is who you are, and who you are wants to feel paramount. This isn't selfish. According to Abraham Maslow, it's essentially coded in your central nervous system. This means if you don't feel paramount or special to each other, you and your partner will find a way to satisfy this feeling in other areas—like education, work, money, parenting, or in an affair."

Olivia put a hand over the letter and studied Oliver. "Is this why you stay at work late? Because you feel more important at work than at home?"

Oliver shifted in his seat and glanced around to see if anyone was eavesdropping. "Well, I don't know. I guess. I never really thought about why I did it. But at work, everyone calls me boss and treats me like I'm somebody, you know?" He looked down and to the left. "But then I get home and I'm just kinda ordered to—you know, do things like take out the trash. I know you're overwhelmed and worn out. It's just everywhere I go, my ideas and opinions are valued—except at home."

She was thinking ahead about the possible collateral damage. "You really feel that way?"

"Not always, but you asked." He took a deep breath. "Okay, let me put it in language that, I don't know, might resonate with you. You know that song 'R-E-S-P-E-C-T'?" Oliver sang it softly in his best Aretha Franklin impersonation. He was so cute in his charm and boyish looks.

"Yes."

"Well, it's all about making someone feel . . . What's that word the letter kept using?" He scanned the paper in his hands. "Paramount—like they're more important than anyone or anything else. Like you're in awe of them. You used to be in awe of me, O, or at least you made me feel that way. I'm sure we all need to feel important, but it's like deeply ingrained in me to want you to be . . ." Oliver paused, struggling to find the right words.

She leaned forward. "Want me to what?"

He let out a self-conscious laugh. "More than anything, I need to feel like you . . . believe in me. I don't think it's a selfish thing either. Maybe it is, I don't know. I do know that whenever you do that—you know, believe in me—I've found myself wanting to be a better man."

Olivia nodded. "So you want me to believe in you, more than even loving you?"

"See, I knew you'd think it sounds silly." Oliver looked away from the table.

"Help me understand." She put her elbows on the table and leaned forward.

Oliver inhaled through the nose and exhaled out the mouth, then studied her. "Okay, let's take your favorite book."

"The Bible."

"Yes, the Bible. Well, this matters so much to me that I flipped through the Bible for answers."

"*You* read the Bible?" She raised her eyebrows.

He tilted his head and smiled. "Some of it. And even your Bible reinforces this point—both the Old and New Testaments."

"Oh? So what'd you discover?" *I can't wait to hear this.*

"Proverbs 12 something, I think verse 4, the writer says, 'A disgraceful wife is like decay in his bones.' And in 1 Peter 3:1, the author says, 'Husbands may be won over without words by the behavior of their wives.'"

"So you're saying you'll get sick if I don't treat you like you're paramount?" She carefully controlled her voice and tone.

"It's not about 'treating' me in paramount ways but making me *feel* paramount. Never mind, I feel stupid talking about this." He picked up his spoon and twirled it in his fingers.

Olivia sighed. "No, I'm sorry. Go on."

Oliver sat back in his chair, increasing his personal space. "Yes, I think it's true. Guys can get physically sick from a lack of feeling respected—sickness is tethered to our emotions, and we're all emotional creatures. I guess what I'm saying is you can win my heart over and over and over again, year after year—anytime you want, really—when you make me feel especially important." He raked his fingers through his hair and turned his body at an angle instead of facing her head-on. "Sorry, I'm rambling. Maybe that doesn't make sense. In fact, don't worry about it."

Olivia had been pressing her lips together to keep from speaking. She tried to understand, but his double standard created a stiffness in her neck. "No, I get it. But if that's how you feel, then you should understand how I felt when I saw all the porn sites you'd been visiting in your browser history. That didn't make me feel very important."

Oliver's neck bent slightly—he rubbed his eyebrow and turned slowly back to her. "I'm sorry, Olivia. There's no excuse. I've said that already."

She quickly shook her head. "So why do you look at them then?"

Five seconds passed.

"Oliver?"

"I don't know. I can tell you this: Whether it's pornography or even affairs, it's rarely about the other woman. You know what a man really sees when he looks at pornography and other women?"

Olivia rolled her eyes and let out a heavy sigh. She couldn't wait to hear the justification. "I don't think I want to."

Oliver leaned in like he held a governmental secret. "We imagine—or at least are hoping—they're in awe of us. I know it sounds stupid, and I'm not talking in an egotistical way but in a way that makes us feel admired."

Olivia sat up and made a choking noise in her throat. "What?" She couldn't help but feel nauseous.

He tilted his head to the side and shook it. "See, this is why I don't tell you things. Men and women are just so different."

Her skin tightened, and she rubbed her nose. "No, no, go on."

Oliver shook his head. "Whatever. Fine. Maybe it's on a subconscious level, I don't know, but guys pretend like those women believe in us, like they . . . want us. You don't have to believe me, O." He flipped his spoon, so it landed on the napkin. "It just is. I suppose that's why all the models in those magazines have the sexy eyes look. It's why a dude sleeps with someone he's not married to—he feels like the woman believes in him. Some girl made him feel paramount. The best thing you can do for a guy is admire him, believe in him, and make him feel important. That's it. Bottom line. There you have it—this is a man's world."

Olivia's throat burned, and she tried not to roll her eyes. This sounded like a lame excuse. Yet Oliver seemed genuine, and this was the most he'd shared with her in months, maybe ever. She hung her head and rubbed the middle of her forehead, eyes closed. She couldn't help but think that this made what she had to reveal a little softer in comparison.

"Are you still listening, O?" Oliver asked.

She looked up and now couldn't help but roll her eyes. "Well, it's no excuse for lusting for them. Ugh."

Shame covered his face. "I agree, and again, I'm sorry, Olivia. Honestly, it'll be a relief to jettison it from my life." He leaned back, folded his arms across his chest, and looked around. "I guess this room is right—there's a feeling we're all seeking to satisfy behind each behavior." He sat up and picked up the spoon again. "Remember when we watched that movie *Cinderella Man*?"

It did not get past Olivia that he was trying to change the topic, but she played along anyway. "Yes. It was okay." She'd been hoping for a little more fairy tale in the movie and a little less boxing.

Oliver leaned forward, and his eyes glowed. "Well, my favorite part of that movie wasn't the boxing, redemption, or love, but when James Braddock, also referred to as the Cinderella Man Boxer, repeatedly said to his wife, 'I can't win without you behind me.'" He took a deep breath to appreciate his own words and managed to lean forward even more. "In that moment, every guy in the theater knew what he was talking about. That's what a guy wants from his partner. When he didn't feel like she believed in him, you could see the disempowered look crawl on his face. The good energy left his heart. It was only when he felt like she believed in and admired him that he became the empowered champ that he always was deep inside."

"Oliver?" She reached across the table and placed her hand on his. "I do believe in you."

*　　*　　*

The iPad flickered at Emma's table. When she saw what appeared on the screen, she quickly rubbed her eyes.

A video of Titus.

Somewhere in the Couples' Castle, Titus knelt in a chapel, tears streaming down his face.

"Titus," Emma whispered, rubbing her fingers on the screen. He was right there and yet a thousand miles away. She missed everything about him, about them. How could she have been so stupid, after everything they'd been through?

I love you, Titus. I made a huge mistake. I was confused and hurt about not having children. I'm so sorry, honey. Please forgive me, and please, please don't give up on us!

"Excuse me, would you like a cup of tea?" The butler appeared at Emma's side.

"How do I get to this chapel so I can see my husband?" She clicked her fingernails against the table.

"I'm afraid that won't help, Emma."

Her head jerked back. "What do you mean? And how do you know my name? Never mind, everyone in this place seems to know things."

The butler spoke like a caring uncle. "Sometimes, when men feel overwhelmed, they hide in their cave to focus on how to deal with it."

"What?" She opened her mouth to criticize the man but stopped short.

"You want to run to him right now, but that's just so you can resolve your own feelings. Maybe he wants you there, maybe he doesn't. Either way, it's in his nature to withdraw in order to figure out what he should do."

She wasn't in the mood for a lecture. She wanted to hold Titus again, if he'd let her, but in order to have a shot, she needed to find him first. *Hello, Mr. Butler? Don't you get that?*

"Was that a 'yes' or a 'no' to the tea?" His smile returned.

She leaned back with slumped shoulders, stared off at nothing, and sighed. "Yes, sure. Thank you."

The butler poured hot tea in her white cup, walked away, and then pivoted. "Oh, I almost forgot—you may want this back."

He whisked away the linen napkin on top of his tray to reveal her model red treasure chest with the key still attached.

*   *   *

Isabella leaned forward, sliding her chair closer. "So after reading that letter, Zeb, let me ask you, 'On a scale of one to ten, how important do I make you feel? And how important is our marriage to you on the same scale?'"

Zeb momentarily forgot all else and wished he'd had his cell phone to record the way she asked the question. The way she made him feel—just with that question—almost made him completely forget that he was going to tell her about Olivia. It made him feel more important than he had in a long time, and he wanted to savor the moment. He put his elbows on the table and his fingers formed a steeple. "Well, when we first dated and got married, you made me feel like a nine. Now . . . and

I don't mean this the wrong way, it's probably because there's so much going on in our lives—it's a three or four. As to the second question, I don't know." He leaned back and looked away.

On a scale of one to ten, how important do we make each other feel? If it's not a ten, how can we make it a 10?

The butler appeared from a set of swinging doors behind them, setting a small pizza in the remaining space on their table.

Zeb glanced over at Olivia and Oliver's table to see if they received the same thing.

"Split it," the butler said.

Zeb looked up from the corner of his eye at the butler, back at the pizza, then shrugged. He grabbed a knife and split it right down the middle.

"No."

Zeb cocked his head back. "What do you mean 'no'?"

The butler grabbed the pizza and walked away.

"What the heck?" Isabella eyes blinked rapidly.

Not more than twenty seconds later, the butler approached again, carrying a new pizza. He set it on the table and, again, directed, "Split it."

Zeb reached for the knife, but Isabella grabbed it first. Starting from the opposite side of the pizza this time, she cut it right down the middle.

Before they could feel satisfied with their decision, the butler picked up the pizza and walked away again.

Zeb couldn't help but chuckle. "This is too weird. And boy that pizza smelled good. I'm so hungry." He played with his napkin, wondering how he might bring up what he had to tell her.

Isabella sat back, looking off into the direction the butler disappeared. "Weird is right."

Their laughter bounced off the walls. Maybe now, while the mood was light, he should tell her. Just as he cleared his throat, the doors swung open, and the butler approached again, setting another freshly cooked pizza in the middle of their table. "Do it again," he said, "split the pizza."

Zeb leaned over and studied the pizza, glanced up at Isabella, then back at the pizza. He sat back and flexed his fingers, curling and uncurling them. "What do you expect us to do?" Zeb eyeballed the butler. He was so hungry he didn't care what happened next. Zeb sliced the pizza into several pieces, grabbed a slice before the butler could react and started eating. Isabella did the same. "Go on," Zeb said while eating, "we're listening."

"Go ahead, eat all you like. My point is . . ." The butler opened and closed his mouth. "I'll be right back. A few moments later, he returned with another pizza, smaller this time, and laid it on the table. "My point is you guys split the pizza just like every other couple—right down the middle. A fifty-fifty relationship almost always ends in a split, however, because a fifty-fifty relationship won't make your partner feel paramount." He stood there like Gandalf the Grey, only in different attire.

"Oh okay," Zeb said. "I see what you're dishing out." He scooted the unsliced pizza across the table to Isabella.

"No, try again."

Zeb's amusement turned to a faint feeling of agitation. "I don't know," Zeb huffed.

Something seemed to click for Isabella. She grabbed the knife and cut the pizza into four slices. She then scooted three slices to Zeb.

"Yes!" the butler exclaimed. "This is what we call the pizza principle. Successful relationships aren't fifty-fifty, one hundred-zero, or even one hundred-one hundred. It's more like a sixty-forty mentality where each partner wants the best for the other partner, whether it's in division of labor, sharing the pizza, or getting to experience things first. You always think and behave in a way where your partner gets 60 percent, is treated better, and feels important. It's a mentality more than a strict number to abide by."

Zeb swapped plates with Isabella so she could have the three slices.

The butler momentarily held his hand over his mouth to cover his smile. "The bottom line is that each person in the relationship needs to feel paramount. It's not just a want, a wish, or desire. It's how you're wired. Currently, you're two strangers living in the same house back home, but by applying the pizza principle to everything in your relationship, and I do mean everything, you'll make each other feel so important that you'll feel like you're falling in love with each other again and again, year after year, in a magnificent romance."

The butler turned, his arms swinging while he walked. Before he made it to the Oliver and Olivia's table, the iPad fired up, and a question scrolled across the screen: "Stimulate feelings of paramount within each other and you'll notice a big uptick in the relationship. Here are some thoughts and strategies to do just that."

Zeb and Olivia glanced at each other, then back down at the iPad. The words continued to scroll:

1. How often do you express appreciation for your spouse? Appreciation is the experience of feeling no lack. When you focus on the lack, you get more of it, but if you focus on what you appreciate, more of what you appreciate shows up. Are you focusing on what your partner lacks or what you appreciate about him?

2. Play the grateful game once per day to make each other feel paramount in the relationship. Take turns saying "I'm grateful for _____," and choose something about your partner for which you're grateful."

3. Carry around a gratitude stone in your pocket, so every time you become aware of it, you're reminded to say something you're grateful for about your partner. If a gratitude journal is your preferred style, go with it. There's always something to be grateful for in your relationship, and the more you're grateful for her, the more you'll have to be grateful for in the relationship and the more you'll feel important to each other.

4. What's paramount is not your career, personal pursuits, or even the children. Your relationship is most important, and when you treat it that way, magic happens, not only in your relationship, but also in your careers, with the children, and in your personal pursuits. A happy marriage generates happiness in other places.

5. Every day someone is praying to experience the relationship you take for granted. Appreciate each other, and treat it with utmost importance.

6. "The deepest principle in human nature is the craving to be appreciated." —William James, Harvard psychologist. Given this, send one text message a day to your partner that makes her feel appreciated. Something like, "I appreciate today you for ____."

7. What if every day you woke up next to a partner who possessed only the characteristics that you thanked God for yesterday? From this day forward, wake up thanking God for three characteristics about your partner.

8. Upwards of 90 percent of women have a low self-image. Your wife needs to be reassured how much you love and appreciate her beauty—inside and out.

9. When you don't appreciate each other, shame enters the picture. Shame lives in the expectations about what you're supposed to be, and it makes you feel the opposite of paramount—small, unworthy, and unlovable. From this day forward, no shaming. Replace shame with making your partner feel special.

10. She wants you to appreciate her like you did when you initially pursued her. The secret of winning your wife's heart back is in the pursuit because she never stops craving your love. There's a part of her that remains insecure, no matter how long you've been together. You think the marriage ceremony put a stamp and seal on her heart forever, but marriage exists for the very purpose of continuing to pursue and love her. Make it a game, if you want, whatever it takes—pursue, pursue, pursue. This will make her feel special.

The iPad went dark again, and Zeb looked across the table at Isabella. He really did appreciate her. He just didn't tell her enough, if ever, anymore. His world was consumed with worry and finances. *And now this thing with Olivia.*

Okay, let's take care of one of those things now. He cleared his throat and tapped the table with his finger. "Honey, I need to tell you something."

Chapter 13

Sixteen Hours

"Look, O, here at the bottom of the letter there are instructions about practical strategies to ignite the passion again."

Nausea rolled through Olivia's stomach. She just needed to tell him and get it over with. She shifted in her chair and promised herself that she'd tell him right after these strategies—no matter what.

"It says, 'Oliver and Olivia, to spice things up, focus on *the way* you talk to each other. If you find yourself angry, apathetic, bored with, or uninterested in, your partner, double-check your communication routines.'"

Is that supposed to be groundbreaking knowledge? She pinched the bridge of her nose and squeezed her eyes tight.

"We are now going to give you the top practical communication strategies for relationships because when you improve your talk, you'll improve your relationship in every possible way. You can see that there are folded papers inside the glass jar on your table. The strategies are written out on those papers. Take turns picking a paper and reading it out loud."

Olivia gave the glass jar a sidelong glance while her hands remained on her lap. She couldn't help but wonder if the notes might help her deliver the news about Zeb in a more amenable way. "Well, would you like to pick the first note or me?"

Oliver rubbed his hands together and then lifted the glass lid. He reached his fingers into the jar to grab the first note. "It says,

EMPHASIZE THE POSITIVES ABOUT EACH OTHER, ESPECIALLY WHERE YOU DIFFER IN PERSONALITY

Anytime there's a difference of opinion, immediately acknowledge how you appreciate your differences. Partners express themselves differently because they are two distinct thinking beings with different thought processes, even when using the same words and syntax. Look, there's a reason there's a kazillion personality tests out there. People are wired differently.

Add to this that all humans are finite and fallible and that contemporary couples are busy and distracted, and you have a recipe for messy misunderstandings in virtually every conversation. So walk into every conversation appreciating what's different about each other, knowing that you can course-correct and disentangle messy misunderstandings along the way. Always stay positive."

Oliver looked up. "Well, would you like to talk through each one as we go along or read the notes first and then talk about the ones we think are most relevant?"

"I don't know. Let's see how we feel as we go along." Olivia sat up in her chair and grabbed four notes from the jar.

"Four?"

Olivia smiled and shrugged. "Okay, it says,

USE THESE WORDS WHEN IN AN ARGUMENT

Be quick to say "I'm wrong," "I'm sorry. Please forgive me," "Thank you," "You're right," "I love you," and "You first." No matter how long you've been together, use these words and phrases often. They just work. Probably because of human egos. Try to be the first to speak them because pride leads to marital ruin.

PICK YOUR ROLES

One area blocks couples from experiencing a world-class relationship: communication. Picking roles helps solve this. Most arguments revolve around the couple disagreeing over what should be done about _____, whether it be finances, where the furniture goes, if the toilet seat should be up or down, paint choice, and parenting. Picking roles solves a lot of this.

Here's how. First, identify some of the major roles in the relationship. Some of these include finances, house aesthetics (where the furniture goes, paint colors, landscaping), cooking/food, couple development (marriage growth), cleanliness (chores), and spirituality. There are more, but that's a starter list.

After you've identified the major roles, have a meeting to decide who will be the CEO, boss, servant-leader, dictator, president, or whatever word works for you guys over the role. This does not mean the person is responsible for doing everything in that role. The servant-leader/CEO could delegate, hire a chef, or whatever she sees fit. The point is whoever is in charge of that role gets vision, decision, and veto power. The person is ultimately responsible for making things happen in that role and the other person serves (yes, guys should submit too!). There's a mutual submission, which means a mutually self-sacrificing love. The leader still asks for suggestions, but she's ultimately in charge of that role.

What's this do? It keeps the couple from killing each other, for starters. Second, it allows each person to maximize his capabilities. It also helps grow respect, love, and kindness. The person in charge learns quickly to use a servant-leadership model instead of a dictatorship. Can you say revolt!

Sit down every Sunday to talk about the role and what you'd like to see done. You can also change up the roles quarterly, yearly, or, heck, hourly if that works for you. This keeps it fresh and the communication gets easier when you know someone is in charge and can do it her way. Suggestions are always welcome, and revolts are always possible. Love supersedes all.

MAKE A BIG DEAL ABOUT HIS
PASSIONS AND PAYCHECK

Verbally make a really big deal about his dreams, effort, and job. If you want him to feel on top of the world and have an enthusiasm for both you and for bringing in streams of income, make sure you tell him in various ways that even if you lose everything, what you care most about is him. He'll *always* carry a big burden to provide—even if you're the primary breadwinner—so he needs to feel like he's a hero regardless of income and your view of gender roles. Communicate this often, clearly, and with authenticity, and he'll give you the world."

Oliver leaned back and folded his fingers behind his head. "So maybe when I come home from work now, I can relax in peace, yes?"

Olivia opened her mouth to make a point, then stopped.

"No, go ahead, say what's on your mind."

She hesitated, then leaned in. "You must admit, without me, you'd sit around playing video games all day."

Oliver twisted his mouth with a sour expression. "You say my videos games are a waste of money, but don't you have a cabinet full of expensive plates we're never allowed to use?"

Olivia sighed. "Those plates serve a purpose."

He sat right up. "So do my video games."

Her head fell, and she batted her eyelids. "What, to help you sit on the couch and become the belch king of the neighborhood? Your belching is its own language."

Oliver smiled, rather proudly. "What, you don't appreciate my burping?"

"Well, you burp and then laugh like it's a great gift to all those around you." She played along with his self-deprecating style.

Oliver raised his hands like the police just surrounded him. "It's true. What can I say? Shall we move on to the next note?"

Olivia nodded.

SHOW HER AFFECTION WITHOUT SEX BEING THE ENDGAME

When you talk to her, use affectionate language like "I'd love to just hold you today," "How can I help?" "Take all the time you need to talk. I'm not going anywhere," "I love you," and "You're so beautiful." Also remember she can feel your energy, and sometimes that energy needs to be minus the sexual overtones. Affection and seduction are not synonymous to a woman.

Olivia leaned back and gave a crisp nod. "Ah, I like that. Should I read it again?"

Oliver rolled his eyes and smiled. "Nah, I got it." He leaned in and picked out a few notes of his own. "My turn."

HEROES AND TOILETS

Talk in ways that make him feel like you trust his abilities. Even when he's driving around in circles! This strategy cannot be overstated, and the lack of it is an Achilles heel in relationships. It's why he gets all crazy with your simple requests about putting the groceries away, mowing the lawn, and putting down the toilet seat. While you're well-intentioned, he's thinking, *What? Does she not think I know how to do that?* The way you talk to him matters more than how and when the honey-do list gets completed. Read that last sentence again.

Show confidence in him without trying to change him. He needs you to trust his abilities. It stimulates those feelings of paramount. When he feels like his abilities are questioned, even in the smallest of things, it leads to conflict and chaos. It may take longer to write a note like "Dear Hero and Man of the House, the toilet seat is waiting for your order to be put down. It's doing its very best to remain in a standing position, and even though it's very tired, it's allegiance is to you, and so it will not rest until you order it to." But it'll spice up the relationship. Do you want him to feel amazing feelings for you? Get creative in showing how much you trust his abilities. This principle is tricky but worth mastering.

VIEW HER TALKING AS AN OPPORTUNITY TO GET CLOSE

Remember the primary reason she talks in the first place—to get close. So if you think she's rambling, getting sidetracked, or lost in thought, remember, it's a great compliment that she's talking to you because it's the way she gets close to someone. Pull up a chair and listen. She's into you.

BOTTOM LINE OR BOTTOM OUT

Sometimes, before you start talking to the man, give him the bottom line of what you're about to say. He cares for you so much that if you don't do this, he may spend the whole time you're talking not listening but instead trying to figure out the real issue so he can fix it for you. We know you don't always know the bottom line before expressing yourself, but it'll really help if he knows because, when he does, he'll be able to relax and enjoy everything you have to say, including topical leaps and side stories, and you'll enjoy talking to him much more without getting cut off and having your feelings invalidated with his problem-solving approach."

Olivia's head flinched back slightly, and her eyebrows squished together. "Is that true?"

"100%." He swallowed his pepperoni pizza, then reached into the jar for a few more notes.

CHOOSE YOUR TOPICS CAREFULLY
BECAUSE THEY SHAPE YOUR MARRIAGE

Choose your subject matter wisely because the topics of your conversations become the themes of your relationship. Most people treat talking purely as a means to describe the day's events, but it is far, far more than that. Your conversation prescribes more than describes. Because talking holds a power to generate your feelings, thoughts, and actions, it winds up prescribing and portending your future.

What this means is that your marriage experience is tethered to your language. It's not what's going on outside of your thoughts and language that determines how your marriage goes, but rather, it's what's inside your brain and language that determines the reality of your relationship, including whether there's sparks and romance. So here are some examples for how to manage the words in your mind and speech to create the ultimate relationship experience:

1. Talk about how things are getting better, what you enjoy, and the day's wins.
2. Use your language to put your relationship in a state of positive certainty and expectancy about your incredible future together, regardless of the circumstances.
3. *Generate good, enjoyable feelings on your own first. Then talk.* The tones and topics of your talking integrate into your emotions, and in so doing, you sculpt and reinforce your relationship with your speech.
4. *Talk intentionally to shape your marital identity.* This is important because everything you do together is a direct result of your identity. Behavior always follows identity. The language you use about your relationship then leads to how you treat each other. If you believe you never get along, it'll become a self-fulfilling prophecy. On the other hand, if you believe that things are always getting better, you're also right. You could begin with

this question every morning: "What if our marriage keeps getting better and it all works out for us?"

5. *Speak in a way that makes you feel the way you want to feel about your partner.* Criticizing your partner for not making you feel a certain way only invites more of the same bad feelings. Your language doesn't even have to be accurate because the words you attach to your thoughts *becomes* your relational experience. How you talk generates your feelings.

6. *Identify words that trigger negative feelings.* Examples include *overwhelmed* in the phrase "I feel overwhelmed," *stressed* in the phrase "I'm stressed out," *never* in "You never help out around the house," and *busy* in "I'm too busy to talk right now."

   a. When you use those words, it intensifies the feelings in you so that it becomes a self-fulfilling prophecy. You become even more overwhelmed, stressed, and busy. So watch for them, and when you feel those words and their accompanying feelings coming on, take a deep breath and rephrase them.

   b. Give the word a better meaning. Examples include substituting the world *full* for *busy* so that when feelings of busyness or stress approach, you remember your relationship is full of so many amazing opportunities that you don't have time to experience all of them yet. You can substitute *sometimes* for *never* so you feel like there's hope and shared responsibility in the home. One meaning leaves you feeling disempowered, while the other causes you to feel empowered.

Oliver looked up and saw O leaning in with her hands clasped under the chin. "Dang, that's some good info."

Olivia studied him and was willing to believe that everything would be all right between them. Without breaking eye contact, she encouraged him to go on.

Oliver licked his lips and swallowed, then looked back at the note. "Where was I? Oh, right . . .

BE AGREEABLE OR BE ALONE

Couples fight because of one reason: ego. We live in a time and culture where everyone wants to be right, even at the expense of ruining relationships. This is just dumb, especially in your greatest relationship. It doesn't mean you can't differ in opinion, it just means that you build every conversation on agreeing with each other's perspective, because that's all it is—you each have a perspective. Be agreeable always.

If you enter a conversation trying to win an argument, someone must lose, and that means your relationship also loses. Hello?! So during the conversation say things like, "I agree. I'm with you. I couldn't agree more. You're right about that. I like the way you think honey." Regardless of how crazy your partner sounds on a subject, the way to bridge your souls and connection is through agreement. It's not manipulation or forgetting about truth, it's about building up the relationship, trust, and agreeing with her perspective. This one strategy will transform your whole relationship. Agree at the beginning of a conversation, agree *in the middle, and agree at the end. Be agreeable or be alone.*

USE LANGUAGE LIKE YOU'RE
ROLLING OUT THE RED CARPET

Want your partner to roll out the red carpet for you? Here's the talking strategy to make it happen: admire him in front of his friends or anyone, really. Use words that make him feel paramount and special, and he'll treat you like you're a rock star, a princess, the woman of the ages."

Oliver sat right up. "Okay, I gotta stop right there. That's so right. Just to be honest, if you did these last two ideas, whooee."

Olivia smiled when he reached across the table to squeeze her hand. She could hear echoes of voices on the other side of the room and the clink of glasses. The vaulted ceilings gave her a sense of peace while the hanging chandeliers reminded her not to hang herself with her own words when she told Oliver about Zeb. She squeezed Oliver's hand, then reached in the jar for notes.

SPEAK LIKE A PARTNER, NOT
A BOSS OR COUNSELOR

Sometimes your partner will want to talk for the sole purpose of emotional therapy—to release her raw emotions. This is natural for a woman and for some men. During these times, she does not want you to "talk-fix" her concerns because it invalidates her feelings.

Caution: Whoever's doing the emotional releasing, keep in mind that yelling, venting, and complaining about anything to your partner is like saying "Here's my stress. It's all yours now. You should carry it instead of me." Talking in this way can have significant repercussions on the couple's stress levels, sleep patterns, and sexual interest. Your partner is not your counselor. Each can play the role from time to time, but dumping emotional baggage on the other takes an emotional toll. It's worse than someone coming into your kitchen, picking up the trash can, and dumping trash all over your house.

Olivia flicked the note down, felt a little light-headed, and proceeded to the next note.

TALK LIKE IT'S A DANCE, NOT
TWO MONOLOGUES

Talking should be a conversation more than two running monologues at each other. It's a dance where two people are interested in each other, with each other, for each other, and assuming the best about each other. In many cases, people treat a conversation to change someone's mind. They focus on their own belief in what they're saying rather than on empathy for the person, engaging in back-and-forth bickering about who's right. That never works. Be more graceful like a dance—where your steps must be congruent and your twirls must be timely. Get in sync with each other or wait until you are. If you talk without getting in sync, it's not a conversation.

WITHHOLD JUDGMENT ALTOGETHER

Talk to each other with mindfulness. This means being fully present without any kind of judgment. In fact, if you can release all negative judgment about yourself, partner, and relationship, your overall satisfaction number will consistently soar.

Olivia tapped her index finger against her lip like she was weighing the pros and cons. "Avoiding all negative judgment. That's a tough one." She pulled down on her shirt. "I like it though. Just think if we tried that in our relationship. You think it's even possible?"

Oliver's bottom lip curled over his top lip, and he tilted his head in a side-to-side rhythm while looking at the jar. "Works for me. So we're getting close to the end of the notes. Should we read the rest of them or . . ."

"Read the rest. Looks like the others are still talking, and Emma over there is reading something. We have time."

When Oliver reached in to grab the rest of the notes, Olivia's stomach churned. She knew it was only a matter of time before she told him about Zeb. She wished she'd just informed him back at the park so that it wouldn't feel so awkward now. She felt like hiding under the table. Maybe she didn't need to tell him. After all, she'd gotten this far without doing so. No harm, no foul. She sat back and smoothed her own hair in an attempt to stay calm.

ASSUME THE BEST

Always assume the best about each other, especially when you're talking to yourself about the other person's actions. It's been said to never make assumptions. This is true, except when it's not. It's healthy to avoid making assumptions, to be sure, especially when you substitute assumptions with empathy and a desire to understand your partner's perspective and feelings. However, there's a more powerful way forward. *Assume the best* in all things about your lover, partner, and friend—when they walk in the door, when they forget to do the dishes, when they are frustrated, always, always, always assume the best.

Don't even let words come out of your mouth until you're in a state of assuming the best about your partner. If you think that takes too long, consider how long it takes to fix things if you assume the worst and say hurtful things. Your thoughts determine your language, your language changes the mood and state of your relationship, and that creates your results. So *always* assume the best.

When you assume the best, the best in the situation occurs. Assuming the best transforms your feelings, and in so doing, you become a magnet that draws the best out of your partner. Your emotional state is always a magnet, drawing unto itself that which it is radiating. So if you want the best possible outcome for every conversation with your partner, always begin by assuming the best.

TALK LIKE YOU HAVE DOG EARS

You talk best with your ears. Listening speaks volumes to the other person, so learn to listen and listen to learn. Much of the problem in your conversations is because, when your partner is talking, you're waiting to reply. When you listen to understand, worlds of wonder and lots of love open to you. Trust that process. People love walking away from a conversation thinking, *I felt so heard.*

There's a reason why the people who separate from their spouses—over 50 percent—fight over who gets to keep the dog. Dogs listen.

USE YOUR LANGUAGE LIKE YOU'RE PLAYING RED LIGHT-GREEN LIGHT

Emphasize what's working. The morning is the most fruitful time because it sets the relational tone for the rest of the day. Simply ask, "What's working between us today?" Even if you haven't done much together yet, the brain will find an answer—and it will set a positive, productive relational tone, kind of like the way you feel when you hit all green lights through the city.

This strategy also stalls potential fights and arguments. Fighting and arguing are like red lights; it stops you dead in your tracks. To get back into a green-light mode, simply interrupt your own argument to ask, "We're disagreeing right now, but what's working between us?" Instead of focusing on the negative red lights, focus on the positive green lights, then get back to problem solving. There's always one thing working, even if it's just the ability to ask the turnaround question "What's working between us?" smack dab in the middle of an argument.

TALK LIKE LOVERS DO, NOT LIKE CRITICS

Criticism never works. You think you're helping each other, but even if you respectfully voice your criticisms, it doesn't work. When you criticize her, it's like her respectfully voicing concerns about your ability to make money. And when you criticize him, it's like him lovingly telling you how concerned he is with your appearance. She'll feel his statement cut into her heart, and she'll carry the wound for days, if not months, even years. The relationship's put on a painful and destructive path. Remember, you married a lover, not a critic.

While Oliver continued to speak, Olivia tipped her head back for a moment and closed her eyes, thankful Oliver had never criticized her like that before.

IMPLEMENT THE TEN-SECOND RULE

When your partner stops talking, wait a full ten seconds before saying anything. Your partner will probably talk again before you make it to ten. You may think, *But she talks a lot,* and while it may be true that women talk on average double what men do, it's generally because they have to repeat themselves to the guy who isn't listening very well.

Oliver moved closer to erase the distance before reading the last part of the final note. "These are workable communication strategies to help create the ultimate relationship experience. You'll be far happier because the speaking strategies make you feel paramount. Of course, you need to *want* your relationship to improve before you can make it a masterpiece. Do you want that?"

The final words cut into Olivia's heart. "I do want this more than anything. I don't want to feel so overwhelmed at home anymore, and I want you to feel paramount. So I have to start by being completely honest with you. There's something I need to tell you . . . about Zeb."

*   *   *

Zeb was rubbing his eyelid when he heard a dinner bell coming from the center of the room. His throat closed up, and he pinched his lips together in frustration about the interruption.

"Sounds like a dinner bell," Isabella said.

Seriously? He had to tell her in this room. No more waiting. The longer this drew out, the worse it felt. If she found out from someone else, that would cause significant distrust.

The butler directed everyone to join the two guests at the center table for dessert.

"Red! Blue!" Isabella called out.

After they all took their seats at the main table, Oliver asked, "Where've you guys been?"

Blue's smile was as joyful as ever. "You first. What takeaways from the rooms are you finding most useful?"

Oliver's eyes widened. "This place is amazing. To be honest, though, we haven't really worked through any of the questions, especially the one-through-ten questions, with any depth."

Blue's smile faded while he adjusted his top hat. "Information without application scores you a low number, while information plus application gets you to a consistent nine."

Oliver put his hands up and nodded. "I know. I know."

Zeb was rubbing the back of his neck. He didn't want to keep this information from Isabella any longer, and he told Olivia that he'd tell Isabella in this room. No more interruptions would get in the way, including this one. He unbuttoned the top button of his shirt and asked Blue, who was taking a sip of water, "Do you think we could get another chance to talk privately with our spouse? You know, like you say, information without application is useless." Zeb clasped his hands together and wore a pasted-on smile.

Blue coughed, pretending his drink went down wrong. "Yes, we will give you all the time you need, Zeb. But let me just give you one of the all-time great strategies to create the ultimate relationship. First, all these strategies you're learning, they mean nothing if you don't generate the right kinds of energy in your relationship. Whether it's physical, emotional, spiritual, mental, or sexual, the answer to a lot of your issues is energy."

"How so?" Isabella tilted her head to the side.

Zeb poked his tongue lightly into his cheek and inhaled a long breath. He grabbed his knees underneath the table to calm himself down.

"Well, for starters, you expend too much energy on the wrong things and—"

Oliver cut him off. "I can tell you how we can save a lot of energy. Someone needs to make refrigerators with see-through doors, then we wouldn't have to open it every ten minutes. Anyone feel me on that?"

Blue raised his eyebrows and went right on. He was passionate about this strategy, even lifting his hands with exaggerated gestures. "Your relationships are energy. So if you want to experience the ultimate relationship, become energy-rich and generate the right kinds of energy toward each other. What Einstein said applies to couples too. 'Everything is energy, and that's all there is to it. Match the frequency of the reality you want, and you cannot help but get that reality. This is not philosophy. It is physics.' So determine what you want with each other, and then generate the energy to make it so."

"Einstein said that?" Oliver pulled on his shirt. "That's gotta be from a blogger who's promoting some new age BS."

Red gave a half shrug that conveyed secret knowledge. "We find this to be one of the most overlooked and underappreciated things from couples who visit the Couples' Castle. The kind of energy you generate affects *everything* about your relationship. In fact, your attitude about a blogger promoting some new age BS is energy—negative energy. Your energy levels affect everything about your marriage."

Everything? Zeb leaned back and tried to shove his hands in his pockets before deciding to pick up a glass of water to remedy the dryness in his mouth.

Red's eyes glistened. "When your energy is low, your relationship satisfaction will plummet. I mean, how exciting is your relationship when your partner is lethargic or has a bad attitude? That's low, negative energy. Your homes shouldn't have an ounce of negative attitude (energy!). Put up a sign that says, "No negative attitude (energy!) allowed here". Conversely, when your energy is good, your satisfaction about your relationship will skyrocket. Guess what type of energy you had for each other in the beginning stages?"

"The high, positive energy." Isabella glanced at Zeb. He caught himself holding his breath and relaxed a bit, taking slow, shallow breaths now.

Red almost stood but stayed seated and placed her hands on the long center table. "Here's what's really occurring in your relationship: After spending considerable time with your partner, you begin to operate from your baseline energy point, but what's needed is a conscious decision to generate your energy levels at all times—just like when you dated, you were energy rich. You were passionate for each other. Wouldn't you like to experience that passion again?

"When you operate from your baseline point, without any conscious decision, you take your cue about how to feel from your circumstances. You get home from work and plop down on the couch, a well deserved rest to be sure, but where's the energy for the relationship? And this occurs day after day, until the relationship becomes a nothingness. When you wait for your circumstances to tell you how to feel, you are a thermometer. We're telling you that if you want the ultimate relationship experience, use your energy to start setting the temperature in your relationship. Be the thermostat."

Isabella's body posture perked up. "Are you going to ask us a one-through-ten question about this?"

"Well . . ." Blue smiled and dropped his elbows on the table.

Everyone waited for it.

Blue cleared his throat and leaned over his plate. "What if you did ask yourself every day, 'On a scale of one to ten, what's the quality of energy I'm bringing to my relationship today?'"

On a scale of one to ten, what's the quality of energy we bring to the relationship every day? If it's not a ten, how can we make it a 10?

Zeb had the leg shakes. These guys were going to keep on teaching and talking. He just needed to pull Isabella aside and tell her about Olivia and his past. Awkward, yes, but she deserved to know the truth. If she found out somehow from someone else, it would be a disaster. As time felt like it was slowing down, he twisted his wedding ring and contemplated what to say.

"Here's the truth"—Red scanned the couples—"there are no marriage problems."

"What about my relationship?" Emma gripped her key. "Surely you've noticed, well, that Titus and I, you know, have some big problems."

Red turned to her left and looked Emma in the eyes. "No. You don't. Because—and this is one of the biggest ideas we hold at the Couples' Castle—there are no marriage problems. Rather, there are just two individuals with their own problems who get together, occupy the same space, and amplify their negative emotions."

A gust of fresh cool air blew in from the arboretum that chilled Zeb to the bone. He pressed his elbows into the sides, making his body as small as possible. He looked all around the table, then behind him. He rubbed his knee caps and bit the inside of his cheeks.

Isabella leaned over and asked, "Are you all right, Zeb?"

He whispered back, "Uh sure. I mean . . . yes." He was oblivious of his own inability to put together a coherent explanation. The only thing he noticed was the cool breeze and how his stomach felt rock hard. He was beating himself up for not telling Isabella about Olivia when they first saw her. Now it was just going to sound fishy.

Red was still talking. "People treat dating, relationships, and marriage like it's about finding someone who will make them happy. But what Maya Angelou's once said is true: 'I don't trust people who don't love themselves and yet tell me "I love you."' There is an African saying which is 'Be careful when a naked person offers you a shirt.'"

"What's that supposed to mean?" Isabella rubbed her chin.

"It means a healthy relationship isn't about finding someone who makes you happy but about being someone who makes you happy. When both individuals are happy, their happiness amplifies and reciprocates like a river of love and passion."

> The way to the ultimate relationship experience isn't by trying to find someone who makes you happy, but rather, by two happy people who amplify and reciprocate their emotions in shared experiences.

A bead of sweat rolled down Zeb's forehead. He couldn't wait any longer. How could he pull Isabella to the side without making this even more awkward?

Blue swirled his glass in front of him before setting it down. "You guys expend way too much energy trying to change each other, and it's a total waste of time. The problems you claim your marriage has are really problems you have in yourself. Instead of polarizing each other with your criticisms and carping, what if you worked more on your own energy and then came back to your partner in a more positive and joyful state. This is the kind of energy that improves your number."

Blue was determined to make his point. "Before each conversation, at the start of each date, or when you find yourself caught in an argument, immediately think in terms of energy, energy, energy. Ask yourself, 'What energy can I bring to this space right now?' Your partner will feel that energy change, and it'll shift the relationship into a new, better direction. Want more passion? More awesomeness? Generate it. You can always generate whatever energy you want."

Zeb picked up the closest thing on the table, a butter knife, for a calming effect. Would Isabella be upset that he didn't tell her right away? Would she believe him that what he had with Olivia was over a long time ago? Would she believe that it was a coincidence that they were here together? Was he overthinking it and would this all seem junior high-ish?

Red leaned in and rested her chin on her hands. "How can each of you make your partner feel important with your energy?"

"Well, we just read a plethora of strategies about talking." Isabella lifted her hands.

"Yes," Blue affirmed, "but it's about the energy it creates. You know that criticism and judgment damages your marriage, but the reason for this is that they create a current of energy that poisons the relationship.

"Even if it's just the quiet critical voice inside your head," he continued, "it creates a crack in the relationship because your partner can feel your energy at all times. Indeed, both partners are always sending unconscious signals to each other, and whatever the partner feels gets boomeranged back to you. So what are you doing that creates poor energy? Here's a starter list of things that create poor energy:

1. Sitting around, watching TV
2. Eating junk food
3. Lack of sleep
4. Thinking negative thoughts

"Then we wonder why we don't feel in love anymore. Those activities lead to poor energy, which gets you poor results. On the flipside, what are you doing to generate amazing energy? Here's a starter list that might help:

1. Drink five liters of water per day
2. Eat clean
3. Sleep seven to eight hours per night
4. Meditate
5. Think positive thoughts"

Red studied her plate like it was a mirror showing her the past. "When you're energy-poor, you're more prone to judge and critique your partner. Judging and criticizing puts your relationship's attention on what you *don't* want rather than on what you *do* want, which is presumably happily-ever-after. Since you always get more of what you focus on we recommend you focus on what you want in your relationship, on how things do and can work, and the positive aspects.

"Become energy-rich! Pay special attention to your language because the language you use creates an energy that determines what kind of relationship you experience. If you use critical, negative, and judgmental language with each other, you'll perpetuate a relational lifestyle that attracts more of just that. Whereas if you speak with positive, romantic and uplifting language, you'll feel what it's like to live in the ultimate relationship." Red picked up a straw from the table and stirred her drink.

"So are you saying it's like a cycle?" Oliver made a circular movement with his hands. "Like when I make Olivia feel appreciated, she feels better, then talks in a more kind way to me, and then I feel better and talk in a more kind way to her?"

Blue spread his hands out as wide as possible. "Yes, and let me ask you, can you appreciate someone too much?" He paused for effect. "Heck no. Everyone loves to feel appreciated—and the more, the merrier."

Red smiled at her partner's enthusiasm. "The relationships that thrive do so because they created a nonjudgmental energy zone for each other. When problems surface, and they will, the thriving couple frames and reframes the problem so that they focus on what they want instead of on what they don't want."

Emma twisted a napkin in her hands. "Can you give an example?"

Zeb felt strained to the limits. He tilted his head to the ceiling and let out a heavy sigh.

"What'd I say?" Emma's hands carved through her hair, held it back, and then released it.

Zeb sat up and blushed. "Nothing. I'm sorry, Emma. It wasn't you." He immediately feigned a smile and felt a dullness in his chest. "Continue, Red. I'm sorry." He sensed the stares of a thousand eyes looking down at him. He wondered if anyone had any antacids available. When he realized there were probably none, he pulled at his collar.

Red eyes were soft, with an inner glow. "Here's how it works: If you speak with kindness to your partner, your partner will feel kindness for you. If you speak words of respect to her, she will believe in you. If you speak romantically to him, he will experience the feelings of romance for you. Your language absolutely creates an energy for your relationship. On the other hand, if you speak angrily to him, he'll experience volatile feelings for you. If you speak rudely to her, she'll experience feelings of rudeness toward you. If you speak impatiently to him, he'll experience feelings of impatience toward you.

"I'm sure you've all heard of Gary Chapman's *The Five Love Languages*. He lists five different ones and then demonstrates how everyone has a primary language and a secondary language. The key is to remember the language that makes you feel important may not be the language that makes your partner feel important. So the goal is to identify your partner's language and speak it often because your partner will respond with greater enthusiasm toward you, and we can all agree that's a good thing." Red sat back, looked up, and rubbed her mouth like she was pondering her own words.

She scooted forward and looked at Emma. "These approaches are far superior to treating your conversations like ping-pong matches where you're slamming the topics into your opponent's face in order to win a point—but lose the relationship."

Blue eyeballed Zeb, whose whole body seemed to shake. "Nor does hiding things help. In fact, hiding things is because of low self-esteem and insecurities. You hide things because you feel like you're not enough to handle telling your partner the truth."

That was the final straw. Zeb had to get it out. Now. His breathing picked up while he rocked in place.

*   *   *

"I know Olivia." Zeb exhaled like he'd been holding his breath under water.

"What?" Isabella wrinkled her brow.

All other eyes darted to Olivia.

"Yes, we all know Olivia." Isabella was so caught up in Blue's words that Zeb's statement sailed right past her. "Sorry about the interruption, Blue. Please continue."

But Blue remained silent.

Zeb took measured breaths, in and out, like a yoga instructor.

Olivia stopped breathing altogether, a bead of sweat falling slowly from her forehead.

Oliver's eyes seesawed between Zeb and Olivia.

Emma sat across them with her head flinched back a bit.

Zeb didn't care about poor judgment or other people's expectations at this point. He set the knife down and pressed his right thumb hard against the middle of his left hand. "No. I mean I *know* Olivia." His teeth bit down on his lower lip.

"What's he talking about?" Oliver asked Olivia, who sat like an unblinking doll in the corner of a little girl's bedroom.

"What do you mean, you *know* Olivia?" Isabella's formerly blank expression grew taut with concern.

He couldn't find the words quick enough. He picked the knife back up and unknowingly tapped the table.

"Zeb, what do you mean?"

"I mean . . ." His voice faded, and he tapped the butter knife on the table. *Tap, tap, tap, tap, tap, tap, tap, tap, tap, tap, tap, tap.*

Isabella grabbed his hand to stop the tapping. "Zeb?"

Zeb inhaled.

"Zeb?"

"Olivia and I have a history," he blurted out.

The air flew out of the room, back into the arboretum.

Chapter 14

Room 6

Well, that could have gone better. Olivia couldn't get the sour taste out of her mouth. It would've been nice if Zeb had given her some warning before just blurting things out. This was supposed to be a private conversation, after all, one that would prevent misunderstanding.

Isabella shook her head, her eyes squinting. "What?"

All eyes on him, a streak of crimson crawled up Zeb's neck. "It was years ago. We were kids, really, but Olivia and I, we . . ."

Olivia was horrified that everyone could hear this. Her hands grew cold, and she wished her blouse were camouflage instead of yellow so she could pull it over her head and hide. A walk in blistery Antarctica would've been preferable to the chill she felt from Oliver's stare.

Isabella had turned her own shade of red. She scooted from the table and stood up, blinking rapidly. "I don't understand?" She looked confused.

Zeb was like a deer caught in the headlights.

What? Now he can't say anything?

Oliver looked stricken. "What's he talking about, O?"

She let her face fall into her hands, everything she'd planned to say forgotten.

"Yes, Zeb. What *are* you talking about?" Isabella rocked forward on her toes, waiting for a clearer explanation.

Zeb stood up slowly, the sound of the chair screeched on the floor. "Honey, I'm just trying to let you know that, uh . . . I just didn't want it to be awkward . . ." He sounded like a cowboy talking to a spooked horse.

Isabella crossed and uncrossed her arms, then shifted her balance.

Oliver leaned over to Olivia and whispered, "Olivia? What's going on?"

She stared at the empty plate in front of her. There was a disconnect where the mind struggled with belief. *This can't be happening! Why did I wait so long to tell him? Now no matter what I say, it all just sounds fishy.* Her face, neck, and ears felt impossibly hot.

A little louder this time, Oliver whispered, "Olivia, look at me."

What else could she say? Would he even hear her right now? The last thing she wanted was a distrusting relationship like Emma's. *If I'd just told him earlier, it would've been awkward but not like this. Trust is everything, and now that's totally under siege.*

Oliver couldn't have leaned any closer. "Look at me, O."

She met his gaze. Still not knowing what to say, her eyes filled with a thousand apologies.

He needed no verbal explanation. Her face said it all. "Are you serious?" He spoke in hushed tones, and his voice broke, and before she could explain, she got the feeling that he did too.

Oliver scooted from the table, rattling the silverware and china, and stood up. He put his hands on his hips while letting out a soft sigh.

Olivia immediately stood and tried to keep the conversation private. "It's not what you think, Oliver. It didn't come out of Zeb's mouth right."

Oliver waved his hand like it didn't matter, but his curling lip and watery smile said otherwise.

Over on the other side of the table, Isabella continued standing—now rubbing her brow like she was warding off a headache. "Honey, I'd rather have not talked about this in public, even if it's no big deal—like you say it isn't."

Zeb had a hard time making eye contact with her. His chin quivered. "I just . . ." His voice cracked while he stared down at the floor searching for the right words.

Isabella glanced over at Oliver and Olivia who were having their own personal conversation, at Emma sitting next to Red, then craned her neck toward Zeb. "And why didn't you just tell me when we first saw the other couples? I mean, we've been here for days, Zeb." Her whisper grew louder. "What am I supposed to think? You *know* her. You *had a history* with her. What's all that supposed to mean?" She leaned closer and lowered her voice. "And why would you humiliate me like this in front of others?"

If I don't say something to make this right, this is going to get way out of control quickly. "Look, everybody, it's not what you think." Olivia found herself with an unwanted spotlight shining on her. She felt her knees lock tight together, and she felt naked, of being on display. Everyone waited for an explanation while she stood like a lame duck president about to deliver a speech.

"It's not what you think," she reiterated, softer this time, searching for the best words.

Isabella shifted her balance and tucked her hands behind her elbows. She opened her mouth to say something to Olivia but then closed it.

A thick wall of ice formed solid between the couples.

Thankfully, finally, Blue stood up and spoke. "Please, everyone, sit down."

Olivia's ribs squeezed when she thought of the looming disaster. She immediately took Blue's advice and sat down. The rest of the group reluctantly followed.

Now Blue was the only one standing, his eyes hopping from couple to couple. "There, now let's allow cooler heads to prevail and give them an opportunity to explain." He scanned the couples again to ensure everyone was calm, then took his seat.

Olivia cleared her throat and glanced around the table. "Zeb and I knew each other when we were in college, practically teenagers."

"And you didn't say anything about this until now because . . . ?" Oliver ran his hand softly through his hair.

She looked at Oliver. "It's why I tripped and fell over in Evermore Park. I couldn't believe that he was there," she said, gesturing at Zeb. "I hadn't seen him in years. And seeing him was like . . . I don't know . . ." Her voice faltered.

"And you 'had history' with each other?" Isabella shoved the hair out of her eyes and pressed her lips together.

You're really going to make me repeat that? "We were just kids, and it never got serious."

Red clinked a spoon against her wine glass, and everyone turned. She held up a napkin on which she'd drawn a circle. "As you can see, there's a circle on this napkin. Let's call it the relationship circle. Now if I asked each person to color in how much responsibility he bears for this situation, how much would you fill in? A dot? Half?"

"What?" Isabella's had fidgety hands, and she jumped to the defensive. "What are you talking about? I really don't think this is the time for a relationship education."

"Ah, but it's the perfect time," Blue responded. "In every argument, each individual avoids taking responsibility, forgetting that when you avoid responsibility, you lose control over the outcome. Would you like control over the outcome?"

Maybe this would actually help get Olivia out of this unfair hole.

"If you want a future that you can craft and celebrate, then you must take responsibility of some portion of the circle in every disagreement." Blue bounced lightly in his seat. "In this case, there are trust issues everyone must take responsibility for. The number one thing all individuals want in a relationship, hands down, is trust. Without it, there's no relationship. So let's allow them to explain some more." Blue nodded to Zeb.

Each spouse must take some responsibility for every tension and argument that occurs. That's what grown ups do.

Zeb squeezed his hands together on his legs while letting out a long quiet breath. "Listen, I didn't know Olivia would show up at Evermore Park." He glanced Olivia's way, then back at his plate. "She tripped, and it was so surreal and awkward it's like, what were we supposed to say?" He looked up and waved his hands. "Then everyone in the limo talked about the Couples' Castle and the excitement of possibilities, and it just grew more awkward to bring up, especially since Olivia and I ourselves hadn't even spoken in years. We didn't even know what to say to each other, let alone to anyone else. I think we both just wanted to talk first, so we did."

"You did? When? Where?" Isabella cheeks were visibly flushed.

"At the waterfall." Zeb grabbed a spoon and began tapping again. "I should've told you then, honey. I'm telling you this now because I just felt like it was the right thing to do. There's nothing to hide. Seriously. That's *why* I'm telling you." He rubbed his forehead. "What I can't figure out is why we're here together. I just felt that if our marriage is going to thrive—and, baby, I want it to—then we need to apply what we're learning here in the castle."

Olivia looked around the circle, each of them sitting there in their dysfunctions, naked for all to see. Emma sat there, alone with them, and watched each person furtively.

Isabella's rigid posture and taut expression softened. "Go on."

Zeb sighed. "Olivia and I knew each other when they first diagnosed me with brain cancer."

Oliver jerked his head back. "You had brain cancer?"

Zeb put his hand up. "Yes. I won't bore you all with the details. The point is Olivia didn't even know I had brain cancer. All these years passed. We go to Evermore Park, and there she is. She sees me and trips." Zeb shook his head. "The whole key and invitation was bizarre to start with, and now we're sitting in a limo with strangers, and I didn't just want to say 'Hey, everyone, I know why that woman tripped and fell over. She and I had history at the beginning stages of my brain cancer, which she never even knew about, we never spoke again, and now we randomly see each other at midnight with our own spouses on the way to some Couples' Castle.'" Zeb leaned back and bit his thumbnail.

Oliver drew in a breath, then released it. "So it's just a coincidence that you're here together? Honestly, that seems a little . . . strange."

"It's no coincidence." Blue moved his head back and forth to crack his neck.

Really?

"Attending the Couples' Castle event is an exclusive affair. We invite only so many couples, always with a purpose. Of course, we brought Zeb and Olivia here at the same time."

Isabella's eyebrows furrowed, then released. "But why? We're supposed to be working on our own relationships."

Blue's eyes told her to calm down. "All of you, and these two in particular, have unresolved issues, and unresolved issues create limiting beliefs about what you can or can't have in your current relationship. The past can cap your ability to flourish in the present when you have unresolved issues. It's like having your leg attached to a chain and ball. It affects your current relationship. Since arriving at the Couples' Castle, these two were able to sort things out and move on."

Isabella rubbed at the middle of her forehead, eyes closed. "What do you mean 'all' of us have unresolved issues? How's that relate to the issue at hand?"

Blue leaned in. "Jealousy. It's always been there deep in your hearts, and we knew you'd never learned to deal with it, evidenced in what we just witnessed. You'll never experience the passion, romance, or the ultimate relationship with jealousy in control because it's a toxic hole that burns through the good of your relationship."

Oliver lowered his brows. "We could've figured out how to deal with those things back home without going through all this."

"You hadn't yet, and better to deal with it here than back home with no coaching. It's always been an ever-present threat to the quality of your relationship." Blue shifted his gaze, giving them an opportunity to dispute him.

"Okay then, what do you suggest?" Oliver's voice was strained.

Olivia felt a lightness in her chest, thankful the spotlight shifted off her and onto Blue.

Blue picked up his wine glass and leaned back in his chair before taking a small sip. "First, you become aware of your jealousy." His eyes darted from person to person. "I think we've accomplished that. Second, you ask, 'Is this feeling an internal insecurity, something I'm lacking, or is this a real trust issue that I need to talk through with my partner?' That's for each of you to decide. Third, in moments of jealousy, your best approach is to focus on what you appreciate about yourself so you'll feel better, and then proceed from that state. Fourth, when jealousy surfaces, lean into care rather than fear. Immediately find ways to show care for you partner rather than imagining fears about your partner's actions. Fear leads to loss, while care manifests gain."

Olivia was impressed with how Blue could pull lists and strategies out of his head on the spot. Plus it kept everyone's attention off her. She tilted her body toward him and asked, "Anything else?"

"Yes. Fifth, or whatever number it is, recognize that you're enough. Jealousy stems from you feeling less than. Your greatest fear is not being enough, something jealousy preys on. Nobody is 'less than,' but sometimes you feel that way, and that's when jealousy rears its ugly head. Sixth, jealousy forces you to go into self-protection mode, but doing that causes you to accidentally block out your ability to receive love. Did you notice how people went into self-protective mode and felt 'less than' just a minute ago? In those moments nobody feels loved." Blue set his glass down on the table.

Red echoed him. "Jealousy's an ugliness that you must move past in order to tap into the life of happily-ever-after. If you never deal with it, it's always going to hover just below the surface, ready to devour your relationship."

"So you put us through this whole ordeal for that?" Zeb deepened his tone, and his nostrils flared.

Blue vigorously shook his head and waved off his comment. "You put yourself through it. Your insecurities and inadequacies prevented you from sharing with each other right away at Evermore Park. And because the rest of the group didn't know how to deal with jealousy, they went through the last half hour of pain. But now you've been equipped with answers and strategies and built up some emotional strength so you can get what you've come for. I can initial your treasure chests now. You're almost ready to handle what's in room 7." He looked specifically at their model treasure chests sitting on the table. "Almost."

Zeb stood and faced Isabella. Caught off guard, she looked up at him from her chair. "Yes, we talked at the waterfall. Because we hadn't spoken all these years, we thought that was the right thing to do before talking to everyone else about it. I'm sorry, honey."

Isabella looked away and scratched her head while biting the inside of her cheek.

Zeb spoke from his heart. "I love you, Isabella. In all our blended family craziness, and through all the past pain, I love you from the depths of my soul."

Olivia couldn't help but think how sweet that was. She wished someone would say something like that to her, but knew it was she who needed to say something to Oliver.

Isabella's eyes watered, and she swiped a tear away.

He stepped closer, barely leaving any space between his black button-down and her green shirt. "I love you, Isabella. With every fabric of my being, I love you. I should've told you immediately. Not doing so led to suspicion and jealousy. I'm sorry. Please forgive me."

When Zeb put a hand on her shoulder, she flinched. After taking in a deep breath, she lifted her chin to keep the tears from falling.

Zeb knelt next to her and spoke in soft and gentle tones. "I'm sorry for not telling you sooner, Isabella. Please forgive me."

She tucked her black hair over her ear, rested her head on his shoulder and lowered her voice. "We both have our darkness, Zeb. Thank you for loving me in mine."

My turn. Olivia could see the palpable pain mirrored in Oliver's brown eyes. She had to own her misstep and reassure him.

She attempted to make her reassurance as private as possible. "I love *you*, Oliver. I'm sorry I didn't tell you earlier. You deserve to know everything. I respect you more than anyone and always will." She put her hand on his shoulder and declared to the group. "I admire this man more than anyone on the planet. He's my man."

The power of reconciliation swirled around the room.

Emma cleared her throat and spoke for the first time in a long time. "Um, guys, I'm sorry to interrupt this Hallmark-card moment, but earlier, the iPad on my table showed Titus in some wedding chapel here in the castle. I need to excuse myself so I can go find him."

Isabella jumped up from her seat, Zeb's hand in hers. "If you don't mind, we'll go with you."

*   *   *

Emma had forced herself to sit still this whole time. While the other couples worked out their issues, she'd clamped her hands in her lap and made herself go through a series of deep breaths. Now that they were really finished, there was an expanding feeling in her chest. She started hurrying to make things happen quicker, including taking the lead toward the exit.

"That's the wrong door. I know a shortcut, follow me," Blue called over his shoulder, already walking toward a different exit.

With a fresh wind in their sails, they grabbed their keys and fell in line. Blue and Emma first, with Red sandwiching the rest from behind. With every step down the long corridor, a new ray of sunshine unfolded in front of Emma. The chilled air only solidified her resolve to win Titus back. She'd beg, apologize again, plead—whatever it took—to demonstrate just how much she cared for him.

Blue turned right.

The last time she attempted to communicate with Titus barriers blocked his eyes and his ears, sealed. It was like he'd walled off his soul. The light in his eyes, gone, just a caged shell of himself. How could she blame him? Her betrayal had cobwebbed his heart.

The group hung left through another room and up a flight of stairs.

There was no eraser big enough to wipe out her mistakes. It would've been kinder to poison him. She was flooded with self-criticism and self-judgment to the point of almost giving up hope and just stopping, turning around, and walking out of the castle forever.

Emma swatted away her doubt and despair and searched deep inside to summon feelings of certainty. *Don't focus on how it can't work. Focus on how it can work.* Maybe Titus was in room 7. Maybe it was their turn to work it out. "Blue, can you pick up the pace?"

He turned to Emma and couldn't contain his smile. With the white cane in his right hand, he began a fast-paced strut.

Emma broke out into a run, darting right past him. "Which way's the chapel?"

"Turn left at the end of this hall. Then it's the next right. You'll see a big brown door with a gold sign above it." Blue stopped to put his hands on his knees and catch his breath.

The other couples passed him as well. When they turned at the final right, they caught up to Emma, who was standing outside the chapel. Above the door hung a big golden sign that dared Emma to enter: *Room 6: Pretend Palace.* On the other side of the door, Titus was praying, raw and uncensored.

Shame hollowed Emma's stomach. *This is my doing. I really am a terrible person.* She tilted her head in a side-to-side rhythm while pinching her lip, then looked at the group. "Should I go in?"

Oliver twisted his mouth, then softly offered advice. "Your relationship with him is already a 'no' if you don't, so you might as well."

Okay. Okay. You can do this, Emma. Take a deep breath. Just one step at a time. Turn the handle, open the door, and take it from there.

The sight that met her when she stepped inside the chapel threatened to undo her. Titus lay on the floor in front of the altar, praying. The sound of heartbreak. He loved Emma more than anything. She was the first girl he ever trusted with his heart. *You're such a failure, Emma.*

She could sense that the couples gave her all the space she needed. They stood huddled in the back, and the room was silent, except for Titus's heaving sobs and desperate prayers.

Achoo.

Everyone shot laser eyes at Oliver. He tucked his elbows into his sides and slowly raised his hands in apology.

Titus froze. He sat up and scrubbed his sleeve over his face, composing himself before turning to look at them.

Go to him, Emma. Take your key and go to him. Walk down that aisle and make one last-ditch effort to save your marriage. Just do it. Don't think. Just do it.

As she made her way up front, she felt a pain in the back of her throat while her thoughts filled with self-loathing. She could see faded frescos depicting famous couples hanging up front and mosaics rich with relational symbolism decorating the side walls between the stained glass windows. The scent of fresh flowers filled the room.

Emma didn't know what Titus was going to say or do. Never mind the couples behind her. This was her marriage, her opportunity, her moment to make things better. She walked until she was a free throw's distance from him.

He stood completely still, staring over her shoulder. His eyes were red and his face stained with tear streaks, seeming unnerved that she had seen him like this. *Say something.*

"Look, Titus. I got the key back."

He stared at her, blinking slowly.

Emma started rocking in place while fingering her necklace for comfort. "We just gotta get it to room 7, and then I think, you know, Titus, I think that, um, everything will be all right then." She let out a slow breath through the mouth.

His stare cut right through her. The loving glow he used to radiate for her was gone. Pain, sadness, and a deep hole of emptiness enveloped him. No begging and pleading would convince him to give her another chance. *You brought this on yourself, Emma.*

Regret crashed over her like a giant wave, threatening to drown her under its weight. She felt a dullness in her chest and sank to her knees, crumpling under his scrutiny. The heat and tingling in her face burned, and the only thing that kept her from completely falling over was the hope that Titus would forgive her. She squeezed the key and tried to remain calm.

"I'm so sorry, Titus. I ruined everything. Please forgive me." Her voice cracked, and her chin quivered with her heartfelt apologies.

"May I help you up?" A tall man entered from a door just to the side of Titus and Emma. He wore khaki pants and a navy blue shirt, unbuttoned at the collar.

Emma rose to her feet, her eyes watery. The man offered her and Titus tissues. "Please have a seat." He gestured toward the front pew, then waved to the couples in the back. "Come and join us. I think you'll want to hear what I have to say."

*   *   *

Zeb felt awkward about interrupting this moment between Titus and Emma. There was a heaviness in his stomach, and he pulled back his head as his shoulders pushed forward. He and Isabella took their seat next to the other couples in the front pew and waited for the man to speak.

"Welcome to the Couples' Castle's chapel. I'm the pastor."

Zeb grabbed Isabella's hand. The pastor seemed like a nice guy, a little scruffy in the face but definitely filled with warm energy.

"Because of our limited time together, truth must come before tact." Instead of stepping up to the podium, the pastor rested on the red-carpeted steps a few feet in front of them. "This is your second to the last room, and it's a special room. This is where you'll understand the most powerful strategy to get the ultimate relationship experience and happily-ever-after. Once you hear it, you'll realize why people have affairs, why marriage partners fantasize about people other than their spouses, what all people crave in a relationship, and what strategies can give your relationship an unfair advantage so that you can make your marriage a masterpiece."

Happy to be past the drama from the previous room, Zeb just sat back to soak it all in. Still holding tight to Isabella's hand, he reached into his pocket with his other hand, took out his lucky half-dollar, and rolled it over his knuckles.

The pastor held a real empathy in his eyes for the couples. "Marriages are no longer only driven by what they need—leave the cave, go get some food, buy a house, build a white picket fence, have 2.5 kids, take vacations, and be content with life in survival mode. Most married couples now experience all this, and they're still not fulfilled. You live in a society where food, shelter, safety, and security are taken for granted. People in today's relationships are discovering that just satisfying those needs doesn't create a consistent happy relationship."

This guy probably counseled hundreds of couples who appeared to have it all in the public eye but remained dissatisfied at home. They probably paid thousands of dollars for his guidance, and here Zeb and Isabella were getting it for free.

"Back in the day, Abraham Maslow developed a 'hierarchy of needs' that showed us what every human being needs to feel fulfilled and happy. It was helpful, perhaps brilliant, to identify and meet these needs. But the problem is most relationships now exist in a world that offers a dizzying array of options beyond what they need, and couples are looking for more of what they want. This isn't a reprimand on either Maslow or contemporary couples but rather an acknowledgment of what kind of world we live in. There's a smorgasbord of options, many of which are exciting, while others derail your marriages from what matters most and distract you from finding true fulfillment, snuffing out the flames of passion. The fact is—and I see this in my counseling over and over and over again—couples crave more."

Isabella leaned forward, a look of intense interest on her face.

"This means what drives your relationship has changed. The old 'togetherness' between couples has evolved into a fragmentation of the family life. Couples grow further apart in their own interests while booking the kids for every activity, and both mom and dad work full time to support every one of those activities and the increasing taxes and mortgages. Their minds scattered and families fragmented, exhaustion sets in, and their relationship gets put on the back burner. This leaves them silently screaming for more in their relationship until they are either left jaded or left scratching their heads about how to achieve happiness when they have everything they thought life had to offer in homes, picket fences, cars, churches, and vacations. When the kids finally move out, the empty nesters don't know what to do because they don't know each other anymore."

The pastor scanned their eyes. "So on the one hand, the old days of providing four walls and a roof, with dinner served promptly at five o'clock, isn't enough anymore. While on the other hand, chasing after more has created marital disasters and heartache. But if accumulating and experiencing everything life has to offer isn't the way forward, what will help?"

Isabella politely encouraged him. "If you know the answer, please share."

The pastor pulled on his shirt and leaned forward, placing his arms on his legs. "The answer is to bring a consistent *newness* into your own relationship." He could see the blank stares he was getting in return. "Before you fall asleep on me, know this is everything to experience a magnificent love. This room exists to show you that you absolutely have a neurological need for new stimuli, variety, uncertainty, and the unknown. Your brain, in particular the substantial nigra and ventral segmental area or 'novelty' center of the brain, *craves* what's new. You know the feeling of passion that flames every now and again? It's because the brain lights up for novelty and experiences a sense of happiness, contentment, and satisfaction."

I wonder if that has anything to do with why my first marriage didn't survive. I kinda just let things go on autopilot, expecting marriage to just work.

The pastor rubbed his pant legs, then looked up. "Newness is why couples crave more and more, even for stimulation outside their marriage. But you don't need to look outside of your relationship to make it work for you. If you want the most passionate and sexy relationship, keep asking, 'On a scale of one to ten, how would we rate the quality of newness/variety in our own relationship? If the answer is less than a ten, what would it take to make it a ten?'"

Right now, an eight maybe. With the craziness that was their blended family, there was always something new going on. Variety wasn't their issue. Maybe there were different kinds of newness. Perhaps it needed to be a kind of novelty they liked.

> On a scale of one to ten, how would we rate the quality of newness/variety in our relationship? If it's not a ten, how can we make it a 10?

The pastor leaned in, hand on one knee. "World-class relationships keep the quality of their newness and variety at a nine. Couples who settle for security and sustenance eventually get bored with each other in today's culture of comparisons and options. Then community leaders tell them they should just be content, making them feel guilty. The truth is, if you want feelings of chemistry and connection, you have to consistently stimulate variety and newness in your relationship."

Oliver leaned over to Olivia and asked, a little too loudly, "Does me sleeping naked all night keep the variety going in our relationship?"

Laughter erupted in the front pew.

Oliver raised his hands and shrugged. "What? I'd rather be cold than hot because I can always put more clothes on, but I can only take so much off before I get arrested."

The laughter continued to bounce off the walls.

"My name is Pastor Mike, by the way."

"Hello, Pastor Mike," they responded in unison, the AA effect setting them off into another laughing fit.

Once Pastor Mike stopped laughing, he cleared his throat. "Look, you live in a culture of abundance, with opportunities and choices everywhere, and each partner in the relationship is turning his or her attention to what he or she wants. Stimulating newness for your partner meets this need and sparks the feelings of romance again in your relationship, eliminating the need to look outside your marriage for fulfillment. When you create newness and variety, your relationship will go from surviving to thriving. No need to feel burdened by this. Just ask yourself weekly, what's something new or some variety I can do this week for my relationship?

Zeb raised his hand. "No offense, but you're a pastor. How do you know this?"

The pastor shrugged halfheartedly. "It's all science, my friend. When you generate feelings of newness and variety in your relationship, you release oxytocin, dopamine, and serotonin to feel great about each other again."

Isabella drew her mouth into a straight line and bit her lip. "But once you've been together with someone for a long time, how can you consistently stimulate newness, like on a weekly basis?"

Normally, Zeb would have been offended, but here, in this place, they were a team. *Ask away, honey.*

Oliver cracked his knuckles. "Yes, I'm sure Olivia feels like there's a lack of newness with me, like she's, to paraphrase the great Mark Twain, 'looked at the mighty Mississippi for so long, it's lost its mystery.'"

"Great questions." The pastor leaned back to stretch his back. "God has put the answer in you already when he wired you with imagination. Einstein said it's more potent than knowledge. Look, you now know the brain thrives on novelty. Well, the key to unlock that novelty is none other than your imagination." He leaned forward, making eye contact with Oliver. "In fact, I'd wager you're already using your imagination."

Oliver stared at his palms as if they held the answers, then looked back at the pastor. "What? How so?"

The pastor touched his temple. "After your brain grows accustomed to your partner, you begin to imagine what it would be like to be with other people. Yes?"

Chapter 15

The Ultimate Relationship Experience

Nobody's going to answer that out loud, bud. Zeb noticed Isabella fiddling with the key and couldn't believe they were only one room away from finding out what's in room 7.

When nobody spoke up, Pastor Mike picked some lint off the carpeted step. "Well, you do." He looked back up at the group sitting in the front row. "Now guess what you're using when you picture yourself with someone else." When nobody took the bait, he answered his own question. "Your imagination! That relationship in your head is not real."

Zeb fidgeted in his seat and rubbed his ear. He couldn't help but wonder if somehow his wife knew his obsessive thoughts about other women when he did have them. He knew it wasn't possible, but the slight paranoia made it feel like it was hotter than it really was in the chapel.

The pastor rested an elbow on his knee and looked at ease sitting on the step. "Think about it. You see someone in your mind's eye and think they're attractive, convincing yourself they might be the love of your life, but you don't visualize them peeing on the toilet or throwing up with the stomach virus. You imagine her always smelling good, but you've never shared a bed with her for two years straight and turned over to be greeted with her nasty morning breath. You imagine what it's like for him to hold you, but you've never dealt with his annoying roller-coaster mood after he comes home from work. You wonder what it would be like to make love to each other, but you conveniently leave out the fact that this involves the same novelty that brought you and your own partner to the bedroom together."

"So our imaginations generate fake relationships?" Olivia sat on her hands and leaned forward.

"While you're imagining them, they're fake. But out of your imagination flows reality."

Zeb studied the faded fresco up on the wall. Some famous couple from the past?

Pastor Mike's eye's followed Zeb's gaze, then turned back around. "You tell yourself a story about how amazing it would be to be with another person, but the whole thing's fueled by your imagination. That's neither bad nor good. It just is. You think how romantic it'd be, how the person would never let you down, the chemistry you'd share, how you'd show him things he's never seen, and how you'd live a dream life together."

Olivia nodded slowly. "But it's all fake."

"It's all fake until it isn't. More couples should heed Logan Pearsall Smith's words when he said, 'Our daydreams would darken into nightmares, were there a danger of them coming true.'" Pastor Mike let that sink in.

Zeb scratched the back of his nape and wished for better mental control over his thoughts. He didn't understand why other women were on his mind when he loved Isabella.

Pastor Mike stood and slid his hands into his pockets. "Every human being is a sexual being, with a strong desire to connect. Throw in the brain's desire for variety and newness and you have the fuel both to keep the human race alive and for infidelity. The remedy is to recognize and refocus your sexual energy. Instead of infidelity, you can either use your imagination to stimulate newness and variety in your own relationship or refocus your sexual energy toward nonsexual goals. Recognizing this is half the battle. Experiencing sexual attraction has a lot more to do with your brain than it does the person you're looking at. Think about it. Once you sleep with the person outside your marriage, you erase the novelty the brain was obsessing about, and before long, you're now thinking about someone else. Solution: Retrain your imagination and refocus your sexual energy."

The pastor slowly paced on the step. "It's never about the person outside of your marriage. What's really happening is you're getting a dopamine hit. Making eye contact with someone outside your relationship floods your brain with neurochemicals like vasopressin that feed you feelings of attachment and lift your optimism about your future with that person, but it's built on your imagination—"

"Fueled with your desire for newness and variety." Olivia sat back against the pew with her hands tucked in her armpits, thumbs visible and pointing up.

Pastor Mike smiled. "Bingo! Moreover, if your imagination is left on autopilot, which so many people do, rarely does life measure up, which is why so many people separate. But you can use your imagination to transform your current relationship into whatever you want."

The pastor approached Titus and Emma and squatted to eye level. "You can also employ your imagination to push through any obstacle. Instead of viewing obstacles as failures, you can, if you choose, appreciate them as an opportunity to strengthen your resolve. It takes imagination though. In the same way you build physical muscle with time under tension, you build solid marriages by overcoming rough patches. Your pain holds within it the equivalent opportunity for progress."

Emma swiped at the tears that fell freely down her cheeks. Titus just stared forward, unmoving except for the muscle ticking in his jaw.

Pastor Mike turned his attention to the group. "With your imagination, you choose what to focus on. Just shift your focus at any time, and when you do, you'll shift your energy, and that'll transform your behaviors, which leads to your ultimate goal—to flourish in an authentic happily-ever-after." He was gesturing with his hands now. This must be what it's like to listen in on one of his Sunday sermons. He starts calm, identifies the problem, and then moves with inspiration to drive home his points.

"You want to make your marriage a masterpiece? Use your imagination to focus on accessing your most powerful, passionate emotional states and on what you desire most for your relationship. The more often you place your imaginative focus there, the more you ignite your neurological wiring to form new patterns and conditioning so it becomes more automatic for your relationship to be in a state of passion and happiness. Put your imagination back on your spouse. It's what you did at the beginning of the relationship, and that's why you felt so alive around her."

Focus your imagination back on your spouse. Let it run wild. It's what you did at the beginning of the relationship, and that's why you felt so alive around each other.

Oliver blew out his cheeks, then released. "This all sounds well and good, but is there an easy way to do this?"

Pastor Mike pivoted, his eyes now beaming with good energy. He snapped his fingers and pointed at Oliver. "Yes. With triggers!" He paced a few steps, searching for the right words. "If used correctly and consistently, they retrain your imagination to create the passionate and ultimate relationship experience."

*   *   *

If Emma could use triggers to earn Titus's trust back, she'd do it.

"What are triggers?" Olivia stole the question straight from Emma's mouth.

Pastor Mike spoke quickly now. "They're physical reminders to access your most beautiful emotional states with your partner. You can place triggers throughout your house, in your car, and at the office— anywhere really.

"One couple I work with put the note 'Bring the Joy' on their entryway door to remind them that when they get home from a long day's work, they're still responsible for the type of energy they carry into the house. The trigger reminds them to choose a joyful state instead of waiting for their partner to bring joy. Before opening the door, their imagination generates a way to bring some joy to the family. They know giving joy begets more joy. They've done this so many times now they could take their note down and still not miss a beat—because they've retrained their imaginations. They could then imagine other things because your imagination never ends. In fact it grows."

Emma started sketching ideas in her head for triggers they could adopt . . . if Titus ever came home again.

Pastor Mike tapped a finger on his lips, recalling another example. "Another couple stuck a note above the sink that read 'New Encouragement,' so every time they see the dishes, they're reminded to speak new encouragement to the other. Still another fastened the phrase 'Dance through Life' onto their TV to remind them that life's not to be lived on their butts in front of a box watching other people live their lives. It's their trigger to get up and dance through life together. Many times they literally get up and dance." He held his arms out wide as if to hug the world, then laughed.

After taking a deep breath in, he said, "To bring things full circle, you can set up triggers to activate newness and variety in your relationship."

Titus raised his hand, and Emma's breath caught.

Even the pastor's breathing slowed. "Yes, what is it Titus?"

The color had drained form Titus's face, and he spoke with a toneless response. "What if we just d-don't feel anything t-toward our p-partner anymore?"

The words felt like a knife in Emma's heart. But she deserved them.

The pastor's arms fell close to the body and formed a grim twist on his mouth. "Well—"

"S-sorry. I'm not quite finished with my question." Titus's eyes barely blinked.

The pastor extended his hand, encouraging Titus to go on. Emma felt nauseous.

"What I mean, and I think I speak for all of us here, g-given what I've seen in our short time together, is that when we first dated, we felt fully alive and experienced a genuine c-chemistry. We c-couldn't get enough of just being around each other, daydreamed of each other when we weren't together, c-couldn't wait to talk on the phone . . . You get the idea. But over time, this faded. My q-question is, is there a way to experience this charged-up chemistry on a c-consistent basis? 'Cause maybe I did something w-wrong—something that circumvented that. I'm talking about even after people have spent c-considerable time— even decades—together. Or will people generally seek out n-new, f-fresh r-relationships v-via a-affairs?"

The pastor looked like he wanted to give Titus a hug. He drew a deep breath and spoke in a soothing tone. "It's been said that love isn't a feeling and that feelings come and go. There's merit to that, but what's totally forgotten in the claim is that human beings always feel. It's to what degree they choose to feel with any particular emotion that's most relevant. Because all your actions flow from your feelings and emotions."

Emma really needed him to get to the point before they lost Titus again.

"How does that apply to you?" Pastor Mike scratched his cheek. "Well, if you stop feeling a positive emotion or stop feeling chemistry with a person, you can, and I'm not trying to tell you what to do, Titus, generate it again without much work."

"How?" Oliver tapped his fingers together.

"Do something."

"Do something?" Oliver's chin lowered and pulled back against his neck.

The pastor held his chin high. "Yes, do something. Take that back, do a lot of something. The key isn't just action but massive action. Action is critical because your feelings for someone follow your actions. The types and proportion of feelings you experience for someone are directly related to the types and proportion of actions you put into motion. So massive action is key.

> The types of feelings you experience for someone are directly related to the types of actions you put into motion.

"Do you see the connection, Titus?"

Titus nodded briefly while looking out into the distant air. "I think so. You're saying when we have n-no feelings, it's because we s-stopped demonstrating anything toward our p-partner."

Pastor Mike sagged against the pulpit on the stage. "Precisely. Jesus once said, 'Where your treasure is, there your heart will be also.' In other words, your heart follows your investment. If you aren't doing anything for each other, you won't feel anything for each other."

"We won't feel *anything*?" Emma looked over at Titus, and she could almost envision him becoming an unfeeling automaton. *I did that.*

The pastor bit his thumbnail. "Yes, I mean no. I mean, you will feel, just not toward your partner. Human beings are feeling beings. You always feel something. You'll just channel the feelings elsewhere."

"So"—Olivia tilted her head to the side—"even if I'm upset with Oliver—not that that ever happens—you're saying if I do something nice for him, my emotions follow because my feelings follow my investment?" She pulled down on her blouse, then scratched her head.

Pastor Mike spoke like he didn't care much whether people believed him. "Yes. Whenever you don't feel love for Oliver, take massive positive action and good feelings will return. The level of your passionate feelings is in proportion to the level of your action. Get him a gift. Then observe how your feelings come rushing back. Write him a kind note and feel what happens to your body. Your emotions flood right back. Contrary to popular opinion, chemistry isn't about the alignment of the stars or controlled by some wizard behind the curtain. You're in control of the chemistry, whether dating or married."

"No, no, no," Oliver protested. "What you're saying makes sense. I'll give you that. But what about the way we feel toward people outside our relationship?"

"What do you mean?" Pastor Mike folded his arms in front of his chest.

Oliver glanced at Olivia before speaking. "I mean, and I presume this is true of everyone here, since you said it earlier that from time to time, we feel chemistry, even sparks of romance, with people outside of our marriage. It seems easy to be around them, definitely exciting, almost like it's meant to be." He shrugged and leaned back, waiting for an answer.

A compassionate smile formed across the pastor's face. "I appreciate your vulnerability, Oliver. What I'd say is this: You're doing the same thing—actions first followed by feelings—with the person outside of your marriage. That's why you feel like it's easy and exciting."

Oliver shook his head. "But what about people we haven't done anything for yet and still feel a connection?"

The pastor took a step down and paused. "I don't deny the connection you feel, but the same thing's still in play. It's just this time your actions are occurring in your imagination. You see yourself spending time together—kissing, laughing, sharing a life together—with your imagination. Then, and only then, do you feel the spark of chemistry. The feelings still following the acts, just this time within the acts of the imagination."

Emma couldn't argue with that. That's the way it had happened with her and Larry. She built up their relationship so much in her mind, and before she knew it . . . She refused to dwell on what she couldn't change. *Titus. Please don't let it be too late to fix things with Titus.* "So you're saying we can feel chemistry with our spouse anytime we want? Just like that?"

"Yup." He took another step down. "Here's another way: Make a list of what partner one should do for partner two, if partner one really felt chemistry with partner two, and then go do that. The results will astound you. Both partners will experience the chemistry again. Chemistry has less to do with the unseen forces of serendipity than it does your feelings following your active imaginations."

"We can do *that.*" Olivia's hand rubbed Oliver's leg. "This just might work."

Pastor Mike clasped his hands under his chin. "Think consistently that it will work, and it will be so because your actions follow your consistent thoughts."

Give the man some big green ears and a walking stick and he'd be Yoda.

He spun around, jumped up the two steps, and slapped the pulpit. "Hey, I have an idea. Would you like to take massive action on what we've just talked about?"

"How?" Isabella stood like a volunteer.

"Well, there's a reason room 6 is a wedding chapel."

"What, you mean we can renew our vows?" Isabella pulled Zeb up to stand next to her.

*   *   *

Olivia held a fist over her mouth to cover her smile. She couldn't believe she was about to renew her vows. A feeling of weightlessness came over her.

Over the next hour, the other two couples pulled out the boxes of pew bows, candelabras, and flowers from the pastor's office and decorated the chapel, while Oliver and Olivia prepared to renew their vows. Zeb and Isabella would go second. Titus declined to renew his vows, but he and Emma did accept the best-man and matron-of-honor roles for both ceremonies.

Forty-five minutes later, the room looked ready for a wedding ceremony.

Servants and lords alike had been notified throughout the castle, and people ranging from five years of age to ninety-five sat in the pews, packed together like sardines. Many walked briskly through the castle's halls and rushed through the chapel doors to claim a seat. The place buzzed with chatter and excitement. People were smiling and seated in full anticipation of two couples choosing to live an authentic happily-ever-after. It was like the castle existed for this moment.

An elaborate sound system played the piano and cello cover of Christina Perri's "A Thousand Years." Oliver, all gussied up in an oversized borrowed black blazer, crisp white collared dress shirt – probably with his Mickey Mouse shirt still on underneath it, and a charming black skinny tie, followed Pastor Mike from the side office and took his place in the front, facing the congregation in anticipation of Olivia's grand entrance.

When the music changed to Pachelbel's "Canon in D," Olivia walked in with an air of royalty, escorted by Blue.

As Red stood in the front row, everyone else did likewise. Then Olivia entered, and applause spread across the room.

She felt alive, full of love. With each step, the breathtaking mosaics and frescos faded into nothingness. A crown of baby's breath held her hair in place, and she could hear her beautiful dress swishing.

Blue gave Olivia a fatherly hug before taking his seat next to Red.

The pastor stood with his arms to his sides. "Wow. Have you guys seen how amazing you look? I mean, really looked? Take a peek, Oliver and Olivia. Not to freak you out, but the people behind you are staring, and do you know what they see?

"Those fascinated with marriage see the wedding dress and the tux and, let's be real, Olivia's hair." Laughter bounced off the walls. "Then there's one group here that sees something beyond what everyone else sees.

"The children."

Olivia felt a tingling in her hands. For the first time in the room, she noticed the small things, like the smell of roses, the pastor's receding hairline, and how one candle burned brighter than the others.

Pastor Mike held notes in his hands. "The children's state of wonder and curiosity sees dreams coming true. It's so mesmerizing to them there might as well be rainbows and ponies in here. Because everything they see—the candles, flowers, suits, and dresses—all combine to transcend what the rest of us grown-ups miss, something more magical than Cinderella at the ball . . . two people in love, like a storybook read to them at bedtime. What you're doing now, to them, is like a fairy tale come true.

"The reason for this is both simple and profound—it's because they see with their imaginations."

Ahh yes, the imagination. I see how you did that, Pastor Mike. Olivia noted how Oliver's eyes were soft, filled with an inner glow. In that moment, she felt like something was clicking for him.

The wedding party was set up in a nontraditional way, with the pastor's back to the congregation so that the congregation could see the wedding couple's faces. "Oliver and Olivia, I'm convinced tapping into your inner child's imagination will give you the ultimate relationship experience. Einstein said, 'Your imagination is more important than knowledge,' while Ralph Waldo Emerson said, 'There are no days in life so memorable as those which vibrated to some stroke of the imagination.'

"You may believe your imagination is just thoughts and dreams and generates no power in real marriage, but your beliefs and your imagination generate more results for your marriage than anything else God gave you. It will help you see the newness, the freshness, in everything, especially in each other.

"Want to improve your number to a nine? Then add variety and newness to your relationship. Imagination is the key to unlock it.

"Like when the two of you hiked in Hawaii together, you stayed on the hiking path for safety reasons, but then, Oliver, with your imagination, you saw another possibility on the other side of the rail. But, Olivia, you felt like you couldn't because you were wearing only a bathing suit and flip-flops, which wasn't very conducive for going off the beaten trail. But you went anyway, didn't you? And you wound up in the most beautiful spot in Hawaii. You stood there overlooking the creamy blue waters, watching the sunset and then staring into each other's souls. It changed how you felt, how you saw each other, forever. Imagination carried you to a real beautiful place where you felt fully alive."

So that's why he asked us about our personal history while the others were setting up for the ceremony. Olivia reached over to hold Oliver's hands. They were soft and sweaty.

Pastor Mike looked relaxed. "A story of marital limitation has been passed on from one generation to the next, and now it's time to tell a different story—one with unlimited love. I wonder if you can capture your imagination right now to do just that. Pretend. Pretend like you're getting married for the first time. Can you feel all those feelings?"

Olivia didn't know if she could feel *all* those feelings, but her heart did feel full. Oliver squeezed her hands, and she could tell that he was holding on to her hands for longer than necessary. A smile genuinely formed and lit his face.

The pastor flipped the page to another note. "What have you always imagined your wedding ceremony to be like? I know you've imagined it even before you met.

"Olivia, when you and your friends whispered in your room about the white dress you'd wear someday, perhaps while watching *Ever After* on DVD, you imagined someone riding in on a white horse and sweeping you off your feet. Or, Oliver, perhaps when they announced the homecoming queen in your school, you imagined one day marrying your own princess. At those times, your unfettered imagination projected a storybook marriage filled with unlimited happiness and unrivaled friendship. Your imaginations dreamed what your wedding day would be like, who the person might be, and the kind of castle you might live in.

"It's your imagination that can take you to your fullest marriage potential. It's the eye of your soul—that part of your thought process situated between empirical evidence and fictional fantasy. It's based on facts but not reduced to them. You two can make your marriage a masterpiece by using your imaginations."

Olivia thought about how much better her marriage would be back home, now equipped with the Couples' Castles' strategies and blueprint. She still longed for room 7 and glanced quickly to the front row to make sure Red was still securing her key. Things were looking up.

The pastor waved his hand around the room. "So color all these facts with your imagination. Oliver, here's your bride. Look at her, really look at her. Use your imagination to see her for all that she is and more. Look at her with more enthusiasm than if the Dallas Cowboys asked you to play quarterback for them. You get to choose how you see Olivia every moment, and you can see her anew, with fresh eyes, every day."

Oliver chuckled at the mention of the Cowboys, then tipped his head back for a moment and closed his eyes. When he opened them again, Olivia felt safe and whole.

"And look at him, Olivia, with the same kind of passion and joy you have when you're reading those Nicholas Sparks novels.

"The best relationships occur when couples use their imagination because that's what creates the freshness, variety, and a never-ending newness within the relationship. So use your imagination to turn your house into a home. Flip on the imagination as you pull into the driveway just before entering your home's front door. See your wife anew everyday. See him like it's the first time again. It's more than possible. To get as much love as you can, love like you never have before. There's absolutely no limit to love because there's no limit to your imagination. So today, right now, pop the top off your imagination and unleash the love God gifted you with."

There was a yearning look in Olivia's eyes, and she licked her lips. Pastor Mike's voice seemed to fade like background noise.

"It's your imaginations that brought you here together, to this day, hoping for what could be. Now you're here, the marriage ceremony, the first and oldest ceremony in the world, a gift from God where you become one as you satisfy the civil requirements and seal the sacred covenant. This is your beautiful marriage. Not one grounded in the authority of the state but in the strength of your imaginative love for each other and God."

Olivia playfully squeezed Oliver's hands, and they exchanged sexy smiles. She felt herself moving closer.

"So, Oliver and Olivia, what do you see when you look at your marriage? It all depends upon the use of your imaginations. It always will. You know what the children see? A storybook marriage of two people who will live happily . . . ever . . . after."

*   *   *

When the two ceremonies finished, it was close to 8:00 p.m., and Emma could sense that everyone was ready to eat and celebrate. She could smell the food from the chapel. Red and Blue dismissed the couples and attendees to an adjacent dining hall where the kitchen staff had prepared the food, buffet style. Emma lost Titus in the transition. Perhaps he was in the restroom.

When she entered the dining hall, she saw round tables covered in white tablecloths strewn with floral centerpieces, china place settings, and champagne glasses. There were artificial potted plants decorating the room and a DJ over in the corner doing her thing. A small table holding a cake was off to the side about twenty feet from a black-clad photographer's flashing camera.

She had a sinking feeling they might be here longer than she wanted. There was only about twelve hours left to find the real red treasure chest. What could possibly be in it? She'd come this whole way to what? Be stalled at a fake wedding reception? She fiddled with her key while struggling with where to sit. Still no Titus, she chose a seat near Isabella.

Throughout the evening, she watched people eat their fill and observed others tapping their forks against glasses to encourage the couples to share a kiss. Titus, now sitting next to Emma, took a sip of champagne each time instead. When Red informed them they'd be sticking around for cake and dancing, Emma felt hopeless. Room 7 and the real treasure chest was all she could think about. She put a cloth napkin on her lap and kicked off her shoes under the table so she could wiggle her toes. Over the next hour, the DJ and silverware scraping the dinner plates grew with such fierceness until she finally excused herself.

If the couples thought partying was more important than finding the red treasure chest, fine. Not Emma. She walked the halls looking for any sign that indicated room 7. All the rooms were locked, no matter which hallway and door she tried. Around midnight, she finally found an unlocked door. Upon entering, she found a corner lamp and turned on the light. She stood in a master bedroom. Shaking her head with disappointment, she locked the door, plopped on the bed, and let out a long-overdue cry. She tried to keep herself awake with the possibilities of what could be in the red chest.

A booming knock came to her door. She sat straight up, heart pulsing. What time could it be? She scanned the room for a clock. Nothing. When the knocking wouldn't stop, she jumped to her feet and cracked the door. It was Red.

"Emma, darling, we've been looking everywhere for you. Have you been here the whole night? It's 4:30 a.m., and we've been searching for you so we can get to room 7. Everyone's in the hall waiting."

No! No, no, no, no, no, no, no. Her breathing picked up. "I'll be ready in two minutes."

Emma shut the door and set her own personal record in getting ready. She matted down her hair, threw water on her face, checked her teeth, used the bathroom, checked her teeth again, quickly pressed down her pink blouse, scurried over to the bed to grab the key, and ran to the door. As she reached for the handle, she hesitated to say a prayer. She closed her eyes, drew in a deep breath to calm herself, and rubbed her wrists. *Now or never, Emma.*

Chapter 16

Room 7

Zeb couldn't believe they finally arrived to room 7. The previous six rooms built an increased assurance in him about his marriage, and his face expressed a supreme confidence, like a glow. He approached the balcony with the large gold barrier they'd admired a couple of days ago.

"Look." Emma pointed to the ballroom. "They're dancing again. Can anyone see the real treasure chest?"

Blue bounced lightly on his feet. "Welcome to room 7."

Blue's tone induced a strange feeling in Zeb. Plus, who dances at four thirty in the morning? Perhaps they were at the wedding and moved to this grand ball room? He studied the details of room 7 through the window, now with a little more angst. "So we're ready now?"

"We'll soon find out," Blue said.

"What do you mean 'we'll soon find out'? What will happen if we aren't?" Zeb's intuition told him something felt off, his inner confidence suddenly waning. Noting his mouth was dry, he licked his lips. A few moments later, Isabella elbowed him to stop biting his fingernails.

Blue motioned with his hands. "Focus on what you want instead of worrying. Haven't you worried enough back home, especially in regards to your finances? Almost every day in your past you worried about your future. But look at you. You made it to the future you once worried about. Some bumps and bruises, sure. But also lots of laughs and love too. All those bumps, bruises, laughs, and love have made you more resourceful than ever to handle anything coming your way; and, now, instead of worrying about what's next, you should focus on making each day your masterpiece with your partner. Room 7 can lead to the ultimate experience of happily-ever-after, if you let it Zeb. If not, well, pain."

Isabella pinched the skin at her throat. "Pain? What's the criteria for being ready?"

"Whether your relationship's near a nine or not." Blue shrugged.

How are we supposed to know if we actually hit that number? Zeb stood like he was in a funeral home line where people pay their respects to the deceased's family.

There was a long pause before Blue spoke again. "Don't look so grim, Zeb. You've been excited about room 7 since you first arrived. I'm sure you'll be fine."

Emma didn't seem to have any reservations. She gripped her key so hard her hand turned a shade of red.

Blue looked at the door that led to room 7, then back at the couples. "Okay, honestly, it's been determined that only one couple is ready. The other two are close and can go, but we'd advise they get one more wrinkle straightened out first."

Before Emma could raise her hand, Isabella shouted, "Is it us? We'll go!"

What are you thinking, Isabella? Blue did say the reward was ultimate happiness, but Zeb had a gnawing feeling about this. He had no idea why his intuition's alarm bells were going off, but he felt trapped and could hear the sound of his heartbeat thrashing in his ears.

Isabella grabbed his hands. "If not now, Zeb, when?"

Zeb removed one of his hands so that he could stroke an eyebrow. "We don't even know if we're the one couple who's ready. Maybe it'd be prudent to go second, you know, after someone else tries it."

She gave him a confused look, slightly shaking her head. "But the treasure chest."

Zeb looked around, embarrassed. "Okay, Isabella." His answer didn't seem to take care of his light-headedness.

She turned to Blue and smiled. "We'll go!"

"But we haven't even told you which couple is assuredly ready. Are you sure you're prepared?" Red asked.

"No," Zeb said.

"Yes," Isabella corrected him.

Blue eyeballed them.

"If they're not ready, we'll go." Emma stepped forward.

A wave of relief came over Zeb. *That's a pretty bold thing to say, seeing how Titus hasn't even agreed to stay married to you. But hey, more power to ya. We'll go after you.*

"So will we," Olivia added, sounding determined. Oliver stood next to her in a wide stance. He didn't look nervous. In fact, he looked more like a football player ready to run through the tunnel and onto the field of play.

What in the world do I have to be nervous about? Zeb looked back and forth between the ladies, concerned a catfight might break out.

"You all seem eager. Of course, this is to be expected, given your journeys." Red lowered her voice. "But it's imperative that you remember the room's success strategies while down there searching for the red chest."

Nausea bubbled up in Zeb's stomach, and sweat broke out on his forehead. "Could you maybe give us a little refresher of some of those solutions and strategies?"

Red gave him an understanding nod. "All couples start out wanting to experience happily-ever-after. Even after hitting some speed bumps, most even want to improve, but few do because they become exhausted with each other, or they think it's too hard or that it'll take too long. They reach a breaking point, believing they've hit the love quota with their partner. But that's because they don't understand that love is infinite. There's always more to access. Improvement doesn't need to take a long time either. There's a misconception that says improvement comes from incremental gains and gradual progress. Sometimes that's necessary, but more often it just takes using the right success strategies. Change happens in a moment. Every couple can experience true happiness no matter how long they've been together."

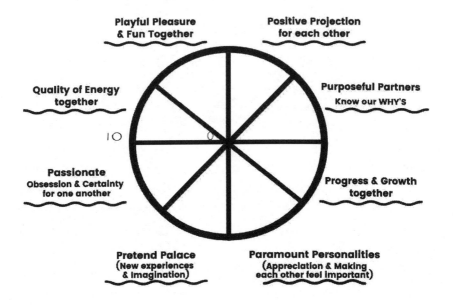

COUPLES' CASTLE GUIDE
To The Ultimate Relationship Experience
Rate your relationship on a scale of 1-10 for each category

Playful Pleasure
& Fun Together

Positive Projection
for each other

Quality of Energy
together

Purposeful Partners
Know our WHY'S

Passionate
Obsession & Certainty
for one another

Progress & Growth
together

Pretend Palace
(New experiences
& Imagination)

Paramount Personalities
(Appreciation & Making
each other feel important)

Our relationship coaching objective is to get you to a 10 on each one.

Blue leaned on his cane and hitchhiked on the idea. "I prefer to think of the previous six rooms like files. You need these files unzipped to flourish in your relationship. In science terms, it's epigenetics, meaning when you unzip the files of positive projection, playful pleasure, etc., there's a connection made between your brain and genes. To experience all that life has to offer in marriage, you want both working in full capacity. Putting the files or rooms into motion changes your brain and body, resulting in a transformed relationship with your partner. Act in the spirit of the rooms on a consistent basis and you'll reprogram your brains and unlock the right genetic expressions to become a world-class couple."

Zeb raised his eyebrows. "Epigenetics? Doesn't sound, you know, uh, very romantic."

Blue nodded. "You don't even have to remember the word 'epigentics' to make it happen, nor is romance up to the fairy gods or some serendipitous alignment of the stars. Some activities in the brain and genes lie dormant and are never expressed or connected, and therefore, you never flourish at a nine, but these files (the rooms you went through), when applied, help you make the proper connections between the brain and your genes so that you can experience the ultimate relationship. When you consistently apply what you've learned in the rooms, you'll shape your brains and DNA so that a wave of positive neurochemicals rushes through you in a way that transforms your thoughts about each other with passion, creates real brain structural changes, and unleashes the quality of your genetic expression to skyrocket your relational success. This is a holistic approach. The point is to amplify your experience by using your brain, genes, emotions, and heart -- all of you. You'll experience new thought networks inside your brain, and you'll become energy rich for one another. In this way, you transform your relationship. Don't worry about the brains and genes talk, it'll all naturally occur when you apply the Couples' Castle strategies."

Oliver saw that the ladies were door-watching. "Um, I don't mean to sound like I'm trying to cut you off, but that all sounds pretty abstract. Plus, I think the ladies are ready."

"Well, we can go now, if you'd like. Zeb just asked to hear some of the strategies again." Blue waited for a response.

Zeb glanced around the room and felt a tightening in the back of his throat. "Yes, maybe if you could just summarize for us and stay away from the abstract, that might be more helpful."

Blue shook his head with disappointment. "How about you tell me the rooms and then I'll summarize? Do you remember what they were?"

Olivia raised her hand to be called on. As soon as Blue acknowledged her, she rushed her words. "Playful Pleasure was the first room. Oh, we loved the massage. Positive Projection was room 2. Um . . . let's see, there was that outside room, Purposeful Partners, where we took different trails. By the way, I'm just noticing these words all begin with the same letter. What's up with that?" She lifted her heels and rose slightly to emphasize words. "Then Progress Patterns with the Asian couple, that was room 4. They were so sweet. However, if I could make a suggestion, maybe store some cots there for the next round of couples. The ground was a little hard, not that I'm complaining. From there, we zip-lined over to the Paramount Personalities room where we ate pizza. Then we renewed our vows in the Pretend Palace room. I got them all, didn't I?" She ran her hands through her hair, flipping her hair back.

"Well done." Blue slapped his leg like a proud grandpa. "Now when you apply the content and main questions of each room, amazing things happen to the point that you'll experience real passion with the love of your life."

Red moved closer to erase the distance. "The room's questions are more important than you think. Not only should you ask them once a week back home, but you'll also need them now for room 7. Let me remind you of what they are.

"*Room 1, Playful Pleasure*: On a scale of one to ten, how would we rate how much we enjoy spending time with each other? And if it's not at a ten, what would it take to make it a ten?

"*Room 2, Positive Projection*: On a scale of one to ten, how would we rate the quality of our positive projection for one another? And if it's not a ten, what would it take to make it a ten?

"*Room 3, Purposeful Partners*: On a scale of one to ten, how would we rate the quality of the purpose of our relationship? If the answer is less than a ten, what would it take to make it to a ten?

"*Room 4: Progress Patterns*: On a scale of one to ten, how would we rate the quality of progress or growth in the relationship? If the answer is less than a ten, what would it take to make it a ten?

"Then there were two questions in *room 5, Paramount Personalities*: On a scale of one to ten, how would I rate how important my partner makes me feel? If the answer is less than a ten, what would it take to make it to ten? And on a scale of one to ten, what's the quality of energy I'm bringing to this relationship today? What can I do to make the quality of energy a ten?

"Then the last question was in *room 6, Pretend Palace*: On a scale of one to ten, how would we rate the quality of newness and variety in our relationship? If the answer is less than a ten, what would it take to make it to ten?"

"So the whole idea is to keep asking ourselves these one-to-ten questions?" Zeb had already heard the one-to-ten idea a thousand times, so it wasn't like he was asking to get a new answer. His intent was to delay their departure for room 7 while he tried to figure out why he felt so uneasy.

> Just think if your relationship was at a 9 or higher with the rooms' strategies - having fun together at a 9, growing together at a 9, sharing purpose at a 9, positive projection at a 9, energy for each other at a 9, making each other feel important and appreciated at a 9, new experiences at a 9. Your relationship would be a masterpiece.

Blue gestured wildly enough that his blue hat fell off, revealing the gray on the top part of his hair. He picked it up, cheeks flushed, and slipped it back on his head. "No. The whole idea is to take massive action for your relationship. Action gets you results. The rooms' questions and strategies are the best kinds of actions to get you the results for experiencing the ultimate relationship, finding the love of your life, and making your marriage a masterpiece." Blue glanced away for a brief time, adjusting his hat. "Taking action is far more important than numbers. The more action you take, the more you train your reticular activating system."

"Our what?" Zeb kept the delay going so that he could scan the room again, including a once-over of the couples. Oliver had his hands in his back pockets, while Olivia craned her neck to hear Blue more clearly. Red stood with a strong posture next to Blue, shoulders back, chest out, and chin high. Titus was deliberately lowering his head to study Blue and Red. Might he feel the same way as Zeb? And Isabella, his sweet wife, she was fiddling with her cuffs and calmly tapping her foot. Impatience might undo her.

"Your reticular activating system or RAS." Red lowered her brows, then lifted her chin. "It's that part of your brain that determines what you pay attention to. Without it, your brain would notice everything and drive you mad. Recall that your brain's MO is to focus on lack and attack; survive, not thrive. So if left on autopilot, the RAS pays attention to things in life that keep you alive."

Is this why I have high blood pressure and stay more focused on my worries and problems? Zeb furtively checked the door and window.

Red placed one hand on her hip and used the other to gesture. "Wherever you go, your RAS scans your surroundings to keep you alive. It searches for what it lacks and how you're attacked. It's why you always think you have a problem in your relationship. Your RAS is designed to look for problems so that you stay alive. It's survival software. But get this, happily-ever-after and problems are not correlated. You can have big problems and still be really happy. The RAS pays attention to only what it thinks is relevant for you, and what's relevant by default, according to your brain, is your survival. Couples argue, fight, and disagree because their RAS, unless otherwise trained to happily-ever-after, seeks to find answers and data to support their point of view about a problem. You point out what you lack, then you attack. This is part of your survival mechanism applied to your relationship."

Blue pointed behind them. "Look over there in the corner of the room. Has anyone noticed the blue pen sitting there?"

Even in all his scanning, Zeb hadn't noticed it until just now.

"And yet you've been in this room twice. You didn't notice it because your RAS didn't think it was relevant for your survival. Let's take it to another level. Close your eyes."

Zeb saw that they closed their eyes. Red waited for him to close his too. He checked behind him one more time and then squinted.

Blue tapped the floor with his cane. "Spin three times."

They all spun around.

"Now with your eyes still closed, tell me all the parts of the room that are brown."

Zeb couldn't recall a single thing, the sofa maybe?

Blue waited, but no one responded. "Open your eyes."

Various shades of brown popped out at Zeb from all around the room—in the ceiling, on the floor, and on the walls. The sofa *was* brown, and so were his shoes. There were variations of brown everywhere.

Isabella jerked her head back while her fingers touched her parted lips. "How did we not notice?"

"You only see part of your experience at all times," Red said. "No matter where you are, what you're doing, or who you're with, your RAS is telling you what to pay attention to."

What else had Zeb missed in life while he was so focused on lack and attack? Did it explain why he hated his job? And how many times was his intuition off? Maybe he was overthinking the current situation. Why the heck was his intuition sending off alarm bells when the hosts had been nothing but kind?

"Our point is you all need to retrain your RAS if you're going to experience the ultimate relationship. How many of you, for example, consciously appreciated your heartbeat in the last hour, day, or week?" Red spread her fingers out in a fan against her breastbone. "You have little, if any, control over your heartbeat, and yet it beats over one hundred thousand times a day. You can train your RAS to be appreciative of things like your heartbeat, and that will change your emotional state so you can take on the challenges of life in your marriage. Train yourself to notice her good qualities. The point is, by default, your RAS determines you pay attention mainly to that what's lacking in your partner in order to survive. Your brain's telling you your partner needs this or that, convincing itself that if he had those things, you'd be safer, more well-off. But there's more to a relationship than surviving. It's where two people share secrets, complement each other's characteristics, and amplify their emotions together in a nonjudgmental way. There's nothing lacking when two people bare their souls in the eternal flame of love."

Zeb felt Isabella clasp his forearm. He looked over and saw her tapping her other hand against her heart. She had a smile that genuinely lit her face, and in that moment, he decided to release his bodily tension. He loved Isabella more than ever, and he'd just been reminded of the rooms and strategies. Now here's Isabella showcasing her gratitude for him. Zeb wanted to drink in the moment, to savor this feeling forever.

Blue wagged his cane. "Because you've traversed throughout the castle's rooms, you now have all the tools and resources to thrive. The challenge then is to condition your RAS so that it pays attention to things that help you not only survive but also to thrive with the love of your life in the ultimate relationship experience. Train your RAS to focus on the rooms' success solutions and quality questions and you'll flip your neurological switch to take massive action and to attract everything you need to transform your relationship into a nine. Where your RAS goes, your relationships goes. Whatever you focus on in the relationship is what you will feel. You want to feel happy in your relationship? Focus accordingly."

> **Where your RAS goes, your relationship goes.**

"Look!" Emma pointed at the couples in the ballroom below them.

They had stopped dancing and were looking up at them.

"How . . . how . . ." Zeb's eyes grew wide with darting eye movements. "Can they see us through the tinted window?"

"Ready or not, it's time for a couple to go down." Red motioned toward the door.

The ladies jumped forward similar to little girls volunteering to play Cinderella at Disney's Bibbidi Bobbidi Boutique.

Blue looked directly at Zeb and Isabella. *Don't call on us first. Please call on someone else.*

"You and Zeb, if you think you're ready." He held his hand out, ushering them to follow Red's retreating form.

"We're ready." Isabella squealed with delight, grabbing Zeb's clammy hand and pulling him after Red.

*　　*　　*

Olivia put her hand on the tinted window, her chest so tight it was hard to breathe. Zeb and Isabella should walk into the ballroom at any moment. Would they find the treasure chest before her and Oliver?

"There they are!" Olivia rubbed her wrists.

They headed straight toward the royal dancers, walking past the fondue fountain and banquet table. After one of the dancers acknowledged them with a smile and a wave during the *bachata*, Isabella and Zeb started searching for the red treasure chest.

Olivia sat down on the sofa and sighed, pulled her hair back in a bunch and let go, then stood tall. "It's our turn, right? Can we go now?"

"Sure. But what we have to say next will be of great value to you." Red raised her eyebrows and offered a questioning gaze.

Olivia bit the bottom of her lip while rubbing her chin. She played the what-if game to understand the repercussions of the situation.

Red waited for a response from Olivia. When she didn't get one, Oliver stepped forward. "Go ahead, give us this 'great value.'"

Red tilted her head at Olivia, waiting for her approval. When Olivia nodded affirmatively, Red let out an uncanny huge breath. "It's called couples' creative dream, and it refers to what you see together *can come true* for your relationship when you see it often enough, deep within your subconscious."

Olivia squinted. "Huh? Maybe we should just go down to the ballroom."

"It's far more practical and beneficial than you think. Trust me, you'll want it for . . . down there." She nodded toward the window. "Would you like to see how it will improve your relationship in every possible way?"

Olivia played and replayed finding the treasure chest in her mind, obsessing over it. "No. I just want to go down there."

"Me too!" Emma added.

Blue softly tapped his cane. "Not if you're not ready, you won't."

The way he said it made Olivia's hairs stand up on her nape. After exchanging looks with Olivier, she conceded her desire and let him continue.

Red's fingers formed a steeple in front of her chin. Couples' creative dreaming is a simple two-step process. First, ask your partner, 'What do we really want in our relationship?' Once you've come to an agreement, then ask, 'What if we acted like the answer is *already* true?'"

"But we *have* talked about what we want, and we don't have those things." Olivia grabbed a fistful of hair again.

Red's steeple transformed into one jumpy finger. "Ah, but what would happen if you sat together in silence for five minutes every day, focusing on your mutual goals . . . just closing your eyes together and seeing the dream life you want to share? And once you see it, you talk about it with each other *as if you were already living it.*"

"Again, this sounds like hocus-pocus stuff." Oliver gave a dismissive nod, crossing his arms in the process.

Blue chuckled at his smugness. "Ah, but didn't you do this when you were graduating high school? Whether you call it couples' creative dreaming or not, you thought about what college would be like - over and over again - in your mind's eye. You talked about it as if it were true. You did the same thing when you were in college dreaming about the next stage of life, marriage perhaps. And those things materialized in your life. But then somewhere you stopped doing this. What if *that* was the conversation you had more frequently in your marriage? Instead of the daily news, politics, or feelings of stress, what if you asked each other what it feels like to live the life you want and answered in a way where you really felt like it was already true?"

"Then I'd say it's living in fantasy." Oliver leaned against a wall, his arms still crossed.

Blue let out a heavy sigh. "Room 6, Oliver, room 6 and the power of imagination. Remember? It's not fantasy. When you summon your imagination often enough, it changes how you feel, and it transforms the expectations your brain holds for your relationship. This is so, so important because your brain is a goal-seeking organism, meaning whatever the brain expects, it seeks to achieve. So if you talk about and expect great things—because you're already answering and living as if they're happening—then your brain expects them to happen and will put your relationship in motion to make it happen."

Olivia's psychology professor in college had talked about a similar idea. "Are you talking about expectancy theory?"

"Yes, and it *profoundly* affects your relationship." Blue moved into their personal space.

Olivia shuffled back a bit. "How so?"

He gestured wildly with great enthusiasm. "Every conversation you have with your partner—every argument, discussion, and planning time—is based on your response to what your brain, in the context of your past relational experiences, expects to happen in the conversation. Your brain determines the meaning of the outside world more than you think, and the meanings you attach to your conversations steer the trajectory of your relationship." Blue drew in a deep breath.

Olivia looked out the window to get a glimpse of Isabella and Zeb. She couldn't find them. *Seriously, I don't see the point of us having this conversation any longer.*

Blue hesitated before speaking, as if weighing his words. "Because your brains have learned what to expect next, when you visualize what you want for your relationship, your brain will expect to make those things happen. It will send signals through the synapses and throughout the body to make it happen. "In this way, couples' creative dreaming is the process to consistently bring about your desired outcomes and future." He looked off into the corner of the room, like he was watching their future play out.

"So I can just sit like Obi-Wan Kenobi and expect my dream life to happen with Olivia?" Oliver rolled his eyes. "No offense, but seriously."

Blue bounced lightly on his feet. "That's just it, this part of your brain doesn't know the difference between what's real and what's not real, so you can use your imagination—based on facts but not reduced to them—to condition your brain to expect and achieve what matters most to you. Couples' creative dreaming isn't some Jedi gimmick. It's neuroscience. The more you see what you want your relationship to become, the more your brain rewires itself to march your relationship in that direction because that's what your brain thinks it's supposed to do."

Oliver blew out his cheeks, then released. "Again, no offense, Blue, but this doesn't sound super practical in our everyday realities back home."

A slow smile grew on Blue's face. "Actually, you already practice visualization."

"How so?" Oliver pressed his lips together and shoved his hands into his pockets.

"In your daydreaming about other women."

Oh please, God, no. Not this stuff again. Don't let them bring up my husband's porn stash if they somehow know about it.

Oliver slanted his body away from Blue. "Um, I don't daydream about other women."

Blue shook his head slightly. "Everyone daydreams about people outside his relationship, Oliver, partly because the brain seeks something new, but my point is visualization works, and having affairs is one bit of evidence. People are visualizing, daydreaming, about other people. Those daydreams don't just exist in some harmless ethereal mental cloud where Cupid sits. No, those visualizations give marching orders to your cells and messages to your sensory factory. And those become plans in your central nervous system that your brain then seeks to carry out."

Blue had their attention.

"All I'm saying is visualize with the one you're with instead, about creating an exciting future together." He paused to consider his words. "Think about how you two came together. It was also through the visualization process. Day and night, you thought about each other, visualizing with your imagination what it would be like to touch, kiss, taste her lips, take long walks, banter, make love, and go on trips around the world. Couples stop doing this on each other after a time, but I'm encouraging you to keep it up because life keeps getting better when you do."

The marital romance waned because the practice of couples' creative dreaming waned. Start visualizing the best in each other again and the romance and feelings of attachment that you experience in your imagination with people outside your marriage will return for the love of your life again.

"So you're basically wanting us to think about each other more often?" Oliver offered a weak smile.

Blue lifted his hands like a symphony conductor. "We want you to build a mental picture together of exactly how you want your relationship to be—the ultimate relationship experience—to visually make your marriage a magnificent love. Then to act as if it was already true. Isn't it accurate that the more you act things out, the more you become those things?"

Olivia crossed her arms over her chest and drummed her fingers impatiently. How much longer until they could go down there to find the treasure chest?

Blue droned on. "Okay, you want practical, here you go: First, figure out ten amazing experiences that if you shared together this year would make you feel like you were in the ultimate relationship." He gave them each a page of paper to look over, titled "Top Ten Annual Amazing Experiences," with blanks below to fill in according to their preferred future. "You can even include drawings, notes, and pictures that showcase your annual dream life. Post those around your house so you both see them often. Reviewing them creates a fun energy and changes the topics of your conversations to what you want. Currently you each visualize randomly about stuff unrelated to your ultimate relationship together. Bring yourselves together and fill this sheet out each year and watch your relationship soar."

Olivia temporarily forgot about the red treasure chest. She wondered if she'd been visualizing the wrong stuff back home. Perhaps if she switched her thoughts to amazing experiences with Oliver, she'd get a better outcome with Oliver.

Red grabbed a poster board from behind the couch. It had a picture of her and a guy in the center, with words and phrases all around it. "One of the most effective ways to transform your relationship into the ultimate relationship experience is with this practical couples' creative dreaming strategy."

"Is that a picture of you . . . and your husband?" Oliver craned his neck and widened his eyes.

Red nodded, then held up the poster board. "Here's what you do: Find a picture of you and your partner, one that you would never want others to see on social media. It should symbolize the couple you sometimes are but don't want to be any longer. Maybe it was taken when you weren't getting along, were full of doubt, or in a season of financial or spiritual distress. Put that picture on a poster board like this and then, around the picture, write the attributes of that couple. List out their feelings. Write down the typical body language of that couple. Do they frown, shrug, and complain? Write out what they eat, drink, and how they sleep—or if they toss and turn from stress. What are their habits? Name the characteristics and emotions of that couple and how they treat each other. Do they speak harshly to each other? Do they interrupt each other? Do they get angry often? Do they flirt with others outside their relationship? Write it all around that picture. Then give that couple a name at the top of the poster board, maybe something like 'The Monsters.'

MARRIAGE MONSTERS

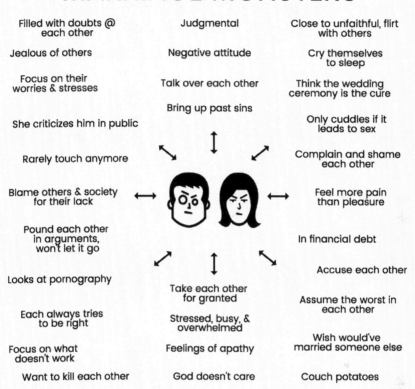

Filled with doubts @ each other

Jealous of others

Focus on their worries & stresses

She criticizes him in public

Rarely touch anymore

Blame others & society for their lack

Pound each other in arguments, won't let it go

Looks at pornography

Each always tries to be right

Focus on what doesn't work

Want to kill each other

Judgmental

Negative attitude

Talk over each other

Bring up past sins

Take each other for granted

Stressed, busy, & overwhelmed

Feelings of apathy

God doesn't care

Close to unfaithful, flirt with others

Cry themselves to sleep

Think the wedding ceremony is the cure

Only cuddles if it leads to sex

Complain and shame each other

Feel more pain than pleasure

In financial debt

Accuse each other

Assume the worst in each other

Wish would've married someone else

Couch potatoes

"Then get a second picture, this time one of you guys at your best. Maybe it was taken of you on vacation, at your wedding, or when you were really happy. Place that picture in the center of a second poster board and write out how that couple feels. What are their emotions? Write down their habits. How do they treat each other? Name the characteristics and emotions of that couple. Do they use sweet nicknames for each other? Do they listen and care? Do they flirt with each other? Do they make time for what matters most? Write it all around that picture. Then give that couple a name at the top of the poster board, maybe something like 'Masterpiece.'

MARRIAGE MASTERPIECE

Opens the door for her	Non-judgmental	Faithful to each other, flirty
Smile & laugh with each other	Practice positive projection	Grow old together, stay young at heart
Know their purpose and are on the same page	Scheduled Sunday night communication about the upcoming week	Worthy of the relationship we expect to have
She admires & compliments him in public		Cuddles
Daily 5-second hugs		Don't complain, blame, or shame
		Make love
Ask the Couples' Castle questions 1-10 weekly		Have fun together, date nights
Let arguments roll of their backs, forgive, and let it go		Great with money
Says 'I love you,' 'thank you,' 'I'm sorry, please forgive me,' 'I really appreciate you,' and 'you're beautiful' to her		Ask better questions
	Treat each other like we did in the beginning	Assume the best in each other
Agree with each other, feel like a team	Self-love and self-care	Alignment with God
Designate project managers for tasks	Feelings of romance and certainty	Peace of mind
Focus on what works	Meet with role models	Healthy, exercise

"Then hang up both poster boards in your house so that every time you see them, it triggers a response in your relationship. They'll remind you every day that you're becoming one of those couples on that day. There are no neutral days. With every thought you think about each other, every act you make toward each other, and every word you speak, you are either feeding 'The Monsters' or 'The Masterpiece.' Whichever couple you feed the most, you become."

"That's awesome outside-the-box thinking, Red." Oliver smoothed down his shirt.

"This isn't thinking outside the box. Couples' creative dreaming is thinking without a box—there are no limitations in your relationship, except the restrictions you put on it."

Tell them. "Hey, guys."

No one answered.

"Guys."

Oliver was saying something to Red.

"Guys!"

They all ran to the window.

Olivia put her hands on the window and scanned the room. "Where're Zeb and Isabella?"

"It's time," Blue said. "Which couple's next?"

* * *

Before taking Oliver and Olivia down, Blue turned to the Parkers. "There's a letter meant for just the two of you over on the end table. After reading it, you can decide what to do."

Emma had an empty feeling in the pit of her stomach. They would be the last to go. Would there still be a reward left for them? She leaped toward the envelope and tore into it. Titus walked close behind, now standing on her right.

With shaking hands, she read the letter aloud.

Dear Titus and Emma,

You've been through some beautiful seasons in your relationship. Can you recall them? Lately, you've suffered some horrendous moments, and should you choose to separate and go your own ways, no one would blame you. If that's the case, the rest of this letter won't help much. If, on the other hand, you're willing to explore whether it's possible to still reach an authentic happily-ever-after for your relationship, continue reading.

First, apply what you've learned from the rooms, especially the one-to-ten quality questions. Ask them of each other every week. They'll certainly help you survive through this trying season, then thrive in happily-ever-after.

Second, there's a time-tested key that'll help the healing process, restore your trust, and transform your number to a consistent nine. Many couples who experience a breach of trust start throwing negative energy at each other. Like a snowball, it builds and builds until it ruins the relationship. The couple becomes so exhausted and exasperated with one another they eventually seek to eliminate the relationship. If your relationship is going to survive, much less thrive, you must generate great energy for each other.

There's one secret solution to make this easier on you. If you try to work things out but don't use this secret solution, you'll only get floods of resentment and regret. So use it.

Here it is: *Your relationship always becomes what you tolerate.* The point is you guys are at ultimate decision time: eliminate the marriage or eliminate the tolerations. It's make or break time for your relationship. There are no marriage problems, just two individuals with individual tolerations that cause problems. This matters because your energy levels for each other shrink or grow in proportion to what you're tolerating in the relationship. Let us explain what your tolerations are so that you can decide what to do.

Emma could feel Titus breathing behind her. *Good, he's listening.*

Tolerations are what you put up with, some are good while others negatively affect your relationship. Think about it this way: You are made up of physical and emotional energy, but you contain a limited supply of that energy each day. Now let's suppose at midnight every night you are given a 100 percent full supply of energy from the Couples' Castle's rooms—pleasurable, positive, purposeful, and paramount energy for each other. Well, as we'll demonstrate below, negative tolerations take your percentage down a notch. At the end of the day, you're either an energy vampire or an energy creator. The vampires separate from each other.

Given that you're unique persons, bound together in marriage, each of you tolerates different things. Depending on your negative tolerations, this can lead to energy depletion until you become jaded, then apathetic with each other. Then it's over.

The goal then is to master your tolerations within the marriage. The more negative tolerations you have, the less energy and passion you'll have for each other. Conversely, the less negative tolerations you have, the greater your energy and ability to create the ultimate relationship experience— even after all you've been through.

Typical negative tolerations might include:

➢ You wake up telling your spouse how much you're dreading the day.

➢ Your spouse routinely complains about your lack of help in the morning.

➢ Your shared breakfast consists of doughnuts and empty calories.

➢ There's no positive emotion in your morning hug, if there's a morning hug at all.

➢ It's not uncommon to have lost keys, missing shoes, and an un-ironed shirt as you run out the door late for work.

This causes mental stress which leads to physical exhaustion. It's only 8:00 a.m., and your energy level is already depleted. Given these few examples, much less all the negative tolerations you encounter with each other, do you think you're going to have much good energy for each other throughout the day?

Well, the analogy is fiction because most couples don't begin with a 100 percent energy reset every day. Given couple's poor sleep patterns, unhealthy food intake, stress levels, "judgmentalness," lack of communication and date nights, and negative talk, many begin with 30–50 percent energy levels, at best."

Emma glanced at Titus from the corner of her eye and swallowed hard. She wanted to be done with the letter so they could go search for the treasure chest, and yet she was beginning to feel that this letter might hold some positive effect on their future. They had nowhere to go but up, right? At least Titus was standing by her. And if Blue and

Red believed they should read it before room 7, then okay. She cleared her throat and read some more.

> For the past few years, your energy level has been even lower because your not being able to have a baby led to tolerations of negative attitudes, shame, blame, and guilt. You tolerated these things in your relationship, and slowly, they eroded your healthy marriage.
>
> The truth is everything you're currently experiencing in your relationship is because you tolerated it—both of you. That includes the unfaithfulness. You either caused it or tolerated actions that led to it, so it happened, and now here you are.
>
> This means, from now on, should you choose to stay together; everything that happens to you in the relationship, you must take 100 percent responsibility for. Eliminate the tolerations, especially the excuses, complaining, whining, and finger-pointing. No resentment, no doubts; only certainty of love and full forgiveness. Given what you're going through, there's no way you can survive if you keep negative tolerations. Both of you are 100 percent responsible. You always have been, but now you can own it and feel liberated, with the power to make this a great love story.

Emma wondered how Titus felt about taking any responsibility for the affair, much less sharing full responsibility. Even to her, that seemed asking way too much. She glanced over and saw him rolling his neck. *Ya, there's no way.* She opened her mouth to argue against the letter, but then stopped—and obsessed about her own flaws and shortcomings.

> Every couple wants a fulfilling relationship, one that provides them with what matters most to them. They want to go through the wedding ceremony and come out the other side living happily ever after.
>
> The little known secret to mastering your relationship and flourishing in happily-ever-after is in eliminating your relationship's sabotaging tolerations.

There's a time in every relationship where these tolerations begin to dominate. It's when conversations become just two monologues—careers consume your attention, dreams get shelved, debt drowns your ability to take vacations and contribute to causes, your sex life flames out, and the method of improving your relationship is based on talking over each other instead of for each other.

The result: your energy is wiped and your relationship put on autopilot or, worse, stuck in mediocrity. The common response is "I'm tired of this."

So you're faced with a choice now: eliminate each other or eliminate the tolerations.

Tolerations are not the same as tolerance. The latter is quite healthy—an acceptance of your partner for who he is without saying whether he's right or wrong. Negative tolerations, on the other hand, drain your energy, weigh you down like a ton of bricks on your shoulders, and prevent you from mastering your relationship and experiencing more of what matters most together.

The good news is you have control over your tolerations. You have the ability to deal with them *before* they destroy your relationship.

Here are some more examples of negative tolerations:

➤ Allowing an affair to become leverage
➤ Not getting up to greet your partner when he arrives home from work
➤ Living in a town where you are unhappy
➤ Prioritizing TV when your partner wants to talk
➤ Staying at unsatisfying jobs just so you can pay the bills
➤ Taking on debt so you can impress people
➤ Criticizing each other instead of caring for each other
➤ Giving too much weight to other people's expectations about your relationship
➤ Stressful conversations
➤ Lack of romance in the relationship
➤ Busyness

➢ Frantic mornings
➢ Lack of a compelling future
➢ No consistent date nights
➢ Interrupting your partner's stories
➢ Lack of sexual interest
➢ Letting in-laws borrow money
➢ Lack of consistent exercise and water consumption
➢ Being unaware of your partner's love language
➢ Uncleanliness and cluttered closets
➢ Emotional baggage
➢ Making incorrect assumptions
➢ Taking things personally
➢ Yelling at each other
➢ Going to bed without a good-night hug and kiss
➢ Playing on your phones while you're at a restaurant together
➢ Not believing in him
➢ Not deferring to her
➢ Negative, pessimistic talk—not believing the best is yet to come
➢ Adultery

Most couples are tolerating—putting up with things that sap their good energy for each other—too often. It's time to consider that your relationship is more important than simply surviving negative tolerations.

If you believe this, then here are steps that'll help you master your relationship with robust levels of good energy for each other:

1. In the next seven days, sit down together and write out fifty negative tolerations.
2. Don't worry about solving them at this point. Just listing them on paper is jarring enough.
3. Fifty will seem like a lot. So on the eighth day, double that. List them all out—turn every stone—how you talk to each other, how you delegate responsibilities,

with what other couples you spend time, with your
emotions. You can add personal negative tolerations in
addition to your marital tolerations because the personal
tolerations drain your energy levels too, causing you to
be less than fully alive when you're with each other.
What are you putting up with that drains your energy,
weighs you down, and distracts you from flourishing in
happily-ever-after?

4. Eliminate them, one by one. List them, take 100 percent
    responsibility for their existence, and then eliminate them.

Eliminating negative tolerations paves the way for
increased natural energy for each other. And as you now
know, the starting place to mastering your marriage and
accomplishing your relational dreams is having robust daily
energy for each other. Currently, your energy for each other
is at an all-time low. Lower energy equals a poor relationship.

It's possible for you to experience the ultimate relationship
together. But you must get rid of all your negative tolerations
immediately.

Emma sensed hope in the letter but couldn't help but worry about the
ticking clock. Surely they wouldn't keep them stuck up there to miss out on
what's in the red treasure chest. She paused the reading because her breath
temporarily bottled up in her chest. She could also feel his tenseness next
to her. He was glancing around the room, wearing an uneasy and pained
look. Emma took the letter over to the other side of the room and crumpled
onto the sofa. She sat quietly with a grave expression, then sighed. Titus
didn't even watch her make the transition. In a lower, more dejected voice,
she read the rest of the letter while he stared unfocused out the window.

Some couples hit a nine every now and then, but their
tolerations sap their energy for one another, and it pulls their
number back down. So they settle for a yo-yo relationship,
up and down, not understanding why. The way to reach
consistency of happiness, which is a mark of world-class
couples, is to eliminate your negative tolerations.

Emma rubbed her eyebrow. *Ya, you already said that.*

This is important. After you list them, the temptation will be to manage them. But you know it won't work. That's what you've been doing, and as the saying goes, "If you do what you've always done, you'll get what you've always got."

Managing your negative tolerations won't help your relationship. Eliminate them, modify them, or change them.

If you're still unsure of how to go about this, here's a short list of suggestions for how to take action:

➢ Write your negative tolerations on paper and feel what your relationship would be like without them.

➢ Dump your negative tolerations.

➢ Deal honestly with them.

➢ Accept responsibility for them. If they continue to bother you, then you're only managing them.

➢ Think about the different life stories your relationship could morph into, then choose your relationship's best story. You have a choice with each toleration—go with the same life narrative or your best story.

➢ Dialogue with each other about your negative tolerations in a positive way.

➢ Give yourself a due date. An example is you decide to sleep in separate rooms until you figure things out with a counselor, but at least you haven't separated.

Whenever you're stressed or feeling challenged, pause and consider current tolerations in life because that's what's bubbling beneath the surface. Accept full responsibility for your tolerations and move on. You can do this. All the best to you in your decision. We at the Couples' Castle care.

Sincerely,
Red and Blue

Chapter 17

Now or Never

Emma's stomach tied itself in knots. How was she supposed to remember everything from the rooms? She couldn't do it. Her head throbbed because her marriage was at stake, and now she was down to her final chance. She scanned the ballroom for the real treasure chest.

It had vaulted ceilings that were embellished with scalloped edging, custom moldings, and painted artwork. She could see high walls with crown molding next to the tinted window where they'd stood looking down. Massive tiered crystal chandeliers glittered in the soft light and circular dining tables with black tablecloths, blue rose centerpieces, and white napkin puffs in wine glasses surrounded the center glossy hardwood floor suitable for the royal dancers. She almost expected wait staff to appear with canapés and fresh wine glasses. *The real red treasure chest is in here somewhere.*

Isabella threw her hands up in an I-give-up gesture and spoke above the instrumental music coming from the speakers. "We've already looked everywhere."

Titus stood over next to the punch table, stirring his drink. How could he purposely ignore their high-stake efforts? Emma inhaled deeply and felt flu-like symptoms—nausea, sweats, and tingling in her chest. It was like he was over there relishing in her downfall. She felt flustered by his inaction, and her mind raced through the possibilities.

"Did you guys ask *them?*" Emma nodded toward the dancers.

"We thought it better to wait until they finished." Isabella shrugged.

Emma felt her face tightening. "But we only have, like, forty-five minutes left."

Isabella raised her eyebrows in a what-do-you-expect-from-me way. "I know. That's why we double-checked *everything.*"

"Has anyone checked inside the baby grand piano?" Oliver pointed its way.

"I haven't," Olivia said.

"Me either." Isabella headed in that direction.

I thought they said they checked "everything." Emma could hear the rustle of dress fabric and the heels crossing the glossy floor from the dancers. One woman acknowledged her with a faint smile while she twirled under her partner's arm.

"It's not here," Isabella called back.

Titus had located the breath mints next to the punch and sat down to watch the dancers. Emma's chin trembled, and her heartbeat seemed to slow momentarily. Flashes of her history with Titus surfaced in her trying to understand how everything led to this moment. While fiddling with her key, she watched the other couples grab their own punch and sit down in resignation next to Titus.

For the first time in her life, she felt totally abandoned.

Emma knew the chest had to be here. They said it was. She scanned the room slowly, still fiddling with her key. She hadn't actually seen anyone check underneath the far side tables, had she? With a sudden burst of energy, she marched over there, bent down, and crawled on her hands and knees. Nothing. She stood up and weaved her hands into her hair and pulled. Titus was now laughing at something, a joke perhaps. It was the first time she'd seen him laugh in a week. Emma's heart felt like it was shrinking while the heaviness in her body caused her to lean against the wall. *Ouch!* Something poked into her back.

She spun around and saw that it was a small door bump to prevent a doorknob hole. Yet there was no door. A button? Immediately, the floor opened up next to her. Out came three silver metal stands, each with a red treasure chest sitting on top, triple the size the one attached to her key. The one in the middle read "Titus and Emma Parker," while the other two displayed the other couples' names. Emma's jaw opened. When she saw that it was covered in shiny diamonds, it felt like her skin crawled up her body and made her light-headed. For a second, she lost the ability to speak, motioning instead at the group who were paying no attention to her.

*   *   *

Titus was laughing on the outside but felt the sting of betrayal in his heart. Every time he noticed Emma's legs, like he did when she'd walked across the ballroom, he felt a bitter tang in his mouth and the need to spit. His whole marriage felt unclean. Hearing his name screamed from across the room did little to change this.

"Titus! Titus! I found it!" Emma rushed across the room, with the real red treasure chest in her hands, and bumped into a table and fell. She jumped back up, oblivious to the small tear in her pants, and ran this time—stopping at a table about twenty feet from him. "Look, Titus! I found it! Here it is!"

Titus's face exhibited a hard expression, almost like he was looking right past her rather than at her. He refused to be bought off with her enthusiasm. A dark mood had settled on him that no one could dispel, let alone the chest.

"Who are you?" The dancers were now standing ten or so feet behind Emma.

Emma spun around to face the dancers. She was practically out of breath when she spoke. "We are couples who were invited to the castle. Upon arrival, we were told there'd be a real red treasure chest in here for us to open, one that contained the secret to an authentic happily-ever-after with our partner, that if we opened it, all would be well again, no matter what we've been through. These smaller ones with the key were given to us in our invitation." She pressed both close to her body.

The eyes of the man dressed like a king widened. The other dancers, three couples in total, stepped slightly forward.

Titus sensed some strange tension and stood up.

Oliver deliberately lowered his head to study them. "And who are you guys? And no offense, but what's with the royal outfits?"

The apparent leader of their group—the kingly-looking one—spoke. "My name's Ryker, and we are couples, the same as you, invited from Europe. And these here . . ." He tugged at his outfit. "We found them back there in a big closet." Ryker eyed the treasure chest Emma held.

"How long you been here? We saw you dancing down here when we arrived." Oliver folded his arms across his stomach.

Ryker's eyes ping-ponged between Oliver and the red treasure chest. "Three and half days. We met in what they call room 7 in the beginning to kick off our journey with a celebration. Since then, we've been going through different rooms. They told us to meet back here in room 1 when we finished, saying there'd be food and dancing."

Oliver tilted his head. "Wait a minute. Did you say *this* . . . is 'room 1'?"

"Yes." Ryker's eyes were dark.

"We were told this is room 7."

"So you say." Ryker drew a short sword from underneath his kingly-looking outfit. "Now hand over that red treasure chest."

Oliver's head flinched. "What, is this a joke? First, the dancing, then the costumes, and now a sword? Ha, ha. Very funny."

Ryker put the sword back under his coat and laughed. He then walked over to a smiling Oliver, practically invading his space. Oliver's smile faded, and he blinked rapidly to repel the man's breathing. Standing toe-to-toe, Ryker threw his hand against Oliver's chest and sent him flying on top of the table behind him. Olivia screamed, while Titus and Zeb rushed to help Oliver up off the table. They looked back and saw the man standing with his fellow couples.

Ryker's eyes were icy cold. "Does it look like I'm joking?"

*   *   *

"I didn't sign up for this." Red shuffled back a step or two from the window.

Blue gently rocked on his feet, humming and observing the couples. His fingers tapped the windowsill like he knew something no one else knew.

"Blue, I didn't sign up for any violence. We've never seen that done here before. What gives?" Red's eyes were bulging, and she did a double take down at Oliver who was just now getting up from the table.

Blue cusped his hands behind his back. "Everything will be all right. Patience."

Red gave him a long side-eye glance, then scanned the group dressed in royal attire. "The automatons look so human. Tell me, do they have consciousness?"

Blue stopped humming. "No, but our team created the closest thing you can get to consciousness. We uploaded a blueprint for an artificial cognitive mind that includes self-interest, improvisation, memory, and an internal voice as an inner monologue.

"Blueprint?" Red's eyebrows squished together.

"Separate blueprints for each. Every one of them is uploaded with back stories that anchor their identity. No fear, they're not allowed to kill, but . . . in this case, they are programmed to induce fear." Blue's eyes widened.

Red shook her head. "The couples look shocked, if not downright terrified." She inhaled deeply. "I don't know if I can agree with this script."

Blue exhaled. "Look, our team of engineers refined them for two years prior to any couple stepping foot into the castle. They only do what we tell them."

"Okay, but how do you *know* what they will do?" Red rubbed her head.

"Because we program them with only so many different narratives, depending on the needs of each round of couples. They look real, but they never exhibit unusual behavior. They are not real because they're not conscious. They simply have scripted and improvisation responses, always staying within their castle loops."

Red couldn't take her eyes off the automatons. "The improvisation part is what makes me nervous. I mean, what happens if they go off script? Did you program that one there to push Oliver onto a table?"

AARON B. BIRD, PHD

Blue rolled his neck. "They won't go off script, but if they did, we can put them in sleep mode and upload new information. As to the pushing, yes, that's part of his improvisation should he hear certain trigger words."

"But look at the couples. Titus's face has turned completely white." The sound of her finger tapping the glass matched the speed of her increased heart rate. She genuinely cared for the couples.

Blue lifted his chin. "Surprise and shock is how you break a pattern. This needs to happen. Titus arrived thinking he was broken because of what Emma did. But he's not broken, his pattern is. The other rooms offered amazing experiences and strategy solutions, but nothing that would break his pattern. It's too thick, too emotionally painful. He needs to be put in an environment like the one he's about to experience where he'll have to decide if staying with Emma is as important as breathing. I'm not saying it'll work, but reconciliation and restoration are always worth the cost. He'll be forced to choose between breathing and Emma."

Red narrowed her eyes, squinting. "So the automatons won't hurt them beyond what we just witnessed?"

Blue remained silent.

"Yes or no?"

He cleared his throat. "They are designed to play off ambient behavior. So if Titus exhibits aggressive behavior, yes, an automaton might reciprocate in kind."

"But it can't injure him. Tell me that, at least." She rushed her words. "Because I can't be a part of something like that. I won't be a part of something like that."

Blue tilted his head slightly, watching Emma fall to her knees. She clutched the chest close to her stomach while shaking her head rapidly. "The units self-correct to their narrative before it gets that far."

Red crossed her arms and faced him. "Always? Look at that guy approaching Emma. What's he going to do? And I remember when I first started here, I heard about the case two years ago."

Blue turned away. "That was in the trial period. It won't happen anymore because we purge their memories after each round of couples so that they cannot build new narratives. Once we bring them back online, they stick to their scripts with minor improvisations."

Red scratched her head. "Isn't there a better way to help? I mean, we've used all kinds of strategies in room 7 before. *They all* worked."

Blue nodded. "Those won't work for Titus and Emma."

Red tilted her head to the side and paused. "But how can it be real for him when they are automatons. What if he figures it out?"

Blue looked at Red, then back through the window. "He won't. Did they figure it out with Pastor Mike in room 6, the Asian couple in room 4, or with crazy eyes Clyde in room 3?" He waited for a response. "And yes, we implanted a fiction, but it's rooted in the truth. This is absolutely real to Titus, more real than the superficial and artificial environments he wakes up to every day back home. Just like those environments play a role in determining his choices, we've set up an environment to force a self-determining choice. By not choosing, he's choosing. We're forcing his hand: His own life or Emma's. By choosing his own life, he chooses to close the door on their marriage, but if he chooses Emma's, he's taking a step toward loving her again."

Blue sniffed. "There's little difference between being lifelike and alive when we are content to follow the scripted stories and patterns passed down from others. In that sense, Titus might be less alive back home than the automatons there. Others are telling him, his own emotional pattern is telling him, to leave Emma. That story is creating an emotional pattern in him to the degree that he's becoming an unfeeling automaton. As he puts up a wall to prevent the pain, he also blocks all love and joy.

"And it's not just Titus. Millions of couples are less alive than they could be. They need to wake up from their relational stupor. They need to get out of marriage mediocrity. They need to break their patterns of pain, come alive, and make their marriage a masterpiece." Blue backed up from the window. "My point is the only way to reignite the flame of love between Titus and Emma is to break through their painful patterns before it's too late. And it might just be too late before he becomes his own version of an automaton, before they walk away from each other for good."

Red wrinkled her nose like there was a bad smell in the room. "This particular narrative just seems dangerous. Did the board really approve it?"

Blue exhaled and walked away, annoyed she'd question his decisions. "C'mon, we need to go prepare for the next round of couples."

Red took one last glance through the window and said a quick prayer for Titus and Emma, then followed Blue out the door.

*   *   *

Emma carefully peeked through her hair at Ryker's face. She'd curled up on her knees and felt the sound of her heartbeat thrashing in her ears. Towering over her, with dark wavy hair and a chiseled chin, he locked his deep black eyes onto Emma's. He'd already taken the chest from her, but when he couldn't get it open, he demanded the key.

Olivia and Isabella inconspicuously hid their keys on the table behind them.

Ryker's eyes narrowed. "You must've done something pretty awful to clutch that key the way you are." He paused and walked in a circle the way a lion looks at its prey. He noticed her glance at Titus. Ryker swiveled his head back and forth between each of them. "What? Did you cheat on him?" Emma hung her head and sighed softly. "Ahh. I'm right. You cheated on him." Ryker looked at Titus again, then back at Emma. "No wonder you want to see what's in this chest. He lifted the chest above his head, then said, "Hand over the key."

The remaining dancers stood just behind him—their faces a mix of curiosity and loneliness. Ryker handed the one with blond hair the red treasure chest Emma had found.

Emma glanced at the key attached to the model chest resting in the palm of her hand before looking up to see Ryker approaching. His sword made a scraping sound as he drew it from the scabbard at his side.

This is the key to my marriage. It could—somehow—lead to bringing Titus and I back together, even after all the mess I've created.

Ryker's eyes were soulless and black. He didn't look like a happy person. Ryker's dance partner, meanwhile, began belittling Emma with comments of adultery.

A wave of shame covered Emma's face when she scanned the faces of all the royal couples. The same dark eyes stared back at her from all around the dance floor, taunting her about her infidelity. She looked for help from her friends, but they were frozen in fear. Chills broke out on her arms. She could see Titus's nose flare and could hear his breathing. He cracked his neck from side to side, then picked up something from a table like he wanted a weapon.

Ryker crouched a bit so that he was eye to eye with Emma. "A pathetic little whore, huh? I don't know why you think that key could possibly help you. Nobody's going to want you now. You might as well hand it over peacefully." He held out his hand, palm up. He was so close she heard his hand open up. She felt a nervous sweat run down her head.

Unless the Couples' Castle had lied to her, this key held the potential to revitalize her marriage. They even promised happily-ever-after. She didn't know what the heck was going on right now, but if she handed the key over, then all hope for her marriage was lost. The hope had to be real. If there wasn't hope, Titus would've never entered the Couples' Castle with her. No, they hadn't gotten along while here, but he did come. That says something. They didn't come this far just to go this far. She couldn't give up now.

A tear dropped from Emma's eye. "No."

She took a deep courageous breath. "Like I said, I was given this key. It's mine, for my marriage. I don't know why you're being so hurtful and cruel."

"Pardon me?" Ryker's cold stare narrowed.

Titus pushed up his sleeves and took a quite step forward.

Isabella and Olivia stood still as statues.

Ryker smirked, then raised his shimmering sword in the air.

Emma's sudden scream bounced off the room's walls. "Go ahead! Kill me! I'm already dead without the key!"

When Titus saw everyone stunned by her scream, he took a giant step onto the dance floor, quietly moving toward them.

"Have it your way, woman." Ryker touched the cold steel tip of his sword to her chin.

She clutched the key to her heart, closed her eyes, and cried. "I'm sorry, Titus. I'm so sorry!"

"Nobody cares about your apologies." Ryker tightened his grip around the sword's handle and pulled it back into a warrior pose.

"Look out!" another dancer cried out.

"What?" Ryker said through gritted teeth.

Like a flash of lightning, Titus positioned himself between Ryker's sword and Emma. "The k-key belongs to us. And if you c-call my wife one more name, I'm going to p-put this fist into your f-face." Titus flexed his fingers and made a fist, his other hand gripping a knife.

*   *   *

Titus could sense Emma's soul behind him crying out for his love. He quickly planned for Ryker's potential punches and strategized ways to overcome them. As his muscles tightened in readiness, he felt an acute sense of purpose rush through his body—protect Emma at all costs, even if that meant sacrificing his own life.

A sly smile formed on Ryker's face. "What, do you still love her after what she did to you?"

Titus could hear his own breathing. "Y-yes. We all have our skeletons. You shouldn't be so c-cruel, and I'd appreciate it if you'd hand over our treasure chest before I have to take it from you. We've c-come a long way to see what's inside it."

Ryker tilted his head, curiosity filling his eyes. He put his hand up to prevent one of the dancers behind him from attacking Titus. Ryker's boots echoed when he stepped forward, coming eyeball-to-eyeball with Titus. "You sure you want to do this?" Titus could feel the cold air from Ryker's nostrils on his face. It was like looking at the devil himself.

"More sure than anything I've ever been sure of in my life." Titus's hair stood up on the back of his neck. He felt powerful, brave, and scared to death.

Ryker craned his neck to look at Emma, then straightened it to match Titus's eyes. "Okay then, if that's really the life you want." Ryker slowly handed Titus the chest, then motioned for the other dancers to follow him from the ballroom, their footsteps echoing in the hall until the faint sound of a door shut left them in silence.

Titus closed his eyes and saw images of Emma and him dancing at the first high-school costume dance when he picked her. His brain flooded itself with the success solutions from the rooms, he took a deep breath, and he made a decision in his heart right then and there.

He turned to Emma—trembling and still on her knees—and reached out his hand.

Her mouth opened, her eyes widened. She grabbed his hand and pulled herself up to face Titus, their bodies almost touching.

The other couples watched in silence until Olivia asked, "Should we open it?"

Titus looked down at the red treasure chest in his hand. "Why? We already got what we came for, didn't we?" He looked back at Emma, put his arm around her waist, and pulled her closer. Her breathing hitched when he softly put her bangs over her ear. Tears streamed freely down her cheeks, and she shook uncontrollably, with joy this time.

"True, but . . ."

"But what?" Titus said, lifting Emma's chin. "Maybe the chest is a symbol to spark our imaginative love for each other again. Someone seemed to know that we would go all out for it and project a meaning on to the treasure chest based on the ultimate relationship we all long for." He tilted his head toward the group. "They knew something we didn't: for couples to experience happily-ever-after, that they'd have to become a couple worthy of the relationship they expect. The chest energized us to meet at midnight in a park, ride in a limo, go through the rooms—whatever it took to arrive in room 7—so we could use the key to unlock the treasure chest. It created an obsession and a sense of certainty in us that an authentic happily-ever-after was possible again—even for us."

With watery eyes, Titus looked back at Emma. "I get it now. There's no marital unhappiness, just two individuals with shared unhappiness— that the ultimate relationship experience are two happy individuals amplifying their positive emotions in a shared happiness with a sense of certainty and magnificent obsession for one another. We don't find happily-ever-after. With certainty and obsession for each other, we bring it out of ourselves and amplify it together with the rooms' strategies."

Emma placed her hand on the red chest. "Titus, your stuttering stopped."

Titus genuinely smiled for the first time in months and lowered his voice. "Emma, we have a lot to work through, but I choose you. We'll walk through this storm together. You're my wife, and I choose to make my relationship masterpiece with you. Regardless of what's in this chest, I choose to live our life at a nine. Heck, maybe even a ten."

As she tried to apologize, Titus placed his fingers over her mouth. "No need. I know." He stepped back and put her hands in his. "I forgive myself, and I forgive you, and I'm sorry for not being there for you. Please forgive me. I'm forever yours, Emma, faithfully. Now will you dance with me?"

Emma shook her head so fast, and her eyes filled with such joyful tears that she could barely say *yes* coherently. Olivia handed her three Kleenexes. "Yes! I love you, Titus! I love you, honey!"

Titus felt such peace.

Oliver was already at the sound booth turning on the music. "This is just like a love story you'd read about in a book. It's just too good not to match it with a song by Journey. Within seconds, the song "Faithfully" flowed from the speakers.

Titus pulled Emma so close that his nose tickled her ear as he whispered, "I've missed you."

Emma rested her head on his shoulder and sobbed with joy. She tried not to cry, given how much of it she'd done in the last few days, but it just felt so good.

As they danced, the other couples joined them, sharing the same smiles, smiles of two strangers learning to fall in love again.

When the song neared its end, Emma rested her head on Titus's shoulder and saw the other two treasure chests across the room. Her eyes widened as she recalled they were for the other two couples.

"Guys!"

The other couples looked Emma's way.

"Guys! Look!" She pointed across the room. "There are two more red chests over there, and they have your names on them. I forgot to tell you in all the excitement."

Before the next song could start, Isabella and Olivia had already returned with their red treasure chests in hand, a little winded.

Before they could open their treasure chests, Emma grabbed her key and inserted it in the red treasure chest labeled "Titus and Emma Parker." She could barely breathe when she turned it. It clicked and Emma slowly opened the top.

She gasped. Emma looked up, then back down. "Titus! It can't be!" She held out the chest for him to see. "It can't be, Titus. Look!"

He picked her up and twirled her around. The other couples looked on, never having seen such happiness blanket a couple in all their lives.

*   *   *

The sun was rising, shining crisply through the weeping willow trees and onto the stream that flowed into the surrounding lake. Emma inhaled deeply, then let out a breath of gratitude.

"Penelope, dinnertime!" Emma called out from the deck that overlooked her gorgeous backyard that included a tree house, flowering shrubs, a greenhouse, and trails that led into the woods.

"She's sure having fun." Titus wrapped his arms around her waist. "Hey, I think I hear the parents arriving."

Penelope came running up. "Mom, can we play for like just two more minutes? My friends are having so much fun!"

Emma and Titus smiled at their daughter.

"What?" Penelope said, unaware of the miracle she was.

"We just love you, sweetie."

"I love you too." She giggled and ran back to her friends.

Emma tipped her head back for a moment and closed her eyes. Her yellow button down shirt mirrored the warm joy that radiated through her chest.

The doorbell rang.

"C'mon. Our friends are here." Titus leaned in to give her a soft kiss on the lips.

He still makes it feel so magical, even after fifteen years of marriage.

Titus opened the front door and bellowed, "Good morning, friends!"

"Right back at ya, partner!" Zeb sauntered in, arm around Isabella's waist. Emma still couldn't get over how in shape he looked these days.

A black SUV pulled into the driveway. Olivia and Oliver climbed out, hollering, "Hey, keep that door open!"

Titus shut the front door in jest, then opened it and waited for them with a big goofy grin.

"You made it back!" Titus welcomed them with a big bear hug. "I think the kids are still alive. Come on in, and I'll get them for you."

"Honey, your friends' parents are here! It's time to come in and wash up for breakfast!" Titus hollered from the deck.

"Okay, Dad." Turning to her friends, Penelope yelled, "Hey, guys, time to go!"

"Ahh, man!" Denzel tossed his plastic sword in the toy bin.

Elizabeth, tall for a sixth grader, and Randal, a short kid in a light blue hat and carrying a cane, came running up together. Johnny and Renee were right behind them.

"Can we do this again next weekend? Please?" Randal pleaded.

"Well, it might storm before then and wipe out the castle," Penelope said with an air of authority.

"We can rebuild it! Please, can we do it again?" Ava ran up alongside Denzel.

"Yeah, that was the best sleepover ever. I've never slept in a tent before!" Johnny added.

The kids made their way up the deck's steps and were met with huge hugs from moms and dads.

"Hey, champ!" Oliver caught Denzel in his arms and tossed him up in the air.

"Good morning, butterfly." Isabella covered Ava's rosy cheeks with kisses.

"Mom and Dad, is it true?" Penelope asked, loud enough for everyone to hear.

"Is what true, sweetheart?" Emma ruffled her light hair.

"The Couples' Castle?"

The adults gasped, quickly glancing at one another.

Emma's eyebrows squished together. "Honey, where'd you hear about that?"

"In this binder full of papers from some seminar about living happily ever after. Oh, and, um, I found your journal in the binder too. I'm sorry, Mom, but . . . I read some of it." Penelope grimaced.

Kneeling, Emma looked her daughter in the eyes. "Honey, that's private."

Penelope studied her shoes. "I know. I'm sorry." She dragged her gaze back up to meet Emma's. "But . . . is it true that you and Dad couldn't have kids back then and that you almost gave up on each other?"

Everyone stared, kids included. The birds sung out a melody overhead, and the wind blew softly on her ears. Emma looked at her daughter like she was seeing her for the first time again. *You don't know the miracle you are, honey.*

"Emma, look." Titus pointed to the backyard, where the kids had built a castle, complete with swords and costumes. "What were you and your friends playing all night?" A slow smile that builds formed across Titus's face.

Penelope shrugged. "We turned what we read in your binder into a game."

"Yeah, it was so much fun!" Randal held up his cane.

Emma's heart felt full, so full, in fact, she thought it might burst. *Thank you, God, for my marriage and my little princess.*

"Mommy, are you okay?" Penelope's face seemed to shine.

Titus walked over and put his arm around Emma.

"Yes, baby, I'm okay." *How could I not be?* "I'm more than okay. C'mon, let's go inside for breakfast. I'm sure your friends are hungry."

They all walked inside and gathered around the table full of pancakes, biscuits, eggs, and coffee. In the pause after the blessing, Penelope asked, "Mommy, the binder said that most couples aren't happy, and a lot of them get divorced. You guys are happy, right?"

All the kids' ears perked up, as if the next generation of couples depended on her answer.

The question caught Emma off guard. She pressed her palms to her eyes to prevent the tears, then let out a huge breath. She was feeling especially emotional after hearing that Penelope had read her journal entry about the Couples' Castle.

Penelope paused and offered a questioning gaze. "Mommy and Daddy, do you have the kind of marriage you want me to have when I grow up?"

Emma interlaced her fingers, put her elbows on the table, and rested her chin on her hands. A tear fell from her eye. "Yes, honey, we do."

"Mom?"

"Yes dear?" The forks and knives cutting pancakes were clanging against the plates.

You didn't answer my question earlier about whether or not the castle is true. And aren't I about the same age as your journal entries about the castle?

After a reflective pause, Emma put her napkin down, then scooted from the table and walked over to the sweet tea china cabinet where they kept their wedding china. She knelt to open the locked door, pulled something out, and set it gently on the center of the table. "Here, honey, here's what you read about in my journal, the red treasure chest."

"Wow! So it is true. There really is a Couples' Castle!"

The childrens' eyes lit up, bulging even.

Emma reached her hand across the table. "Here's the key. Inside you'll find what we saw when we first opened it at the Couples' Castle, plus something else we put in one day later."

Penelope took the key from her mom, leaned over the pancakes, and opened the red treasure chest

Penelope's eyebrows raised. She reached in and pulled out an old paper titled "Emma Parker's Blood Work: hCG hormone confirmed," then reached in and pulled out a twelve-year-old positive pregnancy stick. "What's this, Mom? And why does it have my name on it?"

Before Emma could answer, Isabella's daughter asked, "Mom and Dad, did you guys get a red treasure chest, too, and if so what was in it?" Olivia and Oliver's kid also chimed in, curious about their red chest.

"Yes we did, kids," Zeb sat there rolling his lucky half-dollar over his knuckles, "and it was the best thing that ever happened to us."

"What was in it!" the kids yelled.

Zeb smiled. "It's supposed to remain a secret."

"Please!"

"Tell you what, I'll flip my lucky coin and if it lands heads, we'll tell you. If it's tails, it'll remain a secret until one day you experience the Couples' Castle."

"Deal!"

As the coin sailed up, Zeb looked at Isabella, Oliver smiled at Olivia, and Titus grabbed Emma's hand. Their hearts were full and each felt they were experiencing the ultimate relationship in a real happily ever after that mattered most to them.

About the Author

The kiss. Without it, this book would never exist. My marriage would never exist. My kids would never exist. The kiss changed my life. It was that magical, that good.

About 90 percent of the time, giving a great kiss to the girl or guy of your dreams needs a strong emotional rapport between the two. The stronger the emotional connection, or what some call chemistry, the greater the pull, like electricity. Without the emotional energy, it's like skipping to the end of a romantic movie to see the final kiss—meh. But if you watch the whole movie and enjoy how the two develop a buildup of emotional energy for each other, you feel the chemistry and charge of that one kiss. That's the same charge and chemistry I felt in the kiss that changed my life—my first kiss. Okay, really, it was a total failure.

It happened when I was in the seventh grade. My dad and I pulled up to an old rebuilt white barn where my junior-high self would attend a summer VBS day camp. As we walked through the front door, I saw over 150 kids sitting at long tables doing arts and crafts. I scanned the room for a place to sit and saw one of the most strikingly beautiful seventh-grade girls I'd ever laid eyes on!

That might've been the first moment of real clarity I ever experienced. Way over on the other side of the room, there she sat in all her beauty. She had that blond curly hair from the '80s, big pink glasses resting on her perfect nose, and bright white angels flying around her singing the hallelujah chorus. Most importantly, there was an empty chair across the table from her!

So I turned and sat next to my guy friends. I was terrified at the thought of sitting next to her, much less anything else. *Just talking to her might make me spontaneously combust*, I thought.

I stole half dozen glances at her before my friends noticed. In fact, I must have fallen into some kind of puppy-love trance because when my friends noticed I was gawking at her, they teased me relentlessly. Remember, we were in junior high! They kept saying, "She's out of your league, dude."

"She's not from our town, so it won't work."

"She's older than you, that's dumb. It'll never happen for you, bro."

But I couldn't shake the feeling that I really, really, really, *really* wanted her to at least notice me. I wanted her to know that I existed. I wanted more than that. I wanted to be a part of her life.

Seeing my fear, my dad, who was also sitting there at the table, gave me a mini pep talk: "Which is going to win out, son, your fear or your faith?" (He was a preacher)

I stood like a champion! My friends' eyebrows arched with curiosity and disbelief. But my knees immediately locked up, my feet felt like cement blocks, and my palms became sweaty. I thought I was going to pass out.

I stood there with two beads of sweat dripping down my forehead, paralyzed with fear and what-ifs. The guys were right; she was out of my league—waaaay out of my league. And there's no way this could work with each of us living in different towns (before the days of cell phones and the Internet). I heard fear's taunts: you'll get embarrassed and people will laugh at you. It's not worth it.

She tilted her head to one side, and I melted. My brain's survival mechanism was wrong; she was worth it, and her smile, even though it was not a smile given to me, gave me the courage I needed.

So I started walking toward her, slowly, awkwardly. I could hear small gasps from my friends.

Thinking I saw her look up, I halted, pretending to be invisible. What if I embarrass myself? What if she doesn't want me to sit near her? What if I smell? (All junior-high boys smell, right?) And what if she slapped me right there in front of everybody for sitting there? My whole life would be ruined!

I need a plan, I thought. I can't just go over there and say or do nothing. *I don't even know what I'm going to say. What will I do?* The answer hit me like a flash of lightning.

Give her a kiss.

Can you see that twelve-year-old boy?

If you're going to kiss your dreamboat, you need guts because it means taking one step at a time through your doubts and fears, then another and another and another—one at a time—then you actually have to deliver the kiss! Whether a romantic one where you make prolonged eye contact or a spontaneous kiss where you suddenly grab her hands and surprise her, this takes courage.

This isn't for the faint of heart, but look, *if you do this,* I thought, *it can change your life,* literally; *and if you don't even go talk to her, then guess what? Someone else will, and you'll watch her fall in love with that obnoxious, no-good rascal who would've shown more courage than me.* That was enough to make me lean into my fears.

I took a brave step in her direction and, in so doing, changed the direction of my entire life. She was all the way across the room, and the other 149 kids doing crafts between her and me became just a blur. I couldn't take my eyes off her. My heart beat thrashed in my ears and I felt my breath bottle up in my chest. She didn't know I was there. Didn't even know I was alive! But I knew she was there, and she made me feel alive, and when I saw her smile again, I stepped into a moment that my future self would later high-five me for.

All because of a kiss.

As I walked further, I became light-headed and my hands went half numb. I even forgot to breathe until someone accidentally bumped into me.

In regaining focus, I pumped myself up to give this girl a kiss—my very first kiss. I just kept putting one foot in front of the other.

The closer I got, the more fear screamed, *You're not good enough. You're not smart enough. You're not in her league. You'll bumble, stumble, and mumble. You're going to fail. Turn back. Turn away. She's not for you. Everyone's going to laugh at you.*

And before I knew it, I was sitting down across from her.

She looked up through her big-rimmed pink glasses, our eyes meeting momentarily. When she ignored me and went back to working on her craft, I felt I dodged a bullet. A chance to breathe. I sat there furtively glancing. No words were exchanged. Clarity pulled me into this, courage got me across the room, and now what I needed was some fonzie-like confidence.

I had to believe this would work out. If you don't have confidence, things like this get awkward, unnatural, and weird really fast. And besides, I'd heard that girls like a man to lead them in their confidence. It's about drawing out the experience.

So I sat there mustering up the confidence, thinking, *How should I give her this kiss? Should I lean across the table? Ask her politely? Crawl under the table and come up the other side? Just tell her?*

I couldn't take the pressure! So I sat up in all my dignity and just asked, "Um, excuse, um, excuse me, um, um, um, excuse me?" She looked up without a word.

Pause.

The blood rushed to my head like I was on a roller coaster. It just rolled off my tongue.

"May I give you a kiss?"

If you look up the definition of *eternity* in the dictionary, you'll find this part of the story.

"Excuse me?" she replied.

Oh boy, I thought, *did she not hear me? Do I need to say it louder? Now more people are listening.*

But here's where confidence is so important; you can't get all weird and shaky. I was committed now. "May I give you a kiss?" She definitely heard this time because *her jaw landed on the floor*!

Typical of a twelve-year-old-boy, I hadn't even thought about what her reaction might be.

I knew I just needed to stay cool. That's what they did in the movies after all. You can't get too excited or fearful. Just calm the pulse during the whole kiss process. Be cool, like the Fonz.

If you're approach to the kiss is uneven, shaky, weird, or nervous, her reaction will match. But even after a sudden, startling, spontaneous kiss, if you remain calm and confident, she will have more of an intrigued reaction, something akin to emotional chemistry. Somehow I knew that it wasn't just about me giving the kiss, but about her feeling something. That's why most kisses can't be rushed. You must build anticipation because with that generates her passion, her emotions—you want her to *feel* something.

So there she was, jaw on the ground. I had clarity. I leaned into courage. I was confident it would work out, and now I remained calm even when her face turned bright red.

And that's when I landed the kiss. I put my seventh-grade hand across the table in the shape of a fist and held it there for a few seconds before dropping a Hershey's Kiss in front of her craft. Like a boss. Her junior-high face blushed for so long that I got up out of embarrassment and walked away.

She hadn't said anything. We were now on opposite sides of the room from each other.

Minutes passed. Hours, days, weeks went by. And nothing. The same friends who laughed at me saw my total heartbreak. Dad encouraged me to call her. I did but no reply. It was in those hours, days, and weeks that I learned junior-high heartache and humility, real nonetheless. I felt failure in a personal way for the first time. I had put myself out there in all my vulnerability. I kinda moped around for a while, feeling sorry for myself.

But I'll never trade in those weeks because that's also when I learned the value of keeping the faith despite felt failure. Why?

Because she called me. Because we went to the junior-high dance. Because I escorted her to the high-school homecoming dance where she was crowned the queen. Because I knelt on one knee to place a ring on her finger to make her my princess. Because we got married. And bought a house together. And had two beautiful kids. All because of a kiss.

Meet Aaron and receive free training and resources from all his work at aaron-bird.com. Aaron is the founder of World-Class Couples Academy.

WORLD-CLASS
COUPLES ACADEMY

TAKE THE COUPLES' CASTLE CHALLENGE

Want to create your magnificent relationship? Take the ten-day Couples' Castle challenge at aaron-bird.com/p/couples-castle. It's fun and life-changing.

DISCOVER DR. AARON BIRD'S PERSONAL WORLD-CLASS COUPLES COACHING

Sign up for either the six-month or full-year world-class couples coaching program. It includes live coaching calls, world-class couples academy masters course, a live makeover, e-mail access, and relationship training on making your relationship a masterpiece. Visit aaron-bird.com/p/couples-castle to get relationship coaching with results.

DOWNLOAD WORLD-CLASS COUPLES ACADEMY FREE RESOURCES TOOLS

For free video training and relationship resources, visit aaron-bird.com/p/couples-castle.

ENROLL IN WORLD-CLASS COUPLES ACADEMY MASTER'S COURSE

To receive the best online relationship training in the world, sign up at aaron-bird.com/p/couples-castle. It's designed to help individuals find the love of their life and couples to create the ultimate relationship experience, make their marriage a masterpiece, and live in an authentic happily-ever-after.

GRAB YOUR COUPLES' CASTLE GUIDE FOR YOUR RELATIONSHIP OR SMALL GROUP

Aaron has created a couple's guide for your relationship or small group to enjoy together. It's the perfect way to create a relationship masterpiece alongside friends and family. Visit aaron-bird.com/p/couples-castle to claim your free resource guide.

BRING THE POWER OF THE COUPLES' CASTLE TO YOUR ORGANIZATION: KEYNOTE, WORKSHOP, RETREAT, AND TRAINING

Looking for the most masterful treatment of relationships to help your group or organization? Dr. Aaron Bird's humor, wit, and clarity of thinking gets you the strategies, solutions, and stories needed to get relationships to a world-class level. It's fun, entertaining, and an event your people will be talking about years later. Book Dr. Bird now at aaron-bird.com and let him give your organization an unforgettable experience in the Couples' Castle's rooms.

Bibliography

For more detailed explanations for the principles used in each of the rooms, see the following:

ROOM 1

Bandler, Richard and Grinder, John. *Frogs into Princes: The Introduction to Neuro-Linguistic Programming*. Revised Edition. New York, New York: Eden Grove Publishers, 1990.

Covey, Stephen R. *The 7 Habits of Highly Effective People: Powerful Lessons in Personal Change*. New York, New York: Simon & Schuster, 1989.

Lomenick, Brad. *H3 Leadership: Be Humble. Stay Hungry. Always Hustle*. Nashville, Tennessee: Thomas Nelson, 2015.

Maltz, Maxwell. *Psycho-Cybernetics, Updated and Expanded*. New York, New York: Tarcher Perigee, 2015.

Maslow, Abraham H. *Motivation and Personality*. (3rd ed.). New York, New York: Harper & Row, 1987.

Ibid. Toward a Psychology of Being. (3rd ed.). New York, New York: John Wiley & Sons, 1999.

Ibid. Religions, Values, and Peak Experiences. New York, New York: Penguin, 1970.

Robbins, Tony. *Awaken the Giant Within: How to Take Immediate Control of Your Mental, Emotional, Physical, and Financial Destiny!* New York, New York: Free Press, 1991.

ROOM 2

Allen, James. *As a Man Thinketh*. Amazon Digital Services, 2012.

Bly, R. "The Five Stages of Projection." *The Four Fold Way: Walking the Paths of the Warrior, Teacher, Healer, and Visionary*, pp. 21–22, edited by Angela Arrien. New York, New York: HarperCollins Publishers. 1993.

Burchard, Brendon. "The Ultimate People Skills: Positive Projection." https://www.youtube.com/watch?v=D46H3OyTVBE. October 3, 2015.

Gottman, John. *The Seven Principles of Making Marriage Work: A Practical Guide from the Country's Foremost Relationship Expert.* Revised ed. Easton, PN: Harmony, 2015.

Gottman, John. *Why Marriages Succeed or Fail: And How You Can Make Yours Last.* New York, New York: Simon & Schuster, 1995.

Grey, John. *Men Are from Mars and Women Are from Venus: The Classic Guide to Understanding the Opposite Sex.* New York, New York: Harper Paperbacks, 2012.

James, William. *The Principles of Psychology* vol. 1. Revised edition. Mineola, New York: Dover Publications, 1950.

Maslow, Abraham H. *Motivation and Personality.* (3rd ed.). New York, New York: Harper & Row, 1987.

    Ibid. Toward a Psychology of Being. (3rd ed.). New York, New York: John Wiley & Sons, 1999.

ROOM 3

Hankel, Isaiah. *Black Hole Focus: How Intelligent People Can Create a Powerful Purpose for Their Lives.* Mankato, Minnesota: Capstone, 2014.

Maslow, Abraham H. *Motivation and Personality.* (3rd ed.). New York, New York: Harper & Row, 1987.

Ibid. Toward a Psychology of Being. (3rd ed.). New York, New York: John Wiley & Sons, 1999.

Mihaly Csikszentmihalyi. *Flow: The Psychology of Optimal Experience.* New York, New York: Harper Perennial, 1990.

Tolle, Eckhart. *A New Earth: Awakening to Your Life's Purpose.* Westminster, London: Penguin, 2008.

ROOM 4

Bell, Greg. *Water the Bamboo: Unleashing the Potential of Teams and Individuals.* Portland, Oregon: Three Star Publishing, 2009.

Dweck, Carol S. *Mindset: The New Psychology of Success How We Can Learn to Fulfill Our Potential.* New York, New York: Ballantine Books, 2007.

Grazios, Dean. *The Millionaire Success Habits.* Phoenix, Arizona: Growth, Publishing, 2017.

Hicks, Jerry and Esther. *The Law of Attraction: The Basics of the Teachings of Abraham.* Carlsbad, California: Hay House, 2006.

Hyatt, Michael. "Thinking About an Affair? Count the Cost: 8 Reasons You Should Run, Not Walk, From Infidelity." https://michaelhyatt.com/thinking-about-an-affair-count-the-cost.html. September 4, 2015.

Imai, Masaaki. Gemba *Kaizen: A Commonsense Approach to a Continuous Improvement Strategy.* (2nd ed.). New York, New York: McGraw-Hill Education, 2012.

Maslow, Abraham H. *Motivation and Personality.* (3rd ed.). New York, New York: Harper & Row, 1987.

Ibid. Toward a Psychology of Being. (3rd ed.). New York, New York: John Wiley & Sons, 1999.

Rydall, Derek. *Emergence: Seven Steps for Radical Life Change.* New York, New York: Atria Books, 2015.

ROOM 5

Chapman, Gary. *The 5 Love Languages: The Secret to Love That Lasts.* Chicago, Illinois: Northfield Publishing, 2015.

Eggerichs, Emerson. *Love & Respect: The Love She Desires; The Respect He Desperately Needs.* Nashville, Tennessee: Thomas Nelson, 2004

Grinder, John and Bandler, Richard. *The Structure of Magic II: A Book about Communication and Change.* Mountain View, California: Science and Behavior Books, 1976.

Harley, Jr. Willard F. *His Needs, Her Needs: Building an Affair-Proof Marriage.* (Revised Expanded edition). Grand Rapids, Michigan: Revell, 2011.

Maslow, Abraham H. *Motivation and Personality.* (3rd ed.). New York, New York: Harper & Row, 1987.

Ibid. Toward a Psychology of Being. (3rd ed.). New York, New York: John Wiley & Sons, 1999.

Zondervan NIV Study Bible: New International Version. Grand Rapids, Michigan: Zondervan, 2002.

ROOM 6

Baggett, Bart. A. *The Magic Question: How to Get What You Want in Half the Time.* Virginia Beach, Virginia: Empresse Publishing, 2016.

Berns, Gregory. *Satisfaction: Sensation Seeking, Novelty, and the Science of Finding True Fulfillment.* New York, New York: Holt Paperbacks, 2006.

Bunzeck, Nico and Duzel, Emrah. "Pure Novelty Spurs The Brain." ScienceDaily. ScienceDaily, 27 August 2006.

Dispenza, Joe. *Breaking the Habit of Being Yourself: How to Lose Your Mind and Create a New One*. Carlsbad, California: Hay House, 2013.

Doidge, Norman. *The Brain That Changes Itself: Stories of Personal Triumph from the Frontiers of Brain Science*. New York, New York: Penguin Group, 2007.

Feldhahn, Shaunti and Jeff. *For Men Only, Revised and Updated Edition: A Straightforward Guide to the Inner Lives of Women*. Danvers, Massachusetts: Crown Publishing Group, 2013.

Goldsmith, Marshall. *Triggers: Creating Behavior That Lasts Becoming the Person You Want to Be*. New York, New York: Crown Business, 2015.

Goleman, Daniel. *Focus: The Hidden Driver of Excellence*. New York, New York: HarperCollins, 2013.

Maslow, Abraham H. *Motivation and Personality*. (3rd ed.). New York, New York: Harper & Row, 1987.

Ibid. Toward a Psychology of Being. (3rd ed.). New York, New York: John Wiley & Sons, 1999.

Maslow, Abraham. "The Influence of Familiarization on Preferences." *Journal of Experimental Psychology* no. 21(1937), pp.162–180.

McTaggart, Lynne. *The Intention Experiment: Using Your Thoughts to Change Your Life and the World*. New York, New York: Atria Books, 2008.

Robbins, Anthony. *Unlimited Power: The New Science of Personal Achievement*. New York, New York: Free Press, 1986.

Suzuki, Wendy. *Healthy Brain, Happy Life: A Personal Program to Activate Your Brain & Do Everything Better*. New York, New York: William Morrow Publishers, 2015.

ROOM 7

Bandler, Richard. *Using Your Brain for Change: Neuro-Linguistic Programming.* Boulder, Colorado: Real People Press, 1965.

Carey, Nessa. *The Epigenetics Revolution: How Modern Biology Is Rewriting Our Understanding of Genetics, Disease, and Inheritance.* New York, New York: Columbia University Press, 2013

Gawain, Shakti. *Creative Visualization: Use the Power of Your Imagination to Create What You Want in Your Life.* Novato, California: New World Library, 2002.

Gordon, Jon. *The Energy Bus: 10 Rules to Fuel Your Life, Work, and Team with Positive Energy.* Hoboken, New Jersey: John Wiley & Sons, 2007.

Kirsch, Irving. *How Expectancies Shape Experience.* Washington DC: American Psychological Association, 1999.

Leaf, Caroline. *Switch On Your Brain: The Key to Peak Happiness, Thinking, and Health.* Grand Rapids, Michigan: Baker Books, 2013.

Maslow, Abraham H. *Motivation and Personality.* (3rd ed.). NY, NY: Harper & Row, 1987.

Ibid. Toward a Psychology of Being. (3rd ed.). New York, New York: John Wiley & Sons, 1999.

Peirce, Penney. *Frequency: The Power of Personal Vibration.* New York, New York: Atria, 2011.

Made in the USA
Columbia, SC
27 June 2018